T0408680

Algerian Women and Diasporic Experience

ALGERIAN WOMEN AND DIASPORIC EXPERIENCE

From the Black Decade to the Hirak

Latefa Narriman Guemar

UNIVERSITY
of
EXETER
PRESS

First published in 2023 by
University of Exeter Press
Reed Hall, Streatham Drive
Exeter EX4 4QR
UK

www.exeterpress.co.uk

Copyright © 2023 Latefa Narriman Guemar

The right of Latefa Narriman Guemar to be identified as author of this work has been asserted by her in accordance with the Copyright, Designs and Patents Act 1988.

British Library Cataloguing in Publication Data
A catalogue record for this book is available from the British Library.

https://doi.org/10.47788/YMOW3830

ISBN 978-1-80413-054-4 Hardback
ISBN 978-1-80413-055-1 ePub
ISBN 978-1-80413-056-8 PDF

Cover image: 'Dzair'—the painting depicts the Algerian ballerina whose picture became a symbol of Algeria's Hirak. Dzair is the local name of Algeria. Image reproduced by kind permission of the artist, Ikram Berkani.

Every effort has been made to trace copyright holders and obtain permission to reproduce the material included in this book. Please get in touch with any enquiries or information relating to an image or the rights holder.

Typeset in Adobe Caslon Pro by S4Carlisle Publishing Services, Chennai, India

In memory of my father and my mother, the first great feminists I ever met.

Maya Ameyar, Marie-Laure Ost Mekbel and Amer Ouali, who died before they could read this book in French as they wished, are also remembered. Dying in exile requires courage, and this work is a tribute to their bravery. I will treasure the stories they told me, as well as their desire to see Algeria become a place where the right to be different is respected.

To my lovely children, Imene, Nadji and Lina, for their unconditional love and patience, which gave me the strength to complete this book.

Contents

List of Abbreviations x
Acknowledgements xii
Glossary xiv
Preface xvii

1 The Birth of a Research Project: Defining a Diaspora 1
Introduction: Women and migration 1
Aims and objectives of the research 5
The feminist framework 9
The research methodology 12
Sampling the network 12
Collecting the data 13
Conducting the fieldwork 14
Transcribing the interviews 15
Defining diaspora(s) and diasporic consciousness 17
Beyond ethnicity: The social constructionist definition of diaspora 21
Dialogism: A feminist approach to women's reconstruction of identity 26
'De-selving' and 're-selving' 30
Conclusion: Diaspora as a social condition and a state of mind 33

2 **The Political Background to the Feminization of Algerian Migration** 34

Introduction: The seeds of conflict 34

Democracy and women's rights in Algeria 35

The rise of a radical Islamist movement in Algeria 38

Causes and patterns of Algerian women's forced migration in the 1990s 42

The impact of the Black Decade on women 42

The making of an Algerian intellectual female diaspora 44

The legal and social situation of women in Algeria 48

Conclusion: The impact of historical events 55

3 **One Woman's Story of Trauma, Migration and Reconciliation** 57

Introduction: 'Lamia's' narrative 57

The gendered sociopolitical origins of personal trauma 57

Collective trauma: The experience of terrorism and counter-terrorism 63

Terrorism and women's oppression 68

The migration process 71

Reaching the UK 71

Arrival in the UK 75

Claiming asylum in the UK 78

The emotional impact of migration 85

Reconciliation and forgiveness 87

Personal reconciliation 87

Reconciliation in Algeria: Politics at home 90

The 'myth of return' 95

Resilience: Negotiating a new identity 97

Conclusion: Coming to terms with the past 100

4 **Fragmented Narratives of the Black Decade: Identity, Transnational Space and Belonging** 101

Introduction: Algerian women in exile 101

Persecution and the decision to leave 102

Rebuilding lives and a sense of self 113
Integration, language and identity 121
Narratives of regaining selfhood 125
The 'myth of return': Missing home but where is home? 131
Perspectives on an Algerian women's diaspora 141

5 **Women of the Black Decade and the Hirak** 147
Introduction: The power of history 147
The course of the Hirak 148
Women in the diaspora during the Hirak 154
Women as political actors: Hopes and fears for the Hirak 158
Can the spirit of the Hirak be sustained? 163
Conclusion: Seeds of hope 171

6 **Final Reflections** 172
Introduction: From networks to a diaspora? 172
The use of the concept of diaspora 172
The focus of the research 174
The elements of diaspora: Trauma, adjustment and the 'myth of return' 176
Justice and truth: Healing the rifts of the Black Decade 179
Conclusion: The Hirak and the mobilization of a diaspora 182

Appendix 1: The Author's Place within the Research 186
Appendix 2: The Characteristics of the Research Participants 190
Appendix 3: Survey Questionnaire (English Version) 192

Bibliography 206
Index 218

Abbreviations

AEDHF	Association pour l'Egalité des Droits Entre Hommes et Femmes
ABC	Algerian British Connection
AIDA	Association Internationale de la Diaspora Algérienne
ALN	Armée de Libération Nationale
ANIE	Autorité Nationale Indépendante des Elections
ASC	Algerian Solidarity Campaign
AWA	Algerian Welfare Association
CEDAW	Convention on the Elimination of All Forms of Discrimination Against Women
CISA	Comité pour la Sauvegarde des Intellectuels Algériens
DRS	Département du Renseignement et de la Sécurité
EP	European Parliament
EU	European Union
FFS	Front des Forces Socialistes
FIDA	Fédération Internationale de la Diaspora Algérienne
FIS	Front Islamique du Salut
FLN	Front de Libération Nationale
GIA	Groupes Islamique Armés
IMF	International Monetary Fund
IOM	International Organization for Migration
MAK	Mouvement pour l'Autonomie de la Kabylie
MCB	Mouvement Cultural Berber
NABNI	Notre Algérie Bâtie sur de Nouvelles Idées
NAC	National Algerian Center

PAGS	Parti d'Avant-Garde Socialiste
PCF	Parti Communiste Français
PS	Parti Socialiste
PT	Parti des Travailleurs
RACHAD	Mouvement pour un Changement Pacifique en Algérie
RAFD	Rassemblement Algérien des Femmes Démocrates
RAJ	Rassemblement Actions Jeunesse
RCD	Rassemblement pour la Culture et la Démocratie
SOS	Femmes en Détresse
SM	Sécurité Militaire
UGTA	Union Générale des Travailleurs Algériens
OECD	Organisation for Economic Co-operation and Development

Acknowledgements

I wish to pay homage to the women who took part in the research that resulted in this book. Their bravery and resilience will continue to be a source of inspiration to me. I hope that friendships built during this study will last until we see a free, democratic and prosperous Algeria, and beyond. Special thanks go to Feroudja, Lamia, Nadia, and Louisa (not their real names) for whom I wish even more success in future. Maya has sadly left this world since the writing of this book. May she rest in peace.

I owe the completion of this book to Dr Fran Cetti, and her encouragement and editorial assistance. No words can express my deepest gratitude to her.

I also want to take this opportunity to say how greatly I value the unfailing support, academic and emotional, of Dr Jessica Northey, to whom I owe particular thanks.

Many others have helped me along this journey. I am privileged to have met Prof. Philip Marfleet, Prof. Gargi Bhattacharyya and Dr Maja Korac, who believed in me and took over the job of supervising me in the middle of my research, and without whose encouragement and guidance this research would have taken a different turn.

I would also like to thank Prof. Michael Collyer from the University of Sussex for his interest in my research and stimulating discussion around the Black Decade. I would also like to express my gratitude to Prof. Anne Phillips, Prof. Mary Evans, Prof. Clare Hemmings and Hazel Johnstone at the Gender Institute of the LSE for hosting me as a Visiting Fellow between 2012 and 2014. It was a greatly enriching experience.

My great thanks also go to my dear friends Gill Evans, Prof. Nicola Cooper, and my former supervisors at the Centre for Migration Policy Research at Swansea University, Prof. Heaven Crawley, Dr Tom Cheesman and Dr Keith Halfacre, for their invaluable assistance and support, academic, technical and emotional.

Finally, to my friends who have helped me throughout this journey—Amel Taleb, Nazim Mekbel, Ghenima Ammour, Omar Lassel, Amer Ouali, Ammar Belhimeur, Roger Laurent, Kader Brahiti and Meriem Mentouri-Tamzali—I thank you for your encouragement and invaluable advice.

Glossary

Note on transliteration

No systematic transliteration has been used through this book and, unless otherwise noted, all translations from French and Arabic are my own. For clarity and to assist the reader in locating names elsewhere in the literature, I have used a very simplified transliteration from Algerian dialect 'Darija' in this book, with no macrons on long vowels or accents on emphatic consonants. Wherever possible, I reproduce the Algerian pronunciation of dialect Darija terms rather than attempting to provide an accurate standard or classical transliteration. Algerian proper names and general expressions in Darija are suggested in the most precise transliteration from Arabic or Tamazight.

Glossary of terms

'Alayha nahya wa alahya namut'	'for it we will live and for it we will die'
'ayadi kharijiya'	'foreign hands'/interference
au bled	Back home
da'wa	The Islamic call
dawla Islamiya	Islamic state
'dialoguistes'	Those in favour of dialogue with the Islamists
'Djeich chaab khawa khawa'	'The army and the people are brothers'
'eradicateurs'	Those who called to cancel the elections won by FIS
Elghorba/ghrib	Exile/exiled

Haraket El Jaza'ara	The (Islamic) Movement for Algerianization
'harragas'	Those who burn their ID or risk their life to migrate
Hirak	Algerian political protest movement
hogra	Strong Algerian word used to describe injustice
'koulou hada bi idniallah'	'all this is with permission from God'
Imra'atu I'ijmâ	Women of the consensus, refers to Islamic legislation
issaba	Gangs working within the Algerian state
'la mithaq, la doustour, qala Allah qala erassoul'	'No charter, no constitution, God said Prophet said'
Laïcité	French word for non-clerical or secular
'le pouvoir'	Refers to the state/government/ policy-makers
les carrés des féministes	The 'feminist squares' organized during the Hirak
mashallah	Holy thankfulness
Ma'arifa	Networks for privileges and empowerment
'machiwaktism'	Refers to a refusal of claiming social justice during Hirak
moujahidin/jihad	Holy fighters/Struggle for Islam
moukafa'a	Reward
'moukawama'	Resistance
madrassas	Islamic schools
mourshidates	Female Islamic guides
niqab or *tchador*	Islamic women's clothing covering all parts of the body
nisf-sake	Islamic male's clothing which shows the calf

Qanat El 'aar	The Channel of Shame, refers to TV Channel El Nahar
rahma,	Clemency from God
'roukoub el mouja'	'surfing the wave', joining the Hirak for other purposes
taouba	Repentance to God
Tekhouin	Accusation of treason
'tayebat al hammam'	Pejorative term meaning 'women gossipmongers'
Ulama	Refers to scholars and followers of Abdelhamid Ibn Badis
'yetbelaouek'	Implied sexual aggression in the context of this book
'yetnahaou gaa'	'They will all go'
Wilaya	Administrative department or province
zawiya	Islamic Sufi order

Preface

This book is about us, the women of an independent Algeria, who once spearheaded the feminist movement in the so-called Third World. We overcame experiences of discrimination and violence to succeed in our studies, assert our citizenship and claim our place in the public sphere. However, during the bloody internal conflict of the 1990s, known as the 'Black Decade', we faced the twin terrors of state repression and political Islam. Many of us were forced to flee, only to end up battling prejudice and racism in the countries to which we fled. Although we forged new lives for ourselves, our response to the Hirak—the huge wave of protests that recently spread across the country—has shown that we did not abandon our dream of a democratic Algeria. I hope this book will help to amplify our voices, and that our narratives will engage and inspire others.

During Algeria's Black Decade, the international community reduced the conflict to a clash of stereotypes: Islamists versus an authoritarian but secular military state. The turmoil in the Middle East and North Africa following the suppression of the 'Arab Spring' was often characterized in the same way, even leading some international figures to applaud the return to military regimes in the region. The Hirak, however, revealed the existence of a third, alternative voice—one that is youthful, secular, humane and feminist—calling for urgent social and economic reforms, good governance, stability and democracy. This voice owes much to those highly skilled, professional Algerian women, many of them activists, who fled during the Black Decade and its aftermath. Although they now belong to a wider, transnational community, they have tried to keep alive their hope for an Algeria free of corruption, injustice and inequality.

This book investigates the experiences of these women. I explain the extent to which the lack of freedom for women, the restrictions associated with the Algerian Family Code, and the heightened levels of violence directed against women during the Black Decade and its aftermath motivated their flight from Algeria. I explore the barriers they faced when attempting to rebuild their lives in the countries to which they migrated, and the barriers they face in returning to Algeria. They have created professional, social and political networks, including online networks, not only to promote their chances of resuming their professional lives in their adopted countries, but also to debate and engage in political changes in their country of origin. I investigate if and how these networks are indicative of a diasporic consciousness and could therefore be mobilized to contribute to the reform of women's position in Algeria. Hence, throughout the main narrative of this book, I interweave my reflections on and research into how these women later engaged with the eruption of the Hirak in 2019, both as a protest movement for democracy and as an imaginary diasporic space in which they could express their hopes for a new Algeria.

Although the fieldwork for most of the research in this book was conducted between 2012 and 2016, I felt compelled to revisit it during the Hirak in 2020. The book itself was completed at a time when the Hirak was still ongoing. The Covid-19 pandemic, coupled with the Algerian state's repressive measures, made it difficult to sustain the marches and protests after late 2021, but online debates continued, keeping its ideas and slogans alive. As I write this, the situation remains fluid, meaning that any retrospective analysis of events would be premature. However, in Chapter Five, I present a brief overview of events as they occurred up to late 2021 from my own perspective as a committed supporter, and through the eyes of those women of the Black Decade who contributed to this book.*

* *The names of the women who participated in the research documented in this book have been changed for reasons of confidentiality.*

1 The Birth of a Research Project: Defining a Diaspora

Introduction: Women and migration

Globally, the number of Algerians living outside their country of origin has almost doubled from the 1990s onward—from three million to seven million (Pison 2015). Yet it is telling that between the beginning of the wave of protests of early 2019, with their message of hope for a new Algeria, and the closure of all borders, including maritime ones, in March 2021 due to the global pandemic, the number of migrants crossing the Mediterranean actually decreased. However, state repression and the detention of hundreds of (mainly young) prominent figures in the Hirak, as well as growing disillusionment and despair of seeing any real change, once again provoked an increase in the number of *harragas* risking the Mediterranean crossing to Europe.[1] According to the InfoMigrants (2021) platform, between the beginning of 2021 and September of that year, more than 10,000 migrants arrived in Spain and the Balearic Isles, all thought to be either Algerians or Moroccans. The Spanish coastguard also reported that on 22 September 2021 the bodies of eight migrants, believed to be of Algerian origin, were washed ashore in southern Spain. One child and three women were among those who drowned.

The numbers of women leaving Algeria, meanwhile, started to increase markedly from 2000 on, in the long aftermath of the bloody internal conflict of the Black Decade, which began at the end of 1991. For many of these women (at least those who participated in my research), however, being far

1. '*Harragas*' translates literally as 'burners'. It refers to those who 'burn' (i.e. destroy) their identity documents in the attempt to flee Algeria.

from home did not mean they were disconnected from their country's politics. Most of the participants used social media to keep themselves informed on what was happening in Algeria, and they connected with family and friends in their homeland at least once a day through platforms like Facebook. The emergence of the Hirak in 2019 consolidated this transnational engagement with their country of origin, as seen in the immediate show of solidarity by large numbers of women in London, Paris, Montreal and Washington. It was an opportunity to celebrate a sense of togetherness in exile, a feeling that had been shattered by the Black Decade.

Indeed, the important role that Algerian women abroad played in supporting the Hirak is, in some respects, an indication of the numbers of women that fled the country during and after the Black Decade. This, in turn, is a reflection of what is known as the global 'feminization' of migration. According to the International Organization for Migration (IOM) (2020), women accounted for approximately half of the estimated 281 million international migrants worldwide in 2019, which equates to approximately 3% of the world's population. In addition, there are an estimated 82 million refugees and 48 million people around the world who have been internally displaced, mainly as a result of conflict, and around 50% of these are women and children (UNHCR 2021). Migrant women also contribute massively to the overall outflow of remittances sent by immigrants to their countries of origin, but they generally end up facing harsher social and working conditions than their male counterparts in the countries to which they migrate. Yet, despite the importance of women in the phenomenon of migration, researchers face significant challenges in the collection, analysis and use of gender-responsive data that adequately reflect not only the differences and inequalities, but also the resilience and contribution of migrant women. Global data regarding highly qualified and professional migrant women in particular are almost non-existent. This book turns its focus on this latter under-researched area.

Migration as a whole not only concerns every country it touches, but also challenges the very notion of the nation state and its constructed borders. This is shown by the 'refugee crisis' at the European Union's external border and at the borders of its nation states—for example, in the migrant camps scattered along the French coast facing the English Channel and on the Greek island of Lesbos, as well as in the deadly risks such migrants take in their attempts to reach 'Fortress Europe'. Between January and June 2021, an estimated 827 migrants died trying to cross the Mediterranean, while in 2020, the number of deaths stood at 1,400. However, the exact number of deaths in the Mediterranean cannot be determined: between 2014 and 2018, for instance, the bodies of about 12,000 of those known to have drowned were never found (IOM 2021).

Although the recent attention focused on migration gives it the appearance of a specifically modern phenomenon, it has always been a feature on the world stage, a manifestation of wide disparities in socio-economic circumstances, and has long been regarded as a potential means of improving life or human security. However, during the post-Cold War and post-9/11 periods, and more recently the Syrian civil war and the return of the Taliban in Afghanistan, migration has assumed new dimensions and patterns. Analysts and academics from different disciplines suggest that a number of contemporary changes have caused the mass exodus of populations, reshaping patterns of population movements (Van Hear 1998). Technological transformations and the emergence of ethnic, religious and nationalist conflicts have resulted in national and worldwide instabilities, particularly in the Global South, furthering population displacement (UNDP 2009). Recently, another force—climate change—has generated a new wave of forcibly displaced populations. Added to this, the globalization of the world market has cemented pathways that encourage the movement of skilled workers and professionals from developing countries to fill gaps in the labour markets of more developed countries (Castles and Miller 2009).

On the one hand, globalization creates the idea that people will gain from migrating to richer and more secure countries, increasing the pressures to do so, while on the other, it propagates negative perceptions and fears in the receiving countries concerning the political, social and security consequences of migration (Bakewell 2008). The dominant political and media discourses on migration, and hence public opinion, in the receiving countries are increasingly subject to political manipulation, particularly around such fears as the loss of national identity (Papademetriou 2012). As Noam Chomsky (2001) remarks, despite the declaration by the USA, the dominant global power at the end of the Cold War, of a 'new world order' promising peace and plenty, it displayed extreme incompetence in managing the social issues that resulted from the recomposition of new states, the creation of new borders and the redefinition of people's identities. Chomsky argues that the problems of identity recognition and negotiation in this new global context increased ethnocentrism and racism in most Western countries. The practices of contemporary globalization have therefore encouraged the rise of racism alongside an increase in the claims of indigenous ethnicities (Solomos and Wrench 1996; Castles and Miller 2009). Translated into policies and social practices, these claims not only result in keeping people excluded in the Global South, but also deepen the disparities suffered by minorities living in the West (or Global North). The rise in nationalism and hostility towards migrants has fuelled the popularity of right-wing ideologues within many European societies. According to James Carr (2016: 2), the 'war on terror', initiated after 9/11, created an 'anti-Muslim racism' that exacerbated an 'Islamophobia in western public opinion that spans centuries'.

The fact that international migration has become such an intrinsic feature of globalization highlights the importance of researching the nature of different migrant groups and communities, including investigation into whether they belong to a network, engage in political discourse and activities with their compatriots, retain a relationship with their country of origin, or entertain the ambition of returning. As Nicholas Van Hear (1998) and Nina Glick Schiller (2009) suggest, globalization has meant the unavoidable creation of new social, political and economic networks among migrants, often spanning several societies. It is the formation of these networks that has been commonly identified as 'transnationalism'—or 'diaspora' if the network becomes involved in projects for change in the country of origin. Any research into the phenomenon of migration therefore demands an understanding of transnationalism, diaspora and exile as not only social conditions but also states of mind, and this can be accomplished by using the concept of diaspora as an analytical tool.

Robin Cohen (2008, 2010) argues that contemporary scholars of migration need to recognize the potency of diaspora as a concept, but they must also be flexible and open to novel uses of the term, acknowledging its global evolution. The research in this book takes Cohen's advice into account. It is based on the assumption that diasporas have captured both transnational and national spaces due to the role they play in social, cultural and economic development, as well as the influence they have on policy debates within sending and receiving societies. James Clifford (1994) also stresses that durability is a necessary condition for the establishment of a diasporic consciousness; it needs to be tested by time as well as by other social constructs. This is because, as Cohen (1997) argues, migrants do not necessarily consider themselves as belonging to a diaspora at the point of arrival.

Although I believe that diaspora is essentially a political concept, and have some reservations about using the term, if only as a prototype, I found Cohen's arguments highly relevant for my research, and took them as a starting point from which to define the concept when using it to study my sample of highly skilled women who fled the upsurge of violence in Algeria in the 1990s. My research was further influenced by the work of Floya Anthias (1998), which is grounded in feminist and black literature (Hall 1990; Gilroy 1993; Clifford 1994; Brah 1996). Anthias considers diaspora to be a socially constructed condition rather than simply a description of a given group of the same ethnicity.

In this chapter, I introduce the aims of my research, explain its feminist framework and detail my research methodology. As this book focuses not only on the migration experiences of a specific group of highly skilled and educated Algerian women but also explores the existence of transnational networks among these women, I decided to use the concept of diaspora as an analytical tool to further my investigations. Hence, I consider the contested nature of the concept itself, and explain the way in which I employed it in my research. Finally, I look at the feminist use of dialogism, and the idea of 'de-selving' and 're-selving', concepts that have been crucial to an understanding of the experiences of the research participants.

Aims and objectives of the research

The importance of the research that underpins this book rests on two facts. Firstly, highly skilled female migrants have frequently been neglected by researchers and policy-makers. Migrant women in general have too often been represented in a stereotypical manner as passive dependents and as 'needy victims' (Morokvasic 1984), ignoring their agency. Secondly, although there is a substantial body of literature on Algerian migrants in France, due to the importance of North African migration there in terms of size and social significance, there has been very little research into the category of highly skilled Algerian women who migrated to countries other than France during the Black Decade and its aftermath. For example, Michael Collyer (2005, 2006, 2008) is one of the few researchers to have carried out significant research on Algerians in the UK. This book breaks new ground by placing highly skilled Algerian women, who fled to a variety of countries from the traumatic conflict of the 1990s, at the centre of an investigation into diasporic consciousness.

By the time I left Algeria at the end of the Black Decade in 2003, I had witnessed the departure of hundreds of colleagues. Students were left without teachers, lecturers or supervisors, and research projects were abandoned, while hospital patients were left without consultants. Even now, the issue of this brain drain in Algeria continues to resurface in press reports and academic research. Once I arrived in the UK, I met Algerian women who had been university lecturers back home and were now scattered across the UK under the dispersal policy introduced by the Immigration and Asylum Act 1999. They often held doctorates from UK universities but had left the country after finishing their studies, and then were forced to return, fleeing terrorism. Despite their UK qualifications, they had had to struggle to adjust to a new culture and rebuild their professional lives. One of the first barriers many of them encountered was the gender-blind asylum process, which does not recognize women's specific persecution. I also knew of many other women who had migrated to France, often graduates of French academic institutions at an earlier date, who were also facing barriers to accessing jobs in their profession, particularly as doctors and lawyers. Meanwhile, the Algerian government has (up to very recently) continued to deny that there was any mass exodus of highly skilled Algerians, particularly highly skilled women, during and after the Black Decade. However, my research reveals the existence of a network of highly qualified, highly skilled and often politically engaged Algerian women who fled the country at the time.

It has also been argued that feelings of belonging to a cohesive diaspora are relatively weak among Algerian migrants because of the significant political, linguistic and other differences within the Algerian community, especially between those who migrated (specifically to France) during the 1960s and 1970s and those who did so in the 1990s (Begag 2002; Sayad 2004). The highly skilled and generally politically involved Algerians forced out of the country during the 1990s contrasted greatly with the rural or low-skilled men (and their spouses or dependents) associated with earlier migration flows (Collyer 2006). It could be argued that in fact several Algerian diasporic networks have been created in different times and spaces, and under different circumstances.

Nevertheless, as Collyer (2008: 694) points out, '[t]he Algerian diaspora has always been a focal point for political innovation and contestation. For the first years of Algerian independence, the ruling regime therefore paid great attention to developments in France and developed sophisticated surveillance methods' to track its nationals living abroad. However, it is true that the experience of women who migrated during and after the 1990s differs from that of women involved in previous waves of Algerian migration, and has often been particularly associated with forms of resistance and solidarity. This can be illustrated by the case of Fatiha and Maamoura, two survivors of the so-called Hassi Messaoud event. On 13 July 2001, at Hassi Messaoud, a southern Algerian city centred on the production of oil, a group of local men attacked, abused and raped more than a hundred women (Kaci 2010). They were incited by a local imam, who issued a call to 'cleanse' the city of 'impure women' (Lezzar 2006). The majority of these women were divorced, widowed or single mothers who had been internally displaced from other parts of Algeria and had come to the city to look for work, and to escape the harsh patriarchal rules they were forced to submit to in their own communities due to their social status (Iamarene-Djerbal 2006). In the eyes of their aggressors, however, they were all 'prostitutes' and a threat to the community (Kaci 2010). Although the majority of these women were silenced and constrained from speaking out, Fatiha and Maamoura managed to leave the country. Once in France, they met Nadia Kaci, an Algerian artist and writer who had left Algeria in the 1990s. Kaci recorded their testimonies and published a book, *Left for Dead: The Lynching of Women in Hassi Messaoud* (2010). This gives a detailed account of the horrors that occurred during the night of the attack, and also describes the juridical and social context of the event, including an exposition of the status of women in Algeria (Lezzar 2006).

Even before the Hirak, there were some political protests that succeeded in uniting different Algerian women migrants, although they appear to have been relatively short-lived. During his fieldwork on the Kabyle diaspora in Marseille,[2] a French city often referred to as the 49th *wilaya* (province) of Algeria, Collyer (2008) joined a march organized in protest at the bloody events of April 2001 in Algiers and other Kabyle cities following the death of a young man in custody in a Kabyle police station.[3] Most of the organizations represented at the protest were composed of Kabyle migrants, but the RAFD (Algerian Rally of Democratic Women), which included women who were not Kabyle, was also present, illustrating that migrant Algerian women do participate in national debates and political struggles despite the implicit (and sometimes overt) gender power relations and regional animosities found in many Algerian political organizations (Lalami 2012). Collyer relates the response of one non-Kabyle woman who had joined the protest:

> One of [these women] told me: 'Some of the Berbers you meet are worse than the *Front National*—they won't talk to you because you're Arab. I've come here today because it's important, but I don't normally hang out with these people.' This woman felt that what happened in Kabylia was of concern to all Algerians. (Collyer 2008: 699)

The events in Kabylia provoked a degree of international solidarity among Algerian exiles, and protests were also held in Paris, Brussels, London, Washington and different towns in Morocco (Collyer 2008). However, whether these series of protests were coordinated by a transnational diasporic network remains uncertain, and Collyer argues that these movements lost the ability to mobilize Algerians living abroad, fading away once the government suppressed the protests in Algeria itself.

By contrast, the story of what occurred after the massacre of Bentalha in September 1997, and its impact on both the diasporic and the wider international consciousness, is an example of the potential for continuity amongst politically active networks. A witness to the events, Nesroulah Yous, was able to reach France, where he organized small meetings to publicize what had happened and tried to inform the wider international community by addressing the European Parliament (Algeria-Watch 2009). It was through one of these

2. Kabyle is a Berberophone area situated in the north of Algeria.
3. *Courrier International* (31/5/2001).

meetings that he met Salima Mellah, a female Algerian journalist based in Germany, who helped him write a book publicizing the massacre, *Qui a tué à Bentalha?* (*Who Killed at Bentalha?*) (Yous 2000). Once it was published in November 2000, parts of the European media began to pay attention to the situation in Algeria, leading to an increase in international public debates about human rights abuses during the Black Decade. Even if the accuracy of some of its details could be questioned, the book's content captured widespread attention and generated a series of public demonstrations in France, Canada and Germany, which were attended by well-known politicians and intellectuals. At the same time, a number of prominent Western intellectuals, including Chomsky (1999) and Lord Avebury (1999), voiced their strong criticism of the Algerian regime, while others such as Pierre Bourdieu and Jacques Derrida expressed support for the intellectuals assassinated by radical Islamists (Grenfell 2004).

I focus in this book on investigating the existence of transnational networks of highly skilled and highly educated Algerian women migrants, and examine their attempts to use these networks to mobilize and engage in political projects for positive social change in the country following the tragedy of the 1990s. I also explore the ways in which policy-making—both in the receiving countries (specifically, immigration policies and policies of integration) and in Algeria—shape or influence the relationship that Algerian women have with their co-nationals in their countries of migration, country of origin and in other countries.

The feminist framework

My initial concern when designing this research was to offer evidence of the high numbers of highly skilled, professional women who fled Algeria during the Black Decade—a female brain drain that was ignored and even (until recently) denied by the Algerian government. Although, based on my observations and experience, there appeared to be a lack of cohesion amongst these women, I was motivated to explore whether the networks they engage in act—or could come to act—as agents of women's development in both their home countries and their new societies. This motivation is essentially what gave my research its feminist underpinning.

It is frequently argued that feminist research should be predominantly conducted by and for women, and should necessarily be related to women's struggles against oppression and gender-based violence, as well as to the enhancement of women's well-being. However, there is a concern that universalizing analyses risk presenting women's oppression as the sole definition of womanhood. According to such a viewpoint, migrant women are generally deemed to lack power or agency. This is particularly the case with women who migrate from South to North, or who come from the 'patriarchal belt', an area that ranges from Asia and the Middle East to Africa (Caldwell 1982)—as do the participants in this book. Feminist refugee scholars, by contrast, have shifted the discourse from 'traumatised and needy women' to women who are also 'resilient and resourceful' (Loughry 2008: 167). My investigation is based on the premise that oppression should be seen as an extremely complex process but one in which women are not totally powerless; they often use their strength and inner resources to resist injustice and inequality.

I would argue that an examination of the nature of these women's lives in exile, how they constructed new identities in their new societies, and whether they have maintained or lost the continuity with their previous identities can help advance our understanding of adaptation. Such explorations can shed light on how achieving success in new and unfamiliar environments relates to its apparent antithesis, the 'myth of return', as well as to other factors such as the mobilization of solidarity.

During my fieldwork and data collection, I realized the importance of the feminist framework in which I chose to conduct this research, particularly the fact that it gave me the freedom to consider different methods with which to explore these women's stories. Exploring innovative methods is not of course specific to feminist researchers: in the field of migration studies, Abdelmalek Sayad (2004) in particular has made a foundational contribution to the study of Algerian migrants in France. His original approach 'builds upon an analytical core of remarkably rich and subtle ethnographic investigation, which supports a strong historical analysis, linguistic and anthropological inquiries and political theory' (Saada 2000). As the fieldwork progressed, however, I became increasingly aware of the need to deepen my understanding of my participants' experiences of trauma and to adapt my research accordingly, and I began to collect narratives of their journeys into exile. This risked reviving my own traumatic memories of the Black Decade and experience of the migration process, which could impact the data I gathered in both constructive and less constructive ways. For example, my personal identification with the participants in my research could potentially prevent me from questioning whether my own experiences would affect or misrepresent the conclusions I drew. I perceived how crucial it was to maintain a reflexive approach throughout the whole research process, and to be constantly aware of how my 'values, attitudes and perception influence the process of research, training, research questions, through the phase of data collection to how the data are analysed and explained theoretically' (Abbott and Wallace 1990: 27). Nevertheless, it was soon evident that the fact that I shared some of their experiences enhanced my ability to empathize with my interviewees. This proved to be rewarding: when they recognized that I had been in similar situations, it appeared to put them more at ease during the interviews. Indeed, my conversation with these women has never stopped; most of them have since become my friends. Not only have I continued to follow their activities on social media, but four years later, with the beginning of the Hirak, I revisited my original fieldwork by conducting further interviews with a number of these women.

When presenting the findings in this book, however, I have drawn most extensively on one case, that of 'Lamia' and her traumatic narrative of the Black Decade, due to its richness and ability to produce new insights; the other interviews serve as an auxiliary means of informing the research. At the end of my fieldwork, I began to consider all the participants' experiences as comprising a general testimony of women in exile, albeit with the particularity of having fled the organized violence and terrorism that affected Algeria during a specific period. However, I found Lamia's story particularly interesting, as it drew my attention to the complexity of views that can be encapsulated in one woman's experience of such horrific events.

The theoretical feminist framework of my research thus freed me from adopting the possibly irreconcilable position of 'neutral' observer, and enabled the research to take the course that it did, although I continued throughout to be aware of the potential hazards of such an approach. For those wishing to learn more about my place within the research project, I have included a summary in Appendix 1.

The research methodology

Sampling the network

To say that feminist researchers use specific methods to conduct research is incorrect: although feminist theorists initially criticized quantitative methods, particularly surveys and questionnaires, considering them to be 'masculinist', they later recognized the necessity to adapt whichever existing research tools would most benefit their investigation. If I was to reveal the existence of a network of Algerian highly skilled women migrants, my first challenge was to discover where exactly they had fled during and in the aftermath of the Black Decade. As there is no known methodology to study diaspora, I decided to experiment with Douglas Heckathorn's (1997, 2007) innovative research method, respondent-driven sampling (RDS), which he used to study a 'hard-to-reach' population when investigating the spread of HIV.

RDS is a method that combines 'egocentric' and 'snowball' sampling techniques based on referral from individuals to other people they are connected to (Heckathorn 1997, 2007). The first points of the network—in this case, myself and other persons I was well connected to—are called 'seeds', who then recruit 'nodes' to whom they are connected by 'ties', a relationship defined by specific criteria. As part of the initial network, I web-recruited six seeds through Facebook, blogs and other personal networks, who were living at the time in Algeria, France, Canada, the UK, Spain and the USA. The seeds were selected to reflect the geographical dispersal of Algerians during the 1990s. They went on to recruit nodes using a web-based process, sending a survey to at least one other person. This method helped me reach 188 participants dispersed throughout 18 different countries—France, Spain, Canada, the USA and the UK returned the highest numbers. It was at this point that my input as a feminist researcher was crucial, as the sampling process is usually driven by the assumption that surveys and questionnaires are tools with which to measure objective social facts through a supposedly detached and value-free form of data collection. To remedy this bias, I designed the survey based on a semi-structured questionnaire which provided the means for making extrapolations about the underlying network structure.

As the survey was essentially used to map and locate participants, and collect quantitative data, it was necessary to use an ethnographic method to find out more about their life experiences. The women who contacted me were asked if they were willing to be interviewed. I also created the Facebook group 'Algerian Women Diaspora', mentioned above, to serve as a platform for announcements about events organized by or related to Algerian women living abroad. The languages of the group were French and English, but Amazigh (formerly known as Berber), Derdja (an Algerian dialect) and Arabic were also used. This process helped me to spot online activists among the French- and English-speaking Algerian women, and in this way I was able to identify the fifteen women with whom I conducted in-depth interviews, face to face in the UK and France, and via Skype in the USA, Canada and Spain.

Collecting the data

All the interviews took the form of a conversation, as this was what the participants preferred, but my questions were always focused on the same three topics cited in the survey: the circumstances of leaving; identity reconstruction, including professional identity, in a new environment; and the desire to return to Algeria (and later on the level of their engagement in the Hirak). For the majority of interviewees, departure was a traumatic experience, and this—to a great extent—turned the interviews into narratives of trauma. Having said that, I felt at every stage of the interview that each participant was bringing me into her own experience, not only of terror and trauma but also of resilience and agency, to demonstrate that she also possessed the capacity to succeed in whichever field in which she chose to study or work.

During the course of my research, I was frequently asked by some of the participants, as well as by other friends and academics with whom I discussed my research, how I was able to ensure that these women had not embellished the accounts of their experiences in their new societies and exaggerated the discrimination, abuse and persecution they experienced back home. My answer was always 'No, I cannot establish the veracity of participants' individual stories, but neither do I need to, because it is not the purpose of the research to establish exactly what happened, but rather to explore how women perceive and articulate their experiences of violence, trauma, exile and diasporic consciousness.' The need for this argument confirms Inger Agger's (1994: 5) suggestion that there is a general mistrust of victims' stories; it is this mistrust which is exploited by dictatorships when they deny the abuse of human rights. In terms of the Algerian tragedy of the 1990s, it appears that uncovering the truth in order to give the victims justice is not part of the government's political agenda, and it continues to be a divisive subject among Algerians abroad and in Algeria itself. As far as this research is concerned, it is the way they articulated and interpreted their experiences of violence, exile and identity reconstruction that allowed me to conclude whether or not this particular group of women had developed a diasporic consciousness.

Laura Ellingson (1998) emphasizes the connections that can be established during the interview process between participant and researcher, especially when they share similar experiences. These connections were evident in my research when participants used phrases such as 'you know that, do you?', 'as you know' and frequently, 'I had to return to study for identical reasons to yours'. I had to invest time in building relationships before undertaking the interviews, which I held sometimes only after several contacts, usually via chat rooms on Facebook or by Skype. This process proved helpful in building confidence between us.

Conducting the fieldwork

Since the purpose of the research was to investigate the extent of solidarity between a particular group of Algerian women migrants who were geographically scattered, I made three trips to France between February 2013 and March 2014, two trips to Algeria in 2019, and another two to France between 2019 and 2020. The first two trips to France were to meet participants who agreed to be interviewed and the third was to present a paper at a conference in Paris. The later trips to Algeria in 2019 and France between 2019 and 2020 were to attend protests of the Hirak in Algiers, Oran and Paris. Knowing that I had a very limited research budget, some women offered to accommodate me. For ethical reasons, I only accepted to be hosted by women I was not going to interview.

When writing this book, I have also included my own thoughts and experiences to complement those of my fellow participants. Due to the fact that I shared this facet of my own identity with the participants, it is relevant to examine here the impact that I may have had on the research during the interview process—and that the research had on me. Initially, I felt that I was ideally placed as an 'insider' to explore the lives of my respondents, particularly those who have had similar experiences to mine. The women I interviewed recounted their stories openly and often emotionally, revealing painful episodes of their experience of political unrest and social oppression, illustrating in the process the collective trauma experienced in Algeria during the Black Decade. Added to this, the decision to leave the country was frequently a painful one. Prior to each interview, I anticipated the sort of responses I would receive, causing me to fear that I would feel a corresponding emotion: sometimes in fact I was directly asked whether I had experienced similar abuse or violence. To answer honestly meant that I had to disclose personal information with no guarantee of confidentiality; nevertheless, I took the decision to do so, as it was important for my research that I engaged with my interviewees in a responsive and reciprocal way (Ramazanoglu 1992).

Answering questions was a key part of the interview process, as the interviews were in most cases conducted in a conversational style. Adrienne Chambon (2008) suggests that this is more likely to encourage women to disclose information related to their experiences. However, there was a risk attached to this: I was aware that if participants did not clarify their thoughts, it was usually because they assumed that I would already be aware of the issue. I also made it clear to each participant that they could pass over any question that made them feel uncomfortable. The shortest interview lasted only thirty minutes and the longest took nearly three hours; however, these were exceptions, and the others took around an hour each. On two occasions, women preferred the interviews to be conducted via email. There were also cases where I had to interrupt the interview and return to it the following day or a few days later. One of these respondents, who lived in a small city in Spain, was the mother of four young children, and such breaks were necessary if the interview was to be conducted at all. Another interviewee told me after I had met her that she felt her story was too traumatic and preferred to write it down rather than speak face to face or via Skype.

Transcribing the interviews

The majority of the interviews were conducted in French, Derdja or English. Because of the sensitivity of some issues, I tried wherever possible to produce a faithful and authentic translation of the responses in French and Derdja, although I retained certain words and metaphors in Derdja in my transcriptions. During this process, I would make a draft transcript a few hours after the interview in order to keep the reflections and emotions as fresh as possible, the better to inform my research. The few times there was an exception to this rule, and my schedule was unavoidably delayed, I ensured I wrote all my first impressions and feelings in a journal I always kept with me immediately after I finished the interview.

The interviews were dialogically constructed in an open-ended process. In analysing the narratives, I was interested by both the told and untold stories, and tried to give meaning to both. Consequently, I deliberately added the non-verbal forms of communication that occurred during the interviews in my transcriptions. Non-verbal communication is often associated with gender and culture, as women are generally more non-verbally expressive than men, particularly in the Mediterranean and North African cultures from which the participants came. In fact, it has been recognized that women tend to have an overall superiority as users and decoders of non-verbal communication in many different cultures (Knapp and Hall 1992). Highly skilled individuals, such as the participants in this study, possess a rich vocabulary and the ability to articulate their experiences fluently; nevertheless, their subtle and spontaneous use of non-verbal communication provided crucial auxiliary information concerning their true feelings and underlying messages.

I also included quotations from the survey in the data analysis whenever I felt it was relevant to confirm or clarify an argument in this way. Participants often added long explanations to their answers, particularly in relation to issues around the lack of recognition of Algerian qualifications, the barriers they faced when seeking access to jobs, their feelings of solidarity or otherwise with other Algerians in their receiving countries, and the barriers they perceived to returning to Algeria. Unlike the citations from the interviews, I have not given names to those who partook in the online survey in order to respect its anonymous approach. However, I detail the characteristics of all of the participants in my research in Appendix 2.

In all, the research framework and methodology I chose allowed me not only to explore these women's experiences, but also to ascertain whether the networks they formed could be considered a potential women's diaspora.

First, however, I had to explore the contested nature of the concept of diaspora itself.

Defining diaspora(s) and diasporic consciousness

Rainer Bauböck (2007) has pointed to the way in which the appearance in different societies of migrants of varying status has made a decisive contribution to what he describes as the emergence of 'inter-state societies'. Cohen (1997: 162) has developed similar arguments, which present the new pattern of migration as 'challenging and transcending the limits of the nation state'. The emergence of 'transnational populations', endowed with multiple commitments to various places but not totally disconnected from their homelands, attracted much academic and policy interest during the last quarter of the twentieth century, focusing on the development of what is called a 'diasporic consciousness' (Van Hear 1998: 4). More recently, Peggy Levitt and Nadya Jaworsky (2007) have tracked changes in the scholarly study of migration which ultimately show that contemporary migrants, supported by new technologies and social networking websites, always maintain some kind of relationship with their country of birth. As a result, new kinds of migrants are appearing, comprising those whose networks, activities and patterns of life encompass both their new societies and countries of origin. Arguably, the Hirak movement is the ultimate example of this. Of the many Algerian women involved in maintaining the flame of the Hirak abroad—for example, organizing online meetings—I would say that the majority belong to those who left the country following the traumatic events of the Black Decade.

According to Cohen (2012), the development of a diasporic consciousness amongst a group of migrants or a minority group always reflects a certain degree of unease with living in the receiving country. In identifying with a diaspora, displaced people are in fact trying to reconstruct and revalorize their notion of an 'imagined homeland'. Diasporic consciousness, Cohen (2012) argues, is not only about recovering an historical memory, but is also concerned with building social networks that lead to the creation of political organizations for which this imaginary homeland remains a continuing pole of attraction and identification. However, Cohen (2008: 1–16) also speaks of 'creolization', a term he uses to analyse the emerging characteristics of people's identity in this global era, encompassing such ideas as 'cultural complexity', 'cosmopolitanism' and 'hybridity'. Creolization, Cohen says, is a notion of the 'here and now', a feeling that lessens old attachments to particular places and roots in an attempt to create a new locus of identity.

As William Safran (1999) points out, it appears that the term 'diaspora' now describes vast categories of dispersed populations who either have chosen to identify themselves as such or have had the label imposed on them. As well as the high number of people belonging to this new group, with their varied historical experiences and collective narratives, and their different relationships with their receiving societies and countries of origin, they are also defined by the different characteristics of their diasporas, unlike the groups designated in diaspora studies' classical phase. Cohen (2010), however, puts forward seven criteria or attributes that identify a group as a diaspora: the action of dispersal and scattering; the collective trauma behind the scattering; the group's cultural flowering within a new environment; the difficulty of integration in this environment; the feeling of belonging to a particular community; the transcendence of national borders; and, finally, the cultivation of the idea of return.

If engaging in transnational practices has been encouraged by globalization, it has also been greatly facilitated by the rise of diverse and accessible communication technologies. Anastasia Christou (2006) points out, however, that real and virtual networks between displaced people become stronger and easier to navigate only if they enable the reinforcement of their identification as sharing a common fate as an 'exiled population'. Subject to permanent questioning, these identifications are part of a process of identity construction focused on what and where 'home' is, a concept that is often considered by scholars of diaspora as describing an imaginary place. As such, the feeling of belonging to a particular place or community is continuously negotiated in the diaspora. On the one hand, Ninna Nyberg Sørensen (2007) suggests that the studies of transnationalism and diaspora can be distinguished from one another by the presence or absence of a relationship to a particular place: not all those who engage in transnational practices, moving between different places, are necessarily diasporic; they may simply be operating as networks of people with a limited feeling of belonging to any particular place. On the other hand, although this separation between transnational practices and diaspora seems defensible, diasporas cannot be totally separated from transnationalism since diasporic engagement in transnational practices has become one of the essential characteristics of a diaspora, and is especially encouraged by the increasing use of online social networking—an area that this book investigates. The so-called Arab Spring and later the Hirak movement in Algeria have provided powerful evidence for this argument.

Nevertheless, it is true that transnational social networking practices cannot necessarily be identified as diasporic; the people engaged in these practices do not automatically develop a diasporic consciousness. Some of these groups operate as networks of migrants who do not place any importance on committing themselves to projects in their home countries, and even less to specifically building relationships with other migrants from their countries of origin. According to Nyberg Sørensen (2007: 7), while transnational practices are supposed to dissolve permanent ideas about identity, place and community, diasporic identity is assumed to be constructed around attempts to 'fix' or 'knit' the sense of identity and community with a particular place, albeit imaginary. It is this process that differentiates diverse displaced groups from one another, allowing only a certain number of them to be elevated to the rank of diaspora (Bakewell 2008). This research similarly distinguishes between transnational migration and diaspora by placing emphasis on the use of the term diaspora as carrying a political sense. However, although the memory of a dispersed people is often based on the same event that caused their displacement, this can later become a source of confrontation and argument rather than a unifying factor. I will explain later how, in the case of Algeria, the cancellation of the electoral process which triggered the tragedy of the Black Decade was seen by one side in the political argument as a military coup and by the other as the army's defence of republican values against radical Islam. These arguments have continued among Algerians abroad. Recently, despite multiple reminders from well-known figures in the movement of the necessity for a united Hirak, denuded of all the opposing political ideologies and resentments of the Black Decade, a confrontation between these two sides still arose in the diaspora, most vociferously in the Place de la République in Paris, where demonstrations in support of the Hirak took place on a weekly basis.

Hence, as Cohen (2012) asserts, the idea of diaspora is provocative: not only does it denote a common trauma, but it also raises the question of who was responsible for that trauma. The sense of 'belonging' to a diaspora is negotiated within this process of identification, whether at a local, trans-local or virtual level, transcending physical borders (Davies 2007), but these negotiations overlap, rival and oppose each other. Thus, the term diaspora is more than a description of a social condition; it also refers to socially constructed political struggles. This definition of the concept best reflects the experience of the selected set of highly skilled and activist Algerian women migrants represented in this book, based on the assumption that these women are strongly connected to Algeria, expressing a continuing interest in political developments in Algeria and a commitment to combatting the abuse of women's rights in the country.

Other groups of migrants may have had less traumatic experiences than those associated with the traditional 'victim diasporas', or their connection with their country of origin may be less significant. Safran (1999), nevertheless, suggests that the continued commitment towards a restitution of 'home' usually occurs as a result of the violence or oppression that forced the displacements of a particular group. Safran's account has the merit of offering a wide definition of diaspora, expanding it to include other minority communities. He believes that the diasporic narrative, usually grounded in an 'imaginary homeland', for which the Jewish diaspora has been the core paradigmatic example, should be extended to describe the experiences of other dispersed populations that retain a continued attachment to a relatively more realistic, existing homeland. The imaginary, desired homeland is not the only common characteristic on which diasporas are based, although, according to Cohen (2010) and Clifford (1994), the retention of a collective memory of home, the idealization of this homeland and an ongoing commitment towards its restitution continue to be among the main factors that characterize diasporas as such.

Thus, although there appears to be a consensus that diaspora cannot be simply a synonym for migration, the exact meaning of the term itself continues to 'provoke and intrigue' (Tölölyan 2011). While taking these debates into account, it is necessary to clarify the basic characteristics of diaspora when using the term, otherwise it risks losing its coherence as a conceptual category. For this reason, I use three of Cohen's (2010) fundamental markers of a diasporic community, as outlined above (collective trauma as the main motivation for migration; difficulties integrating into the receiving society; and the cultivation of a 'myth of return' to an often idealized homeland, which assumes a political character), as the starting point from which to address one of the fundamental questions of this book: to what extent can those highly skilled and educated Algerian women who were uprooted and dispersed following the traumatic events of the 1990s be called a diaspora? The question, however, will be explored using a feminist lens. This specific focus entails an engagement with the social constructionist theories of diaspora.

Beyond ethnicity: The social constructionist definition of diaspora

According to Anthias (1998), it was Stuart Hall who helped open the concept of diaspora to other groups, forging the path followed by the constructionist critics of classical theories of diaspora, and allowing the addition of class and gender as essential features. Anthias claims that Paul Gilroy's *The Black Atlantic* (1993) represented another turning point in the development of the theoretical arguments highlighting the importance of diaspora as a social condition. Gilroy charted the establishment of a diasporic consciousness among migrants in multicultural and multi-ethnic societies, and paved the way for other writers on transnational migration, displacement and resettlement to consider diaspora as a heuristic device to better understand the relationship of migrants to others, to their receiving societies and to their homeland (Anthias 1998).

Social constructionists aim to deconstruct two of the major factors delimiting and demarcating the notion of diasporas: the first is the nature of the relationship of displaced people with their homeland and the second is the ethnic/religious bonds that link dispersed communities to each other. The social constructionist view is grounded in the fact that identities have become deterritorialized, deconstructed, reconstructed and more flexible in response to displaced people's social situations (Hall 1990; Anthias 1998). Social constructionist theorists attempt to respond to this complexity. Even though earlier scholars of diaspora now agree to some extent with these critics, they initially expressed the fear that this approach would empty the concept of meaning and, more importantly, of its analytical power (Cohen 2008). Cohen (2010), however, later reconsidered the question, claiming the beginning of a phase of unification for a study of diaspora that encompassed the social constructionist critiques.

As we have seen, the increasing complexity of the idea of 'belonging' created by the deterritorialization of identity is an important phenomenon in the composition of diasporas, particularly for those groups who have been repeatedly displaced. Nevertheless, there is a broad consensus that ideas of home and a commitment to a homeland are powerful discourses when defining diasporas in general. Thus, the phase of consolidation in diaspora studies, as Cohen (2008) explains, has been marked by an adapted reaffirmation or reconsideration of the diasporic idea, one that includes both classical elements and other common features that best describe the experiences of contemporary migrants. According to Hall's (1990) argument, the concept of diaspora involves a new conception of identity that seeks to go beyond the essentialist debate on ethnic/racial and cultural identities. Diaspora studies have now refocused their attention on transnationalism as a dynamic process relating to ethnic commonalities, while at the same time recognizing differences and diversity such as gender and social class (Anthias 1998).

Through looking at the experience of a selected group of Algerian women in this book, I interrogate the proposition that 'diasporic experiences are always gendered' (Clifford 1994: 313). Avtar Brah (1996), Floya Anthias (1998) and Yasemin Nuhoglu Soysal (2000) claim that the etymology of the word 'diaspora' refers to the migrant's social condition, which is constructed from multifaceted identities informed by both their past and current circumstances, as well as their future hopes. I know from my own experience that migration is a non-linear journey, but one that is always marked by resistance to the process of forgetting the homeland when negotiating a sense of belonging to a new society. Brah suggests that home can be both the place we come from and the place we settle:

> Where is home? On the one hand, home is a mythic place of desire in the diasporic imagination. In this sense, it is a place of no return, even if it is possible to visit the geographical territory that is seen as the place of origin. On the other hand, home is also the lived experience of a locality. Its sounds and smells, its heat and dust … all this, as mediated by the historically specific everyday of social relations. (Brah 1996: 192)

Brah (1996: 180) therefore strives to disconnect the idea of diaspora from the obsession with its necessary relationship with a physical homeland, suggesting a difference between a 'desire for home' and a 'homing desire'. For her, if home is seen as a place of origin, it can also be interpreted as being a transnational and sometimes even fictional space. People are also increasingly beginning to identify themselves with members of other groups who have been through similar experiences: for example, professional networks; gay, lesbian and transgender networks; and even virtual networks, constructed via the internet.

The work of Anthias perhaps delivers the most powerful social constructionist critique of the classical view of diaspora, revealing its obvious neglect of internal identity divisions among ethnic groups. In her article, 'Evaluating Diaspora' (1998), she draws attention to the fact that the classical discourse is gender-blind, and asserts that this failure to recognize gender and other diverse identities within diasporas seriously hinders the concept's potential as a device that enables a fuller understanding of the complexity of migrants' experiences. The issue of gender is particularly important, given the increasing amount of research that illustrates the ways in which it shapes the experience of migration and displacement. According to Anthias (2001), adaptation to new and sometimes hostile environments involves the invention of new identities that must constantly be recreated or reinvented. As we shall see later in this book, in the case of Algerian female migrants—whose lives have often been difficult, if not traumatic, even before the process of migration—the reconstruction of new identities involves a process of constant negotiation between vulnerability and resilience, which also relates to their experience of the migration process itself, particularly if it was unexpected or if its circumstances were dangerous or difficult. Female migrants' experiences in general, particularly if the migration is forced, are constantly being shifted from one stage to another, forever in limbo. This accords with my findings: according to the testimony of the respondents to my survey, not to mention my own personal experience, it appears that migrant women are engaged in a process of constantly building, negotiating and reinventing identities from multiple sources and out of multiple resources, and this often leaves them with an almost schizophrenic feeling of ambivalence. There is, however, a need to also recognize migrant women's resilience, agency and ability to cope with change; the extent to which their gender helps in asserting agency is one of the subjects I investigate. Overall, as Anthias (2001) stresses, it is important to recognize the significance of the gender-specific impact of the migration process on women.

Meanwhile, the focal point of Soysal's (2000) critique of the earlier concepts of diaspora is the fact that the experience of migration is a dynamic process rather than a vector between receiving and home countries, or simply a melancholy desire for home. Such ideas fail to recognize the multi-connections migrants have within their new environment or their aspirations to fully practise their new citizenship. This affirms Rina Benmayor and Andor Stoknes's (1994) argument that migration is not a linear but a dynamic process that responds to the individual's aspirations. However, while taking this into account, my main argument in this book is that, in the case of the women under investigation, their access to citizenship and citizenship rights is based to a significant extent on the politics of gender in both their countries of origin and their new communities.

The way migration has been politicized in the West during the last two decades has resulted in the increased presence of a stereotypical representation of the 'other', and this representation highlights a crisis in national identity, particularly in some European countries, that questions the principles of citizenship. In light of this, the feminist literature on nationalism, nation and gender is crucial to understanding the role of gender in the formation of the notion of citizenship, nationalities and nations, not only in the West but also in the countries of migration. This was most clearly evident during the immediate post-colonial era (Yuval-Davis and Anthias 1989; Moghadam 1994), and has particular significance for the Algerian background to my research. I would argue that it has also been evident among the Algerian diaspora during the recent Hirak, as seen in Chapter Five.

It is undeniable that newly independent countries often limit their principles of autonomy and freedom to the public sphere—a space in which women, as protectors of the private sphere, are not permitted (Moghadam 1994). It could also be argued that codes of conduct controlling and dominating women in different societies are universally grounded on patriarchal institutions that define the politics of gender, even though these may differ from one society to another (Yuval-Davis 1997; Guemar 2011). Yet this policing of women is also seen in many contemporary political movements and in many sociological theories, in which women tend to be allocated the role of the bearers of a 'collective identity' (Yuval-Davis and Anthias 1989; Moghadam 1994). Theoretically, as well as symbolically and physically, women are all too often still required to carry the burden of representation of cultural and religious values, and the traditions and symbols of their communities. Yuval-Davis (1997) has extended this view to explain that nations are undeniably considered as expansions of communities and families. She claims that women's main role in society was, and in some cases still is, considered in many nationalist discourses to be that of carrying out the tasks of reproduction, both of the nation's citizens and of its ideology, and argues that these theories justified the exclusion of women from the public and political arena, confining them to the private sphere. However, the politics of gender, in the context of both colonialism and post-colonialism, is constantly wavering between the dichotomy of private–public space, as in the case of Algerian, Iranian and Afghani women. Valentine Moghadam (1994), for example, relates gender to other identity struggles, arguing that it modifies and mediates religion, class, ethnicity and race.

In the context of diaspora, this feminist argument joins other social constructionist critiques which argue that the concept should avoid the essentialism of the traditional discourses based only on ethnic and cultural identities. Clifford (1994) investigates women's experiences of diaspora by questioning whether or not they reinforce or conceal gender subordination as dictated by patriarchal rules. On the one hand, female migrants often strive to maintain connections with their religious and cultural traditions, which tend to reproduce patriarchal structures; on the other hand, new roles and opportunities in the receiving countries' public spaces are potentially opened up to the diasporas.

Assia Djebar (2002) recounts that, under the French occupation, Algerian women created networks of solidarity despite their differences. They had to fight two enemies, the colonizer and the indigenous patriarchy, creating in the process two distinct strategies of resistance and solidarity. Later, during the Black Decade, women were faced not only with patriarchal rules but also with radical political Islam, an even more extreme form of patriarchy (Lalami 2012). The highly skilled Algerian women who were forced into exile during this period consequently developed a sense of self-awareness that later, as seen during the Hirak, enabled some of them to create efficient networks to help overcome their divisions and ease the pain of exile. In this book, I seek to verify the feminist and social constructionist arguments by exploring the networks and experiences of these women, in terms of both their social class and gender.

Dialogism: A feminist approach to women's reconstruction of identity

One unavoidable issue that became central to my investigation is the question of how women migrants reinvent their identities in the effort to adapt to their new environment. If there is a desire among women to integrate into the new, albeit sometimes hostile, societies in which they find themselves, and to create a new sense of 'home', it is often mediated by a resistance to the process of forgetting their country of origin. Adaptation is not accomplished without experiencing an ongoing duality between the individual's self-perception and others' perceptions of this self. I have chosen to explore this question of identity through a Bakhtinian dialogical approach (Pearce 1994; Hajdukowski-Ahmed 2008).

The term 'dialogism' is used to denote that every instance of discourse is defined by its relationship to other instances—to a past to which it responds and a future which it anticipates; it is a constant process that engages with and remains informed by other voices, seeking to either alter or inform them. Dialogical statements are always involved in an intense relationship with the other's words; they are always addressed to a listener and anticipate a response, aware of the other's consciousness. Dialogism therefore is not simply a description of different perspectives on the same world but involves the sharing of completely opposite views and perspectives, affirming plurality and diversity. Hajdukowski-Ahmed (2008) cites Mikhail Bakhtin's statement that there are always varied standpoints from which to see and respond to the external world. Hence, Bakhtinians view identity construction as a dialogical process: it cannot be unified in a particular view of the world but is formed through language in the course of social interaction.

Although Bakhtin did not specifically address gender, Bakhtinian feminists have used his approach to define gender identity as socially fashioned through language by means of a dialogical process. This theory is in broad agreement with those of black, post-colonial and Latina feminists, as well as scholars in refugee studies, who seek to promote an understanding of the importance of agency when working with women from diverse backgrounds (e.g. Mohanty 2003; Forbes Martin 2003; Hajdukowski-Ahmed 2008). In this regard, the Bakhtinian feminist approach enables a better understanding of both the specificity and complexity of the identity transformations women experience as a result of forced migration and relocation. Most importantly for this study, it has enabled researchers to identify and validate 'the power of agency', so that even when women have suffered torture or abuse, the dialogical approach helps reveal moments of resistance (Hajdukowski-Ahmed 2008: 53).

Dialogism, which views the process of identity construction as continual and relational, involving questioning, reacting and repositioning oneself, seems to be particularly suitable for understanding the experiences of those highly skilled Algerian women who fled the country during the traumatic Black Decade. It helps to reveal the process of identity fragmentation and reformulation that occurs during the journey into exile—that is, losing an identity and gaining a new one, or what has been termed the 'de-selving' and 're-selving' of exiled women (see below for a fuller explanation of these terms) (Hajdukowski-Ahmed 2008: 38). It also shows how a displaced group of people creates continuity out of chosen common identity markers, leading them to create networks of solidarity and to mobilize a diaspora. The psychosocial scholar Renos Papadopoulos (2005) explains that the negative reactions identified with trauma are not the sole emotional response of people who experience oppression, violence and forced migration. As this book suggests, participants react differently to different stages of their journey, varying from the most negative and vulnerable responses to the most positive and resilient. Perhaps the most interesting and most recent part of the journey of the Algerian women whose experiences are the foundation of this book has been their involvement with the Hirak, not only as a protest movement but also as a diasporic space, and its effect on their relationships with each other, with their home country and with women's conditions there.

Papadopoulos investigates the etymology of the word 'trauma' and explains that '*titrosko*', the original Greek word, comes from the verb '*teiro*' ('to rub'). He argues that the different meanings of '*teiro*' in Greek—'to rub in', 'rub off' or 'rub away'—have dialectical implications. Depending on their personal characteristics and their environment, a wounded person could have two opposite dialogical responses to their experience—either a negative one, 'rubbing in' the wound, or a positive one, 'rubbing off' or 'rubbing away' the experience, which disposes people to positively recover from their injury (Papadopoulos 2006: 26). The positive reactions and resilience of the women who participated in my research demonstrated an aptitude for healing. My study in fact suggests that the meaning that people give to the suffering they experience as a result of political oppression, violence and exile depends on diverse factors that can best be addressed if their gender and cultural background, as well as the context in which they now live, are taken into consideration. Frantz Fanon's (1986) work on Algerian women's participation in the struggle to free the country from French colonial rule, for example, led him to conclude that women confronted by war, conflict or exile almost inevitably transfer the inner strength they develop through their struggles in the private sphere to the public sphere. It appears that the Hirak was an opportunity for Algerian women, both in Algeria and in the diaspora, to revive their reputation (built during the War of Independence) of courage, determination and resilience. It offered a physical and moral space which allowed Algerian women coming from various viewpoints to celebrate—for a time—a united identity, as well as to recall the historical importance of their presence in the fight for a free and democratic Algeria.

However, the experience of forced migration and the loss of homeland often leads to the loss of a locus of identity that can enhance a person's sense of their own value as shaped by their direct environment (Papadopoulos 2006). In the particular case of Algerians exiled following the rise of radical Islam and the terror of the 1990s, positive external valuation was lacking from within the community itself, which was divided around the question of who killed whom and who did what during the conflict, as well as from the countries to which they fled, where newcomers from Algeria were frequently regarded with distrust and associated with terrorism. Dialogism explains how such women may have constructed a new idea of home, one that is idealized or imagined, in a dialogical process in which the ideal replaces the real and the abstract replaces the concrete.

In the case of Algerian women, and perhaps more generally for many other women forced into exile, their new societies' attitude to gender differ greatly from their countries of origin. To give an example, the highly skilled Algerian women who moved to countries in which the idea of gender equality is mainstream sometimes found they had to renegotiate power relationships within their marriages in a way that was not necessarily in their husband's favour. During her ethnographic research with professional and activist

Algerian women who left during the Black Decade for France and Canada, Myriam Hachimi Alaoui (2010) found that loss of social status, due to the barriers to rebuilding professional careers, led to the destabilization of the respective married roles they had negotiated in Algeria. In some cases, these new conditions, as well as the open discourse on gender equality in the receiving country, gave women the opportunity to see their spouses from alternative perspectives. Husbands who may have appeared open-minded and supportive of their wives' political activism and professional careers 'back home' can lose these qualities in exile. Indeed, the growth of women's inner strengths in order to successfully adjust to their new environment does not always favour the previous patriarchal pattern. If, in the country of origin, it is socially and customarily agreed that women can occupy public space, this will usually be limited by 'safeguards' and laws to prevent them from gaining 'too much' freedom. Once these social safeguards are no longer available, men can feel deprived and powerless, and may attempt to take back control over their wives and daughters. Alaoui (2010) remarks on the high number of divorces among the women she interviewed. This particular example shows that women have to constantly adjust to new kinds of familial relationships as a consequence of the new economic and community roles they inhabit during the process of adaptation to a new environment, implying that identity breakdown and reformation does not progress in a linear way but remains open to diversity and a multiplicity of roles, as well as to context and negotiation.

Dialogism helps us understand that identity transformation for women who have been separated from home, kinship and other identity markers does not only provoke trauma and a loss of self but also the negotiation of new forms of self. It is important to underline the need to understand every woman's experience(s) and how these affect their aptitude to develop agency and survival mechanisms. Cohen (2012) explains that even when people are able to organize their journey and predict what they might find in their new environment, it often turns into an unknown and uncertain situation that calls for painful readjustment, and this inevitably involves a process of 'de-selving' and attempts at 're-selving'.

Based on the work of Papadopoulos (2006) cited above, I would argue that in situations of conflict and war, the loss of a sense of home remains the main reason for trauma among people who are obliged to flee, whether they seek asylum (international protection under the 1951 Refugee Convention) or take other routes. Here 'home' becomes the metaphor that not only describes a physical space but also represents the continuity of the individual's relationship with the outside world. In this sense, it has physical, social, cultural, historical, linguistic, psychological and religious meanings (Papadopoulos 2006). It is also the root of family life, with all its positive and negative memories. The particular circumstances of the journey and arrival make professional women realize that they have also lost their social status, along with their personal belongings, their immediate and/or extended family, and their language. The guilt of having left behind family members in danger and a homeland in flames further contributes to the trauma. For this reason, many exiled women from the Black Decade, at least many of those who participated in this study, feel the need to continue to campaign for women's rights in Algeria and to help their compatriots build a just and democratic nation, regardless of gender. When, nearly two decades later, in 2019, an ailing president tried to run for a fifth term in order to perpetuate the status quo, these women felt as humiliated as did their sisters still living in Algeria.

'De-selving' and 're-selving'

When uprooted from their original homes, displaced people lose a part of their original selves. However, when combined with the position of vulnerability during the migration process, due to their gender, not to mention the gender-related violence and harsh patriarchal rules many have previously been subject to in certain societies, women's experience of migration is often far removed from that of their male counterparts. The psychological impact of a woman's experience is so intense that it could be seen as a process of 'de-selving'.

According to Hajdukowski-Ahmed (2008: 37), the key point is that de-selving 'does not mean the loss of identity and culture, but rather the gradual erosion of agency'. The implications are psychological, social, economic and political. Not only does it mean that a woman must reinvent herself and learn to inhabit an identity as the 'other' in a new society, but the psychological trauma that she encountered when she left her wider family and community can cause her to lose her sense of herself—she is de-selved. It appears, then, that the de-selving process actually begins when a woman is oppressed or abused, and continues when she flees the country; indeed, it continues up to the point when she is given the right to fully participate in normal day-to-day life in her new environment. However, many migrant women are denied administrative status in the receiving country, making the de-selving process even more complex. The whole process requires a continuing response to change, demanding ever more energy and internal resources to deal with intense dialogical experiences, which can also involve violent and racist forms of labelling. In fact, Pamela Sugiman (2008) believes that many migrant women arrive with little awareness of racism and do not consider themselves as 'racialized' beings. Hence, the discrimination and racism women often face in their new countries can have a traumatic effect.

In terms of this book, the testimonies of individuals about their experiences of the process of de-selving and re-selving constitute a vital narrative resource for my research into the impact of the Algerian Black Decade on those highly skilled women who fled the country and now live abroad. For this purpose, a diaspora seems to be the most appropriate space in which such narratives can be shared, a space that allows the ventilation of resentments in order to find the ability to forgive and to heal. This again involves a dialogical process. For many of us, taking part in the Hirak from abroad gave us the opportunity to highlight the need for the creation of such a space, one in which the identity, selfhood and agency of Algerian women who have been forced to migrate can be constantly reshaped and renegotiated—driven as it is by the need to face the challenges that arise from the experience of dislocation, including the need to develop social ties in a new environment as well as back home.

Exiled women often develop their own discourses, rejecting the identities that are forced on them in the receiving country by generating their own 're-selving narratives'. According to Hajdukowski-Ahmed (2008: 49), as part of this process, they face a continuous dialogical struggle between victimization and resistance, between being a helpless victim and an empowered survivor, between the 'here' of their present and the 'there' of their past, between what they say and what they are silent about, and between perceiving a situation as a challenge or as an opportunity. Once granted immigration status or citizenship and given the chance to gain or resume their professional careers, women can regain some kind of agency, on condition that they are able to avoid what Hajdukowski-Ahmed (2008: 39) terms 'pseudo-re-selving', which may arise when they attempt to rebuild their new identity under extremely 'asymmetrical power relationships' within their new society. There is little doubt that the Algerian women in this research aspired to free themselves from the old patriarchal rules as soon as they became more aware of their new society's commonly accepted values of gender equality and freedom. Some women I met during the course of this study seized the opportunities offered them in order to affirm themselves, whether as professional women or as political activists, or simply as 'themselves'.

In his famous work *The Suffering of the Immigrant*, Abdelmalek Sayad (2004) points to the fact that it is important to research the historical conditions of being an emigrant from Algeria, and being viewed as an immigrant in France, to better understand the sadness attached to what is known in Algeria as '*elghorba*'. This term derives from '*ghrib*' (the Arabic word for 'alien') and is the most common Algerian term used to describe migration and exile. Sayad's work, originally titled *The Double Absence*, has been considered so important that it is now applied to an understanding of the social conditions of migrants in general. Drawing from this work, Emmanuelle Saada (2000) points out that the success of what is called the process of re-selving and the creation of a new home in which women feel settled always depends on the immigration and citizenship policies of the receiving countries, which are invariably gendered. Thus, there is far more research into and evidence of the de-selving impact of being a migrant woman than the process of re-selving, particularly as many migrant women find themselves in a liminal state when they lack the legal status that would allow them to exercise citizenship rights. This equally inhibits professional, highly skilled women from starting a new academic or professional life, and can in turn undermine the sense of agency of even the most determined and resilient.

In his *Reflections on Exile*, Edward Said notes that exile is an 'unhealable rift between a human being and a native place, between the self and its true home' (2000: 173). Explaining this statement, John Barbour (2011: 736) believes that being in exile is equal to constantly being reminded that you are not where you are supposed to be, and that this experience pertains to 'a present condition of absence from one's native land'. Although the Hirak came at a time when all the women who participated in my research had attained citizenship of the countries in which they lived, and the majority were settled in their new careers, their desire to participate in the protest is evidence that an element of truth in both Saada's and Said's observations continues to resonate with them.

Conclusion: Diaspora as a social condition and a state of mind

It appears that the Hirak was able to, as Hajdukowski-Ahmed (2008: 41) puts it, 'open up a space for developing agency' from which 'transforming opportunities [can] emerge'. As the Hirak was ongoing at the time of writing, it would be difficult at this point to see the decision to take part in it as evidence of a re-selving process, although it could be argued that it offered a platform for re-selving. However, as mentioned above, evidence of the re-selving of exiled Algerian women is limited due to the lack of research, particularly in relation to the specific group of women who are the subject of this book. Such research is dependent on an understanding of diaspora not only as a social condition but also as a state of mind. I believe that this can be accomplished by using the concept of diaspora as an analytical tool, but on condition that it is used to enable a fuller understanding of the complexity of these migrants' experiences. This complexity is also related to the specifics—historical, social and political—of the situation in which they found themselves in Algeria and which precipitated their flight. I investigate this more fully in the following chapter.

2 The Political Background to the Feminization of Algerian Migration

Introduction: The seeds of conflict

This chapter addresses the historical conditions in which Algeria's Black Decade occurred. I explain how the post-colonial regime of the FLN (National Liberation Front) imposed the doctrine of 'one land, one language and one religion' on the country, ignoring the legitimacy of the diverse national movements that had contributed to the liberation of the country from French colonial rule. However, in the 1990s, the fall of the Soviet Union and the discrediting of Soviet communism had significant implications for the FLN, both politically and economically. This was particularly the case as it took place around the same time as the collapse in the price of oil, which had a severe impact on Algeria as a major oil producer (Evans and Phillips 2007). The oil crisis fed into the concurrent global downturn, which exposed the corruption and bad governance of many one-party states, including Algeria. The IMF, World Bank and WTO shifted their focus from economic failure to failures of governance, and imposed the introduction of democracy alongside the liberalization of capital markets as a condition for financial aid (Jordan and Duvell 2003: 32).

The first part of this chapter addresses the question of how these factors helped the emergence of the FIS (Islamic Salvation Front), a political party with a radical Islamist ideology. It first offers a definition of what is commonly understood by the concept of democracy, and its relationship to the lack of development and political participation that women experience in a predominantly patriarchal society, and goes on to describe what provoked the tragedy of the Black Decade following the victory of the FIS in the first democratic elections to be held since liberation. It gives a brief illustration of how the Islamist movement evolved to become the main pole of resistance against colonialism, and how it later became radicalized due to the imposition on Algeria of market reforms coupled with liberal democracy. This was the situation in the country after the cancellation of the electoral process in 1992, almost two decades before the advent of the Arab Spring in Tunisia and Egypt in 2011. The chapter's second section explains the impact of these events on the lives of Algerian women, and how—and to what extent—they influenced the decisions of many highly skilled professional women and female intellectuals to leave the country.

Democracy and women's rights in Algeria

This section takes a brief look at the meanings given to the terms 'democracy' and 'human development', and then examines some ideas about how the two relate and how this relationship affected the democratic process in Algeria during the 1990s, the failure of which plunged the country into bloody internal conflict. I argue here that the Algerian experience is particularly pertinent as it illustrates how the process of democracy, initiated during the 1990s with the encouragement of international institutions, witnessed the emergence of religious fundamentalism in the form of extremist political Islam, one of the most menacing aspects of which was the hostility it bore towards gender equality and women's rights.

Algeria is part of the North African region that demographer John Caldwell places in a 'patriarchal belt'. As mentioned in the previous chapter, this refers to an area that ranges from Asia and the Middle East to Africa (Moghadam 1994). Within this broad, cross-continental region, social structures are shaped by the institutionalization of restrictive 'codes of conduct' for women (Yuval-Davis 1997). Many of the women in this book experienced severe social restrictions and sometimes physical violence, as well as the heavy patriarchal responsibility placed on them to transmit Algeria's cultural and national identity to the next generation, and this played a part in their decision to leave Algeria. However, as we will see later, it is arguable whether the FIS victory and the subsequent outbreak of terror was necessarily the starting point of this process, or its defeat the end point.

According to John D. Stephens et al. (1992), the Western definition of democracy is essentially a liberal one: democracy means a system based on free, fair, regular elections and universal suffrage. This first, quite limited but widely used definition of democracy is, for example, associated with the World Bank, which sees it as more or less equivalent to good governance (Leftwich 2005). However, democracy is more generally taken to imply the protection of freedom of speech and basic civil rights, meaning that citizens have the ability to hold their rulers to account and their government is obliged to hear the voice of the people rather than represent its own or other powerful interests. This given meaning of democracy implies processes that go beyond the state itself and regular elections, and is in some ways a sociopolitical definition; the focus is more on the purpose of the democratic process as a system of protection from arbitrary governance than simply its institutional features (Stephens et al. 1992: 43). One of the consequences of any authoritarian and military regime is the restrictions laid on women in their use of public space and their right to 'access the city' (Chapter Three gives a more detailed account of this concept). Consequently, the more civil society is organized, the better the process of accountability and the responsiveness of decision-making is likely to be, and the more women benefit.

During the 1980s and 1990s, and following the end of the Cold War, many developing and Eastern European countries were obliged by international institutions to take steps towards instituting political pluralism, liberal democracy and good governance (Jordan and Duvell 2003). The official reason given for requiring such changes was that these were 'good things' in themselves, and were also likely to make it easier for those countries to make rapid gains in development. However, democracy should also ensure that all citizens are equal and have reasonably equal access to social services, regardless of gender or other distinguishing group characteristics (*UN Human Development Report* 2002). Serious problems arise when democracy is introduced alongside the implementation of neoliberal policies of structural adjustment and economic reform that exacerbate inequality, as was the case in Algeria.

It is important to note that, since Algeria's independence, political decisions have always been handled by the military, imposing the FLN as a dictatorial single-party system (Roberts 2003: 90). As the UN Human Development Report cited above states, dictatorships tend to be poorly informed and out of touch; they often misjudge their citizens' capabilities and needs. This was surely the case for the Algerian regime, which claimed it was in a better position than its citizens to know what was needed, meaning it had to take 'hard' decisions on behalf of society, such as the cancellation of the 1992 elections. Furthermore, dictatorships frequently argue that the electoral process and other forms of democratic politics tend to cause disturbances and political instability which impede foreign investment and economic development (Przeworski et al. 2000). The post-colonial socialist ideology of the Algerian state was supposed to ensure economic independence and growth, rebuilding a country destroyed by 130 years of French colonial rule. However, the FLN adopted the motto 'development first, democracy later', which it based on the country's post-colonial economic and social realities of unemployment, deprivation and lack of education (Roberts 2003).

The FLN's development strategy was financed by oil and gas revenues, which represented nearly 98% of Algeria's exports. During the 1960s and 1970s, this led to Algeria boasting one of the largest state sectors in the developing world; access to education, including higher education, health care and social protection was universal, and was widened to include women, despite the fact that patriarchy was still firmly rooted in Algerian society. At the same time, however, civil society, academic freedom and individual liberties were suppressed. Almost all of the 'mass organizations' and trade unions were linked to the FLN and were placed under the supervision of a branch of the Algerian army and the internal security services, the Securité Militaire (SM), later known as the Department of Intelligence and Security (DRS), whose remit was to support the implementation of state development projects (Evans and Phillips 2007). This situation encouraged corrupt members of the regime, including army officers, to use their positions of power to acquire wealth and privileges (Roberts 2003). This trend, which continued for many years, greatly affected capital investment in development projects, particularly from the 1980s on, as well as the amount of financial assistance allocated to social services, housing and health care.

Despite repression, activists of all types—social democrats (FFS), the socialist/communist left wing, and various manifestations of political Islam and (mainly left-wing) feminists—began to oppose state policies, denounce corruption and demand democracy. During the late 1980s, following the fall in the oil price, Algerian citizens grew increasingly frustrated as the standard of living fell. On 5 October 1988, a strike organized by one branch of the UGTA union degenerated into general rioting in Algiers and other cities (Addi 1991). The army bloodily repressed the riots and many protestors were killed or arrested and tortured. On 10 October, Ali Belhadj, a radical Islamist imam and Arabic teacher, called for a demonstration to denounce the repression that had taken place a few days earlier (Kepel 2002). An impressive turnout of 20,000 people responded to his call and marched to Bab El Oued, one of the poorest neighbourhoods in Algiers. The army intervened and once again responded with bullets, causing more deaths and injuries.

In the meantime, the World Bank and other international institutions decided to withdraw their support for dictatorial governments, including Algeria's, and began to pressurize developing countries to introduce democracy (Leftwich 2005). In response, the Algerian authorities adopted a new constitution in October 1989, and a multi-party system emerged, leading to the emergence of sixty political parties, including Islamic parties, formed out of the various political tendencies (Stone 1997). However, by this stage, the majority of Algerians appeared to believe that only a fundamentalist religious movement such as the FIS would be capable of effectively changing the status quo (Roberts 2003).

The rise of a radical Islamist movement in Algeria

As many scholars of migration, diaspora and identity studies assert, we need to understand the conditions that precede and follow on from the (often traumatic) event that lies behind the decision to migrate, if we are to fully understand the creation of networks of solidarity and the development of a diasporic consciousness. In the case of the women in my study, the backdrop for their decisions was the terror of the Black Decade. For this reason, it is important to provide a brief insight into the political, social and economic conditions in which the fundamentalist Islamist movement in Algeria developed in its radical and violent form, and why, despite this, it was able to win the first democratic elections to be held in post-colonial Algeria. It is beyond the scope of this book to explain in any depth the origin of political Islam, or its radicalization and espousal of violent forms of terrorism within Algeria itself.

The fundamentalist character of the movement was revealed in its use of slogans such as the *da'wa* (the Islamic call) for a *dawla Islamiya* (Islamic state) in which '*la mithaq, la doustour, qala Allah qala erassoul*' ('[there is] no National Charter and no constitution, but only Allah and the Prophet legislate') and '*Alayha nahya wa alahya namut*' ('for it we will live and for it we will die'). This violent and nihilistic language encapsulates the ideology of the members of the FIS, who were chanting slogans like these during their marches and rallies in the years before the cancellation of the electoral process in 1992. The euphoria generated by these slogans recruited thousands of Algerians to the FIS, often young men who had already been nurtured in a patriarchal environment in which they played the role of guardian of their female relatives. However, I myself also witnessed the radicalization of women—neighbours and colleagues—and have drawn the conclusion that it is perhaps the imbalance of power between social, political and economic factors, specific to each society, that is the fundamental trigger of radicalization. As Olivier Roy (2016), the French philosopher and expert on political Islam and its links to terrorism, asks: does this represent the 'Islamisation of radicalism or a radicalisation of Islam?' According to Roy (2016), terrorism arguably has its roots not in Islam but in the psychosocial background of the individuals concerned. These (mainly) young people, full of energy and frustration, often feel disconnected from their parents' generation whom they consider too traditional and politically amorphous. In the Algerian case, many young people, attracted by the radical neo-Salafist discourse of imams such as Ali Belhadj, broke with the peaceful version of Sunni Maliki Islam espoused by their parents, which had been predominant in the Maghreb (North Africa) for centuries (Samraoui 2003).

That said, a fundamentalist discourse proposing the creation of an Islamic caliphate as an alternative to the nation-state system had first gained traction and begun to spread in the Middle East during the nineteenth century as a reaction to colonialism. The discourse became dominated by the Saudi Wahabi doctrine, which later spread to Pakistan during the 1970s as a consequence of its instrumentalization by the USA and Saudi Arabia in their efforts to combat the USSR in Afghanistan (Kepel 2009). In 1928 a movement called the Muslim Brotherhood emerged in Egypt, whose self-proclaimed aim was to free the country from British colonialism, take power and imbue Egypt with Islamic values. The assassination of its leaders—Hassan Al-Banna in

1949 and Sayyid Qutb in 1966 were turning points that pushed the Brotherhood towards political violence and the creation of a clandestine armed wing, mainly funded by the Wahabi King Saud of Saudi Arabia (McDougall 2011). The ensuing repression that Egyptian president Gamal Abdel Nasser unleashed against the Brotherhood was deadly.

Meanwhile, in 1940s colonial Algeria, an Islamic movement of *ulama* (Muslim scholars) emerged, whose main purpose was to oppose the French secularism imposed in colonial schools (El Tayeb 1989). The leader of this movement, Abdelhamid Ibn Badis, an erudite Algerian from a conservative bourgeois family, had studied in Egypt and Tunisia and returned home influenced by the Brotherhood's ideology. He established *madrassas* (Islamic schools), in which an Islam with a neo-Salafist orientation and the teachings of the Quran were taught to young Algerians. Despite being a descendant of the Amazigh Zirid dynasty and his recognition of Algerians' Amazighity, Ibn Badis declared 'Arabic is our language, Islam our religion and Algeria our land' (El Tayeb 1989). Since Algerians are at least 90% Muslim, the *ulama* played a crucial role in the Algerian movement of national liberation, which used the twin pillars of Arabism and Islam as mobilizing concepts (McDougall 2011). Following independence in 1962, the regime consolidated Ibn Badis's declaration, imposing Arabic as the official language of the nation and Islam as the religion of the state, the latter governing Algerians' private lives in matters of inheritance, affiliation, marriage and divorce. By contrast, it simultaneously engaged in imposing a rigidly 'socialist' industrial and agrarian revolution, detached from the Islamic values to which most Algerians are deeply connected.

Arguably, the process which led to the emergence of radical Islam in the country can, in some ways, be dated from 1962, with the rise of opposition to the lack of academic freedom within educational institutions and the exclusion of religious programmes and ideas that did not conform to the official discourse of nationalism and socialism. At first, however, this indigenous movement was not radically Islamist. Boutheina Cheriet (2004) mentions the Djazarist movement, Haraket El Jaza'ara (the Movement for Algerianization), led by Malek Bennabi as being 'far from fundamentalist or violent'. Bennabi, an engineer educated in France, expressed his desire to reform Islamic thought and adapt it to the diversity of Algerian culture, including its Amazigh and

North African dimensions. His movement grew in popularity among Algerian students during the 1970s and 1980s. But although Bennabi was not persecuted, the regime disregarded his ideas; instead, Arabic and religious education were taught by teachers 'imported' from Egypt and Syria—another element to consider when researching the development of political Islam in Algeria. There were also dissenting voices from inside the FLN itself, such as Mohamed Khider, who in 1965 railed in his magazine, *Humanism Musulman*, against the 'Western clothing of Algerian women' and the 'socialist policies' of the FLN (Khider 1965, cited in Roberts 2003: 9).

To implement its policies, the Algerian government turned to its supporters in the PAGS (the Vanguard Socialist Party), including university students who were affiliated to the party. Students of Islamic and liberal tendencies found themselves excluded from public debates, particularly during the consultations around the first National Charter in 1976. As a consequence, Islamist students started organizing amongst themselves in campus prayer rooms, preaching political Islam and distributing Qutb's seminal Islamist text, *Milestones*, and the videos of Abdelhamid Kichk, a radical Egyptian preacher and scholar of Islam. Arguably, the political wing of the radical Islamist movement, the FIS, which went on to contest and win local elections in the 1990s, arose out of these embryonic beginnings. However, by 1979, an underground Islamist armed movement (Mouvement Islamic Armée) had also emerged, dedicated to the imposition of an Islamic state by force. Around the same time, in 1980, the Berber Cultural Movement (MCB) appeared, agitating for the official recognition of Tamazight as Algeria's national language. Both movements resonated with Algerians, particularly on the question of the monopoly exercised by the party in power over religion, language and other markers of diversity. The FLN responded with repression, and the leaders of both movements (including, among others, Ali Belhadj of the Islamist movement and the MCB's Mokrane Ait Larbi) were imprisoned and tortured.

It is interesting to note the similarity with what happened during the Hirak in Algeria in 2019. The effects of 9/11 and the ensuing 'war on terror' had moderated the discourse of Rachad, a movement linked to former members of the FIS, who now presented themselves as 'moderate Islamists'. Rachad and the MAK are the two groups who stand out as the most influential bearers of what developed into two key political strands in the Hirak: political Islam and the claim of Amazigh identity.[1] The response of the Algerian government has not changed, and the repression unleashed against these two movements during the Hirak has included placing them on a list of terrorist organizations, imprisoning their members in Algeria and sending international arrest warrants for those who live abroad.

Returning to 1984, this was the year in which the Family Code was implemented (I will return to the Code in more detail later in this book), which suppressed women's rights and their access to citizenship. It was a political move by the government to try to appease its most conservative adherents. Despite this, many members of the government did join the radical Islamist movement, including Abbassi Madani, who later became leader of the FIS. This party's rapid growth in Algerian society led it to win the country's first democratic elections since independence, in December 1991. When the regime cancelled the elections on 11 January 1992, claiming it was acting to protect the republican nature of the nation state, the FIS and its supporters reacted violently, revealing the existence in its ranks of an armed group that was ready to fight for power with or without elections. The ensuing decade of violence was the backdrop to the exodus of Algerians that followed.

Causes and patterns of Algerian women's forced migration in the 1990s

The impact of the Black Decade on women

There has been little research on the Algerian Black Decade of the 1990s, as well as a lack of literature and statistics relating to the ensuing mass exodus and the numbers of people internally displaced during that period and in its aftermath. It has been argued, however, that the feminization of migration from Algeria only started to rise after 1999, a fact that was illustrated by the survey conducted for this study. Indeed, more than half (53%) of the respondents to this research left after 2000. Around a third (38%) left between 1996 and 2000, and only 18% left between 1990 and 1995. Nine declared they had

1. The MAK (the Movement for the Autonomy of Kabylia) emerged out of the MCB. A radical separatist movement in the Kabylia region, it was established in Paris in 2001 to assert Kabyle (it only focuses on the Kabyle region) self-determination.

left before 1990 but could not go back to Algeria because of the instability and violence.

Alaoui (2010) indicates that the Algerian economy may have suffered to the tune of tens of billions of dollars during the conflict. A significant portion of this loss may be accounted for by the forced dispersal of a large number of highly qualified men and women, the intellectuals or professionals who were the most educated and skilled members of the Algerian middle class. The victory of the Islamist party in December 1991 was perhaps the first event that sparked their fears. When the regime decided to cancel the electoral process and declare a state of emergency, this class was divided into '*eradicateurs*', those who agreed with the cancellation, and '*dialoguistes*', those in favour of allowing the democratic process to take its course and engaging in dialogue with the FIS. The *dialoguistes* predicted that cancellation would lead to civil war, and were later proved correct (Alaoui 2010: 271). It is important to mention that women in the latter group did not necessarily support the FIS; rather, they were in favour of democratic continuity, in the belief that only democracy could produce the rule of law and give women the opportunity to exercise full citizenship (Moghadam 1994). For such women, halting the democratic process was more likely instead to ensure 'the continuity of the traditional structures of power' (Chomsky 1999: xv).

At that time, the feminist movements and organizations found themselves at a low ebb in terms of activism (Ghezali 1999; Lalami 2012). Their main focus had been the patriarchal institutions dominating the whole of Algerian society, but in addition to these public and private struggles, the political situation brought women to the forefront of the conflict, subjecting them to persecution from both sides. The battle over the elections culminated in the Black Decade. In the preface to *An Inquiry into the Algerian Massacres*, Noam Chomsky (1999) called for an independent international inquiry into the conflict, describing the situation as 'a reign of horror'. According to Alaoui (2010), the rise in violence in that period, added to the bad governance of the country during the 2000s, was responsible for a huge rise in the feminization of migration over the years from the Black Decade on (from about 36% in 1982 to 51% in 2010). The phenomenon was particularly noticeable in Quebec. The Canadian province became a place of exile for thousands of Algerian women, most of them highly educated, who had been politically involved in the various sides of the conflict. Alone or with their families, these women fled the persecution of not only the fundamentalists but also their own communities and, in some cases, the Algerian security services. The investigation conducted by Alaoui (2010) in both France and Quebec reveals that the majority of these women had been, to varying degrees, involved in women's rights movements in Algeria; some had even chaired trade unions and/or local organizations fighting for women's rights. They had initiated or taken part in sit-ins and protests in the major cities of Algeria to counter the rise of the fundamentalist movement and denounce acts of intolerance and violence against women, and the increasing numbers of terrorist attacks. This had made them visible targets for all sides in the conflict. Fearing for their lives, concerned about the future of their children, and finding their inferior status and the social pressures to which they were subjected no longer tolerable, these women took the path of exile—mainly to countries like France and Canada but also, as my research revealed, to other countries, where they hoped to find some sort of protection.

It is important to mention that although these women saw themselves as political exiles, their legal status was hostage to the gender-blind international refugee regime and asylum policies in the countries to which they fled. Even though France was traditionally the main receiving country for Algerian migrants, it was difficult for women who fled the conflict in the 1990s to be recognized as political refugees (as defined by the 1951 Geneva Refugee Convention). In fact, the French government turned a blind eye to the failure of the Algerian government to protect its citizens from the armed Islamist movement. According to Alaoui (2010), the French authorities supported the idea that the suspension of the electoral process, considered by many to be a military coup, was justified by the need to protect the republican nature of the Algerian state and its citizens against fundamentalism. This study, however, does not have any pretentions to entering into the controversy over the involvement of the French government in the conflict, which remains undocumented and difficult to assess objectively.

The making of an Algerian intellectual female diaspora

Although some sources claim that the feminist movement in Algeria started in 1940 (Smail Salhi 2010), this is contested, and there is still uncertainty about the exact date of its inception (Knauss 1987). Peter Knauss (1987), a political scientist and Africa expert, states that Algerian feminism began in the first half of the twentieth century, when a middle class, which had graduated from the French colonial education system, began to emerge. This class comprised highly skilled Algerians, generally from the *petite bourgeoisie* (doctors, midwives, lawyers, pharmacists and so on), who were mainly concentrated in the big cities. By contrast, the majority of the country remained very conservative, attached to strict Islamic rules and an indigenous patriarchal culture, partly because they had been deliberately kept in a backward state by the colonial system. It was from the new middle class that an Algerian intellectual elite emerged, and with it, nationalist and progressive movements including a feminist movement (Gadant 1995). Although there were fewer highly educated women than men, women of this new social class, particularly those living in rural areas, were encouraged to further their studies, remove their veils and fully participate in the Algerian liberation struggle.

Dazzled by the number and the quality of women who had joined the struggle for independence, Frantz Fanon (1968, 2001), the Caribbean philosopher and revolutionary who supported the Algerian revolution, declared Algerian women to be the pioneers of 'Third World' feminist movements. Decades later, however, women in Algeria found that many of the rights they had won in the intervening years had been compromised by the implementation of the 1984 Family Code, based as it was in *sharia* law (Lalami 2012). This made polygamy and the husband's right to repudiate his wife official, and ruled that a woman could not leave the country—or even the conjugal home—without her husband's permission, and that even once she had obtained her husband's permission to work, she still required his further permission to move from one workplace to another. This law had a huge impact on the careers of professional women, especially as attending conferences and meetings or networking outside the university or workplace are crucial steps towards attaining a more senior position.

Thus, the beginnings of the brain drain of Algerian women can be dated to the aftermath of independence, around the 1970s. As it was a silent and gradual phenomenon it is not well known and is poorly documented. The cases of three highly qualified women, Assia Djebar, Fadéla M'Rabet and Malika Mokadem, who chose to leave Algeria soon after independence because they could not live and work in such unsatisfactory conditions, provide telling examples of this flight of women intellectuals. The first and most prominent, Assia Djebar, a celebrated novelist and member of the Académie Française, was the only female professor of contemporary Algerian history to work at the University of Algiers after the 1960s. Jane Hiddleston (2006: 248), a specialist on the work of Djebar, writes: '[Her] novels are clearly focused on the creation of a genealogy of Algerian women, and her political stance is virulently anti-patriarchal as much as it is anti-colonial.'

Another important Algerian feminist of that period, Fadéla M'Rabet, not only held a doctorate in biology but was also a communist activist and the author of a number of books on Algerian women. M'Rabet was suspended from her job as a science teacher because her work criticized patriarchal attitudes towards young girls. Her radio talk show, devoted to answering the questions of young women, which often revolved around their experience of social oppression, landed her in trouble with the Algerian government and she was forced to take the route of exile to France in 1967. As M'Rabet herself explains:

> My generation fought for dignity, both in Algeria and France ... This really embarrassed the government to the point that they blocked all mail addressed to us. I was even called by the Minister of Information at that time, who told me that I was too impatient and that he was willing to sacrifice women to save the revolution. (M'Rabet 1983: 35)

In fact, it is often the case that newly independent countries renege on their principles of autonomy and freedom, and deny access to the public sphere, particularly to women, who are seen as guardians of the values of the private sphere and are not allowed to step outside this role. Valentine Moghadam (1994) explains that the ideology of nationalism adopted by these countries used women as symbols of collective liberation and role models for the new nationalist patriarchal community. Mahfoud Bennoune (1999: 23), for example, considers the fate of Algerian women in the armed liberation struggle: despite their full participation in the liberation army, their status was quickly reshaped 'by the urgent needs of the male to restore Islam as the religion of the state, Arabic as the unique language and themselves as sovereigns of the family'. Women who opposed this restoration were accused of being disloyal to the nation and to Islam, and were 'sent back to their private spheres' (Hajdukowski-Ahmed 2008: 42).

The third example is Malika Mokadem, who also left Algeria during the 1970s. She trained as a medical nephrologist but is also a well-known feminist and novelist who has received numerous literary awards. The majority of her novels are overtly critical of the attitude of Algeria's patriarchal society towards women. Of course, there are other similar cases that could be mentioned; these highly qualified women are just the most prominent examples of numerous women who fled Algeria due to the constraints placed on them following independence. As explained above, these restrictions were based on deep-rooted patriarchal customs that were officially legitimized by Article 2 of the Algerian constitution, which declares Islam as the religion of the state and promulgates a family law which confines Algerian women to the role of second-class citizens. It seems that Fanon's optimistic vision, when he declared women's emancipation in post-colonial Algeria as a model for the 'Third World', rapidly faded (Guemar 2011).

During the political and economic crisis of the 1980s, which led to the rise of Islamist movements, unveiled women with access to the public sphere were singled out for censure (Bennoune 1999). The strict cultural and religious codes stating what is deemed proper behaviour for women imposed boundaries that kept them in a position of powerlessness. As such, they were placed in a vulnerable position that often made them the first victims of political, economic and social repression, as gender-based boundaries, being neither immutable nor stable, are constantly contested and transgressed, and thus transformed 'across spaces and time' (Crawley 2001: 6). By taking the journey into exile in the 1960s and 1970s, the three Algerian feminist academics cited above paved the way for a larger exodus of female intellectuals, which reached its peak during the post-Black Decade period. The courage it took to leave Algeria during the crucial era of post-colonization and national reconstruction, and the fact that despite the social burden imposed on them as women they managed to rebuild successful professional lives in exile, meant that many younger Algerian women considered them role models.

Algerian sociologist Hocine Labdelaoui (2012) stresses the problematic lack of data concerning the migration of Algerian women. Nevertheless, according to statistics published by the OECD (Organization for Economic Cooperation and Development) in 2008, this migratory flow evolved as follows: from 6.45% in 1954 to 32.31% in 1975, increasing to 42.35% in 1990, and finally reaching a peak in 1996. Other sources, however, reveal a further important increase in the feminization of Algerian migration commencing in 2000. The move into exile, following their resistance to the harsh effects of Algerian patriarchy, was the common trajectory followed by female intellectuals.

The legal and social situation of women in Algeria

This phenomenon, however, failed to raise concern about women's situation in the sphere of Algerian political decision-making. This lack of interest is closely linked to women's status in the country; policy-makers do not appear to consider the situation of women as an essential social issue. As French-Moroccan journalist Zakya Daoud (1996) pointed out in an interview: 'As soon as [it was] created, the Algerian state refused to give itself the tools to exist.' Comparing Algerian with Tunisian family law, which at the time allowed more gender equality in practice, Daoud went on to explain that Algeria was now paying the price of the bloody conflict of the 1990s. As mentioned above, although the Algerian constitution (Article 29) makes no distinction between men and women, the Family Code subjugates women to the authority of men and to Algerian patriarchal customs. Consequently, the equal constitutional rights of women are nullified in practice by a family law that is built on the hierarchical organization of Algerian society. The policy-makers have always turned a blind eye to this schizophrenic reality, which consists of giving women equality with one hand and taking it away with the other, and feminist efforts to challenge the constitutionality of the Family Code continue to be ignored (Lalami 2012). This duplicity is confirmed by the attitude of the Algerian government towards the ratification of the international Convention on the Elimination of All Forms of Discrimination Against Women (CEDAW). At the peak of the conflict, in May 1996, Algerian policy-makers, in keeping with the patriarchal values which constitute the cornerstone of the Family Code, put forward reservations to some of the Convention's articles on the pretext that they were incompatible with Islam as the religion of the state (Article 2 of the Algerian constitution). This legal and constitutional incoherence severely hampered the professional advancement and self-development of Algerian women. The journalist Salima Tlemçani (cited in Evans and Phillips 2007: 108) denounced this betrayal, saying, 'the promises made to women have not been kept'.

The Tunisian historian Latifa Lakhdar (2002), a specialist in Islamic thought, has produced a study called *Imra'atu I'ijmâ* (*Women in the Mirror of Muslim Orthodoxy*), which skilfully deconstructs the orthodox vision which keeps North African Muslim women imprisoned in an unchanging model. Lakhdar explains that a dogmatic conception of the foundations of Islamic law, built on a literal reading of the Quran, has produced a religious discourse that essentializes women. This construction, claiming to draw its legitimacy from the divine word, 'places the woman in the sacred space. And we know that the sacred defies history and always seeks to remain outside historicity: that is already the greatest tactic of marginalization' (Lakhdar 2007). As explained earlier, however, violence towards women was already institutionalized in Algerian society, carrying the seeds of future conflicts (Lalami 2012).

The growth in the number of highly qualified women migrating from Algeria from the 1970s on was partially the result of the difficulties they faced in achieving personal development and successful careers, due to the constitutional status of women and their inferior social position. However, it has only been in the first decade of the twenty-first century that studies and reports, such as those of Fatiha Dahmani-Lovichi (2006), have revealed the extent of the growing feminization of Algerian migration, especially the significantly greater numbers of female journalists, academics, medical doctors and university lecturers leaving the country. The state/fundamentalist crisis, accompanied by the high level of assassinations of women around the mid-1990s, corresponded with the first great wave of women's migration (Alaoui 2010), but the crisis only amplified and highlighted the ongoing phenomenon of violence against women, rendering it more visible. However, it is clear that Islamist terrorism targeted women first, especially educated women, and triggered the migration of whole families towards safer countries. The assassinations, kidnappings and rapes of women by terrorist groups also caused a deep sense of shock in the collective psyche of Algerian society and left no other form of escape apart from fleeing—for those who could afford it. Thus, on the basis of the available data, it is clear that the post-1990s recorded the highest flow of migration of women, especially educated women, and it can be deduced that violence was the immediate although not always the main reason for this vast female brain drain.

Looking deeper into the history of contemporary Algeria from a gender perspective and comparing two crucial periods for women's rights—namely, the post-independence and the post-Black Decade periods—it is clear that the phenomenon of female migration is much more complex than it first appears. It has manifold causes and needs to be closely scrutinized. The rise of fundamentalism and terrorist acts against women undoubtedly had a catalytic effect on the mass feminization of Algerian migration, but they served to amplify an already ongoing subterranean trend. One could argue that instead of being the main cause, the Black Decade simply swelled an already existing migratory movement of Algerian women, a movement that society and especially policy-makers did not want to address because it required a more insightful and critical historical analysis of the ingratitude of the post-independence state towards those women who had wholeheartedly participated in the War of Independence (Dahmani-Lovichi 2006). This led to a growing awareness, especially among highly qualified women, that independence had not brought the freedom that women expected; they felt betrayed. The growing exodus of professional women can therefore be linked to Algeria's contemporary history and its programme of 'nation-building', and the way legislators dealt with the place of women in the post-colonial nation state. This migratory movement later coincided with a further debasement of women's status resulting from both radical Islamist-based violence during the Black Decade and the inertia of the Algerian government when it came to offering women effective protection against it. Even recently, for example, Hafida Mansouri, a nurse in her thirties and a Hirak activist, was murdered by her neighbour, who set her on fire before burying her body. Although it was reported that the cause of this horrific crime was her refusal of his marriage proposal, it is more likely that her murder was linked to the fact that she had broken the social rules and refused 'the code of conduct imposed on her' by participating in the Hirak movement in a city known for its conservatism.[2]

2. Available at: https://feminicides-dz.com/feminicides/feminicides-2022/liste-des-feminicides-2022/ (accessed 19 January 2022).

Thus, two important periods of policy development in contemporary Algeria were arguably the crucial turning points in the history of Algerian feminism: namely, the post-independence period and the war against civilians in the Black Decade. These periods were vital in women's history if we consider the way they affected their lives. Although the latter period was known on an international level as the 'Decade for Women' (Kabeer 2013), in Algeria it was instead the decade *against* women. There are some important similarities between these post-war and domestic-conflict periods that are worth underlining if we want to shed light on the trend of the female brain drain in Algeria. During these two unstable moments, the definition of the nation state was at stake, and from this perspective, so was the place and role of women in society. Daoud (1996: 153) comments that 'the Algerian woman became an issue at stake in the societies in conflict', and adds that the fierce political battle over the definition of the state 'was concentrated and organized around the dialectic of honor'. Algerian women were the greatest losers in this fight since they could not intervene in the process of policy-making at that time. In both eras, the Algerian regime imposed its patriarchal and conservative views, excluding the question of women's rights. This resulted in the sacrifice of women for the sake of the political and material interests of the male-dominated power structure.

During these two periods, women faced great violence, and the very fact of their existence was effectively denied. Although aware that they were always the most exposed members of society—as is the case for women during any conflict—Algerian women struggled and resisted with great courage during the war of liberation and the conflict of the 1990s. After independence, Algerian women had believed they would gradually gain access to equal rights with men through education and a change in the Algerian mentality. Even if some chose the route of exile, the majority remained in Algeria in the hope that they would see society evolving from a patriarchal system towards a modern social organization. Knauss (1987) explains that the dilemmas thrown up by Algeria's brutal colonial heritage placed a burden on Algerian women: they were caught between the process of reclaiming their Amazigh and Muslim identity and participating in building the new nation.

Yet for a time after the war of liberation, it did seem as though women's hopes were to be fulfilled: during the presidency of Houari Boumediene

(1965–78), the construction of a new nation based on a socialist ideology was linked to the decision to encourage women to study. Bourdieu explains in his *Algerian Sketches* (2013) that many Algerians at the time were convinced they should give priority to their children's education, not only their sons' education but also their daughters'. This was particularly important because for a long time it had been said that education ruined girls: to send a girl to school, to teach her French, was tantamount to encouraging her to adopt European customs and habits, tempting her with the chance of escaping her father's authority and later her husband's. Working-class families, however, especially those in urban areas, began to encourage their daughters in the same way as they did their sons, to go and 'get instruction' (Bourdieu 2013: 199); working-class fathers decided that you could trust educated women, and came to believe that young women must be brought up to go out to work and not simply stay at home as before.

However, women and girls were never allowed to reach their full potential. Natalya Vince (2014) claims that Algerian women, despite their active participation in the country's liberation from French colonization, were very quickly 'relegated to the kitchen' in post-colonial Algeria, and even during the struggle. Although many participated in the frontline combat against the French army as nurses or soldiers, their male counterparts expected them to also do the domestic chores—in other words, to also carry out 'women's duties'. As the personal testimonies gathered during this research confirms, Algerian women have, in a sense, never really left the kitchen: professional women have the household and children to attend to as well as their studies and work. Following independence, women were encouraged to enter health care, education and the civil service, if only because Algeria was in need of rapid development and lacked professionals in every field, from fashion design to medicine and education (Bourdieu 2013). There was no taboo on women studying science and technology, and hundreds became scientists and researchers (in my own case, for instance, in non-destructive testing, a field that is usually a male preserve even in the developed countries). For this reason, it is arguable that although Algerian women failed to prevent the implementation of the Family Code, they are often more politicized than most of their Western sisters on comparable issues.

However, even before the cancellation of the electoral process in which the FIS, the Islamist party, won the highest number of votes, the social atmosphere in the country had become increasingly unfavourable to unveiled,

French-speaking professional and working women in general. Women known to be communists active in the PAGS or standing for political parties other than those with Islamic tendencies were particularly singled out for censure. Martin Evans and John Phillips (2007: 168) cite the testimony of a woman who was standing for the FFS (Socialist Forces Front) in the region of Kabylia: 'There are threats against my children and myself [...] when I drive around, people gesture at me as if they are going to cut my throat. But I will not let them intimidate me.' According to Evans and Phillips (2007), during the elections on 26 December 1991, Western journalists present in the polling stations in Bab El Oued, a part of Algiers where the FIS was firmly implanted, reported seeing women wearing the *niqab* or *tchador* voting several times. Once the ballot papers were counted there were accusations of fraud. This incident shows how the daughters, wives and mothers of the Islamist leaders were used during the electoral process, although it appears that left-wing and liberal political parties also used 'their women' to influence the cancellation of the electoral process.

There were a large number of women present at the social democrat FFS rally in Algiers on 3 January 1992, which called for a vigilant stand against a military coup, but six days later, thousands of women also demonstrated against the eventual victory of the FIS, fearful of what would happen once it gained access to legislative power. Undoubtedly, many women were concerned by the pronouncements of the leaders of the FIS at the time. For example, they warned athlete Hassiba Boulmerka, the first woman from an Arab or African nation to win a world track championship—and the first Algerian to win an Olympic medal—not to run with bare legs in front of an international public. Indeed, following the first electoral round, a prominent leader of the FIS declared that 'from now [on], Algerians are advised to change their way of dressing, eating and behaving' (Evans and Phillips 2007). Women were the first to perceive this declaration as a specific threat. Yet many observers and political actors, including journalists and sociologists, considered the cancellation of the electoral process to be a military putsch, not only against the FIS or political Islam but also against the left-wing activists of the FFS, including feminists, as well as those civil servants who might take advantage of democratic institutions to denounce corruption and claim a voice in the political debate.

In addition to the political violence of the regime and the physical violence of the Black Decade, the Algerian authorities showed no willingness to protect women from rape, ill treatment or assassination by either side during the conflict. Worse still, a few years after the end of the bloody civil war, in 2006, the Algerian government negotiated an amnesty (discussed in greater detail in Chapter Three), excluding women's associations from the debate, particularly the mothers of the disappeared. Yet these mothers were the only social group to maintain their demand for justice and truth regarding the hundreds who disappeared during the Black Decade. The group held a vigil every Wednesday in a public spot in Algiers for more than twenty years, despite police attempts to impede them, on one occasion beating up its chairwoman. Although the majority of the disappeared are believed to be men, unverifiable sources have also denounced the disappearance of hundreds of women and girls. Unfortunately, there are no records and all research on this topic is fiercely suppressed. It was due to such actions by the authorities, particularly the introduction of the amnesty, that increasing numbers of educated women became convinced that far from improving, the situation was reverting, and that once again they would have to pay the price. It seemed clear that any negotiations would be at their expense: for example, the Law of Reconciliation rehabilitated those terrorists who agreed to lay down their arms, without giving their victims justice, especially their women victims. As a result, the majority of highly educated women, aware that the Algerian government had sacrificed them in order to placate the fundamentalist opposition, began to see leaving Algeria for a safer country as the only way to survive.

The history of women's struggle for emancipation in Algeria has therefore been long and difficult. By the end of the Black Decade, women's optimism had turned to pessimism. Even if the beginnings of a civil society, triggered by the 1989 constitution, witnessed a flourishing of numerous feminist associations, which has continued up until recent times, women still faced and continue to face numerous obstacles on their way to liberty. Every Algerian government has put impediments in the way of women's exercise of full citizenship. The implementation of the Family Code in 1984 (due to pressure from the radical Islamist and conservative tendencies already existing in the ranks of the FLN), and the different reservations placed on the ratification of CEDAW in 1996, clearly illustrate the lack of any political will to encourage the emancipation of Algerian women. In February 2005, women welcomed certain amendments to the Family Code, particularly the nationality code, which reformed or cancelled articles that impeded the right of the children of a woman with a non-Algerian husband to Algerian nationality. This surely was a moment when the limitations of the patriarchal system were challenged, and it was considered a victory against the whole North African patriarchy. However, Algerian women continue to fight for the complete abolition of the Family Code and its replacement by a civilian code that treats men and women equally, as specified by Article 29 of the Algerian constitution. It is clear that the Family Code, seen in its wider context, exacerbates the challenges that all Algerian women face, professional women in particular. According to feminist lawyer Nadia Ait Zai (2010: 22): 'The family law inspired by pure Islamic tradition is the main obstacle to the emancipation of women. It even generates violence towards women as men's and women's relationships are based on subordination and submission.'

There is sufficient evidence to show that the Black Decade was the nodal point of the wave of highly skilled women's departures, giving the trend more visibility, and it is hardly surprising that the peak year for women's migration to France was 1996, although the steady rise in the number of highly qualified Algerian women leaving the country continued: the growth rates rose from 1.18% between 1990 and 2000 to 2.7% between 2000 and 2006 (Bouklia-Hassane 2011). Although the politics of the receiving countries and their fluctuating needs for highly skilled migrants is also a factor to consider when examining the phenomenon, Bouklia-Hassane explains that the growth in the feminization of highly skilled migration is more telling than that of other categories of Algerian women migrants, because it is a significant sign of continuing dissatisfaction with and intolerance of the conditions women live in. In fact, nothing really changed for women, even if the bloody conflict has long since ended. Violence and discrimination towards women, which are seemingly deeply ingrained in Algerian society, have been implicitly justified and legitimated by the official amnesty, since the victims of the Black Decade did not receive any justice (Lloyd 2006).

Conclusion: The impact of historical events

The violence that occurred during the Black Decade was rooted in Algeria's historical conditions and the events of the late 1980s and early 1990s. This period shook the post-colonial one-party Algerian regime. The fall of the Soviet Union and its ideological underpinning, the collapse in the price of oil which led to economic instability in the country, the imposition of the liberalization of markets by the international financial institutions, with the subsequent rise in inequality, all contributed to weakening its hold. These factors affected all of Algerian society and contributed to the emergence of the FIS, a political party with a radical Islamist ideology, from among the different political trends opposing the regime. The Islamist movement had evolved over time in a mainly Muslim society to become the primary pole of resistance against colonialism, turning radical under the one-party authoritarian regime and violent in the face of the pluralism imposed by the neoliberal international institutions. The ensuing tragedy of the Black Decade followed the democratic victory of the FIS and the cancellation of the electoral process. These events had a dramatic impact on the lives of Algerian women, already severely constricted by legal and social restrictions, and they certainly influenced the decisions of many highly skilled women, professionals and intellectuals to flee Algeria. The following chapter looks at the story of one such woman.

3 One Woman's Story of Trauma, Migration and Reconciliation

Introduction: 'Lamia's' narrative

This chapter follows one woman's story of surviving the Black Decade in Algeria and her decision to flee the country. As such, it represents an important contribution to the analysis in this book by offering a very immediate way of understanding the impact of terror on women's lives, as well as illuminating not only their struggles but also their agency when constructing new lives in exile. 'Lamia's' story also has the particular merit of highlighting the importance of justice and truth in achieving forgiveness, healing and reconciliation between Algerians. Although it is too early to judge, the alleged failure of the Hirak to identify leaders for the movement or address the tensions within the movement itself, including the lack of agreement among Algerians living abroad, could be partly a result of the unhealed societal fragmentation and traumas of the Black Decade.

The gendered sociopolitical origins of personal trauma

Most of the participants in this study had lived in Algeria during the first half of the 1990s and left from 1994 onwards. Lamia stated that her reasons for leaving were complex:

> Right, the reason why I left? It was a cocktail of reasons. I was an English teacher, and as a teacher, I had difficulties finding a job in Algeria. I lost my job and it was very hard for me to find [another] job after [my cousin] was killed. Maybe it was difficult because we have the same name. But no, it wasn't only that...

During this period, only the government-run secondary schools taught English. Jobs in the educational sector had fallen victim to IMF restrictions, and a successful application to the Ministry of Education was dependent on knowing someone influential, having a relative in the sector or being part of a network, none of which applied to Lamia, like most of the women who took part in this research. *Ma'arifa* (networking) was—and continues to be—a vital tool for accessing all kinds of services in Algeria, including local authority housing and health care; women in particular find difficulties in accessing *ma'arifa* (Talahite 2000). In a report published by the University of Virginia, Jonah Schulhofer-Wohl (2006) states that from 1993 the country was on the verge of bankruptcy and in the process of rescheduling its public debt of $9 million in an attempt to boost the economy. At the same time, hundreds of public buildings, such as schools, workplaces and hospitals, were burned down by the GIA (the Islamist armed forces). As a result, regionalism, family connections and recommendations from a father or male relative became vital resources in the attempt to access increasingly limited employment opportunities or public services. This inequality was rife throughout the education system. 'Wahiba', another woman I interviewed in London, revealed the effects of the unspoken prejudice in universities at the time against young women who came from outlying villages and towns to study, and who, due to lack of connections in the city, had to live on campus:

> I used to feel sorry for those girls [who lived] on campus. You know, they may go out with the boys, but when it comes to marriage, parents will never allow their sons to marry a girl who has lived on the university campus. Often, girls were left pregnant or had to go for illegal abortions. This, in the majority of cases, would prevent them from going back to their villages or smaller cities.

On 10 December 2013, Ennahar, a private Algerian TV channel, later called 'qanat *qanat El'aar*' ('The Channel of Shame') by the Hirak, broadcast a documentary purporting to show the lives of female students on the campus of Algiers University. The documentary used material based on a secret investigation into the students' private lives; some were shown smoking and drinking. The documentary was condemned by Algerian feminists, as well as by Algerian women abroad, who believed it degraded the image of female students.

Although it triggered the indignation of many Algerian students and their parents, and the political parties condemned the programme, it was later reported that several fathers summoned their daughters home in the middle of the academic year, cutting short their education. According to the testimonies of female students, many of them were subjected to physical and verbal abuse from male passers-by in the street after the broadcast. It seems that it placed all female students living on campus at risk of sexual aggression. This is surely a regression from the situation immediately after independence that Bourdieu (2013: 199) refers to, in which 'people [were] beginning to realise that going to school, there's education, and with education, you can trust a woman'. As for Lamia, it appears from her narrative that, before she moved to the UK in 1994, she spent more than three years living on the university campus, until she was forced to leave. She did not give any details about this but simply said, 'I wasn't allowed to stay anymore, so I went to stay with my auntie.' Lamia never went back to her village.

Lamia's framing of her reasons for leaving Algeria is very revealing: 'What really triggered my leaving was the loss of hope, complete loss of hope, after I lost my cousin.' The violent assassination of her cousin could be an example of what Renos Papadopoulos (2007) calls the 'devastating event' that provoked her departure, a concept he uses in his work with traumatized refugees and asylum seekers in Europe. He explains that the discourse on the trauma of forcibly displaced people tends to emphasize the main 'devastating event' that forces people to flee, such as violence, persecution, war or internal conflict. Although it is recognized that this event is usually the main cause of symptoms of post-traumatic stress disorder (PTSD), earlier crucial experiences, which make up what Papadopoulos (2002) calls the 'phase of anticipation', are generally ignored. However, this phase may have been marked by suffering from discrimination and/or violence, both in the public and private spheres. As seen in the example of the students, Algerian women were subject to both collective and individual oppression, and the experiences related to this oppression were potentially traumatic.

Maryanne Loughry (2008: 169) describes the traumatic experience as something that becomes encapsulated in the 'psychological world' of the victim. The degree of the damage resulting from this experience therefore depends on both external and internal factors: the extent of continual persecution in the public sphere, and the emotional trauma the victim might have suffered since her childhood in the private sphere (Agger 1994). Eugenia Weinstein et al. (1987) emphasize the importance of considering the process of dissociation when seeking to understand trauma, because the dissociative process is also an essential part of subsequent reactions to it. Loughry (2008) describes how by dissociating, the victim establishes a partial disintegration of their ego in order to avoid overwhelming anxiety, which would lead to a total breakdown. Lamia echoed this experience when she explained that in Algeria 'I wasn't myself' and 'I wasn't allowed to be myself', which suggest two types of oppression, external and internal, that are most likely linked.

This is also reminiscent of Tovi Fenster's (2005) feminist interpretation of Henri Lefebvre's concept of 'the right to the city'. In her critique of Lefebvre's work, Fenster (2005: 217) looks at women's everyday lives and 'their reflections regarding their sense of comfort, belonging and commitment to the city they live in'. According to Mark Purcell (2003), there are two essential points that underlie Lefebvre's concept of the 'right to the city': first, the right of all citizens to fully and freely use the urban space they live in, and—most importantly—to feel secure in their everyday lives and activities; and secondly, the right to participate in policy decision-making regarding the design of the urban space, as well as its management, maybe through an electoral process. Although Lefebvre recognizes the right to be different as integral to exercising the 'right to the city', his critics argue that he overlooks differences such as gender and culture. Fenster (2005) argues that a dominant, homogenizing power such as patriarchy shapes the 'right to the city', and this affects women's right to use and participate in urban public space. Crucially, without employment and the ability to freely occupy public spaces, most Algerian women would be denied any 'right to the city'. Of course, in Algeria, as elsewhere, the larger cities have a different social environment than the smaller towns and villages, particularly when it comes to women's rights and public participation—more women from larger cities took part in the Hirak, for example, than did women from more rural places. However, even in a larger city, it is almost impossible for a single woman without male 'protection' or contacts to establish herself. Although the Algerian government offers an unemployment allowance, the amount is very small, and women do not have equal access to local authority housing. According to Fenster (2005), it is important to understand the full impact of the restrictions of the 'rights to use' both in private and public life in cities such as Algiers.

There is also a large body of literature suggesting that a person who experiences physical and psychological violence loses a sense of self. Indeed, a few of my participants mentioned having experienced sexual harassment in their workplaces before their departure from Algeria. Lamia, for example, recounted:

> I applied for a job with a private oil company. Anyway, before I left that job, saying, 'enough is enough', one of my superiors in the same [department] was trying to flirt with me, if you like. He was inviting me to … He was about fifty-five and I was twenty-five years old … euhhh … [A gesture intimating that this was not acceptable]

If one of the key achievements of the feminist movement is that women are finally able to provide an exact political definition of what sexual harassment consists of, it is clear from such a case as Lamia's that this goal has not been met in all parts of the world, and especially not in Algeria. What are the boundaries between flirting and sexual harassment, abuse and bullying? Lamia is from a culture, in particular a village culture, in which a woman is not used to being—and is not allowed to be—in touch with men who are not direct relatives. She told me, for example, how her mother had to stay inside the house every day of her life, and was not even allowed to open the door to the postman if her father was not at home.

It is important to also mention the widespread discourse against women in the workplace which flourished as a consequence of both the rise of the Islamist fundamentalists and the anti-feminist backlash in Western countries that influenced the so-called secular and democratic Algerian spheres. The instability and insecurity of working for a private company may also have placed many women in a vulnerable position, particularly when forced by lack of opportunities into working in the informal labour market. In general, women almost never reported sexual harassment to the police or any other form of authority, often through fear of being blamed for the harassment. According to Moghadam (2011: 114), '[i]n Algeria, the problem of sexual harassment was recognized as a part of the larger problem of violence against women, which had been the subject of a survey conducted by "Collectif 95 Maghreb Egalité"'. However, legislation to protect Algerian women from domestic violence and abuse was only adopted by the Algerian Assembly in March 2015, and the law was blocked for more than eight months before it was adopted by the Algerian Council of the Nation. Although women's organizations and lawyers welcomed its adoption, it remains the case that there have been no acts or official circulars to ensure that the law is implemented (Smail Salhi 2013).

Regardless of the conflict between the army and the Islamists during the Black Decade, post-colonial Algeria has never been a state governed by the rule of law, and the relationship between the authorities and its citizens has always been dysfunctional, not to mention the fact that the Family Code places women in an inferior position. Hence, a woman who experiences sexual harassment commonly suffers in silence, often developing a sense of self-recrimination based on speculation over the way she was dressed or how she must have behaved in order to have attracted such attention. The ability to defend herself is hampered or extremely difficult to implement, and this can become a source of personal destabilization: her self-confidence is eroded, resulting in the negation of her right to talk about her experience or to complain, as well as a diminished sense of self. As such, sexual harassment is not a minor violence; it must not be underestimated.

In Algeria, sexual harassment in the workplace increased following the economic crisis that began with the end of the Cold War. The brutal restructuring of national enterprises and the capitalization of the Algerian labour market during the 1990s caused the loss of thousands of jobs, and women were the first to be affected. Employment in public and government services, including education, health care and universities, was frozen due to IMF directives, which only ended in 2000. Although the impact of restructuring and privatization mainly affected men, as the national companies that were privatized were very male-dominated, the high level of redundancies following the 90-11 Labour Law placed a burden on employment in government agencies. The restructuring imposed by the IMF austerity programme also opened national companies up to partnerships with foreign companies, placing pressure on and encouraging corruption in the labour market, further hindering women's access to employment, promotion and training. If an educated woman manages to be recruited in such a situation, it is likely that she will find herself in an exploitative environment in which she will have to take on a huge workload, differing in quality and degree to that of her male co-workers, regardless of her level of education. Moreover, it is important to recall here that during the 1990s the Islamist party, the FIS, had on several occasions publicly coerced women workers into giving up their jobs so they could be filled by men, the supposedly legitimate breadwinners of the family. Even recently, in one of the football anthems famous for having triggered the Hirak, young men sang: '*They build a prison, the women are working, and Chabiba* [a young man] *is sleeping. Let me go, my heart is bleeding, in a wooden boat* [i.e. migrate].'[1] There is an underlying sentiment, not exclusive to the more conservative or Islamist factions of society, that the structure of the family and—by extension—of society is deteriorating, and one of the signs of this is the inability of men to fulfil their expected role as breadwinners. The frustration of the young men, vocalized in their football chants during the Hirak, is a ripple of the same pressures that faced Algerian society back in the 1990s.

Collective trauma: The experience of terrorism and counter-terrorism

Although it was hard, Lamia found a job, revealing her determination to overcome her difficulties. However, this brought with it further risks: 'I was travelling every day from the city. In fact, when I was working as a high-school teacher, it was the period when terrorism was at its highest peak, the "hottest" time.' In addition to the terror that affected all Algerian citizens indiscriminately, such as bombs in public places and the shootings and massacres of entire groups of citizens, women suffered particular troubles, especially those who refused to veil themselves. The mothers, sisters and wives of members of the police, army or other state institutions were especially at risk due to their relatives' positions, but sometimes simply because they were women. Women known to be family members of young men suspected of joining the armed wing of the FIS also suffered persecution and harassment at the hands of the police. Educational institutions and universities known to be female-dominated suffered the most attacks. Even before the cancellation of the elections, the

1. This song was translated and presented by the author at a roundtable on the Hirak at St Antony's College, Oxford in June 2019.

FIS had won a majority in local elections and in rural areas where women and girls were already under a great deal of pressure to conform in dress and behaviour to strict Islamic rules. The targeting and harassment of foreign-language teachers, particularly those who taught French, was common. In reality, the threats levelled against these women had less to do with anger at a colonial legacy and more with installing an atmosphere of fear in order to force women to leave their jobs and evacuate the public space.

There were also areas—'hot' areas—in which women were in even more danger: violence was generalized, and every day there was a new terrorist attack, directly affecting everybody. As Lamia recalled:

> One day I was walking down la Rue d'Ardu. I was going back to my auntie's, and suddenly we heard 'tatatatatata', a gunshot … It was an attack, followed by a big battle in the middle of the city. Oh my God, we panicked.

Witnessing violence can have a severe impact on a person's mental well-being. According to Jan Seeley (2008: 11), terrorist attacks are deliberately designed to provoke intense fear, shock and intimidation amongst a large number of people; their psychological effects are more harmful than a natural disaster due to the fact that they are caused intentionally by other human beings. The bomb attack on 12 August 1992 at Algiers airport, for example, not only shocked the Algerian people but also instilled in the entire population the sensation of continuing threat and fear. A short time earlier, on 29 June 1992, President Mohamed Boudiaf had been assassinated while addressing the public, and live images of his assassination were broadcast into every home. Although the exact date of the terrorist attack that Lamia mentioned is not clear from her story, there is a high probability that it took place after these two events, which had already damaged Algeria's collective consciousness in many ways.

Lamia recounted that she was walking down one of the busiest streets in the city when suddenly what she had always feared happened. What follows in her narrative is a very detailed, intense description of a terrorist attack:

> We found refuge in the first boutique in front of us, and there was a woman, she was with her two kids [and she was] panicking. She held one [child's] hand but the other one was outside the boutique [because] when the owner [let] us in, all the women [ran inside] and the owner closed the door. The poor woman, she managed to get in with only one of her boys. She was

> sobbing loudly and the man shouted at her: 'Stop crying. Either you come in or [go] out. Don't go back to look for the other one.' ... In a way, he was right, because if she had gone out, she would have received a stray bullet. We were lying down in the fitting room of that boutique ... 'tatatatata'. We stayed until everything had calmed down and we were safe. In the end, her child was in the boutique next door; another woman had taken him in with her, so he was safe.

Although she said nothing of her own feelings at the time, Lamia vividly remembered the woman sobbing and the sound of the bullets, repeating the noise loudly. It is important to recall that it was only after 9/11 that the international community was made aware of the high psychological impact of a terrorist attack that can appear to come out of nowhere (Seeley 2008).

Even after spending twenty-five years in the UK, the question remains as to whether Lamia has recovered from her trauma. As she explained, '[w]henever I hear a siren, I re-experience the terror I felt in Algeria, and the memories intrude into my daily life in the UK'. The extent of this is betrayed by the fact that even when telling her story from exile, she kept returning to the different events—sometimes private, sometimes public—of indiscriminate terror, the fear of sexual violence, and the experiences of oppression that have traumatized her the most:

> I remember once I was walking down the street, and someone was walking behind me. [It seemed] to me that he was following me. Because, you know, in Algeria, as a woman, with or without terrorism, you are always followed by men, you know, '*yetbelaouek*' [implied sexual aggression]. And that has always been the case, even before the terrorism. So, for me, that guy was one of these men, and I was convinced that he was holding a knife, because while I was walking I remembered that one day, near my university campus, there was a girl walking on the street and she was wearing a skirt, not very short—you know the shortest you can wear in Algeria, to your knees and that's it—and there was a guy walking very closely behind her, and suddenly he slashed her legs with a razor. We were told it was because she wasn't wearing a *hijab*.

It is interesting to note that at the time of analysing Lamia's narrative, a national debate around the acceptable length of a woman's skirt was taking place in Algeria following an incident in the University of Algiers' law faculty, when a candidate for a law proficiency examination was denied entry by a security guard because her skirt was 'too short'. The Algerian slang word '*yetbelaouek*' mentioned by Lamia translates literally as 'they aggress you'. It is used for antagonistic situations, either when men try to pick up a woman or when they insult them if they consider the woman to have 'invaded' their territory—that is, the street.

Lamia gave a further account of her everyday experience of harassment and fear:

> One day, I was in a bus coming from Bezerga towards Algiers, and we were stopped at a checkpoint. Two soldiers got on the bus to check [the passengers]. The route was so 'hot' that there was one checkpoint after another ... There was a man sitting next to me, he was very old, maybe a peasant working in one of the fields around there. The soldier asked everyone to get off the bus except for the women—you know, all of that bullshit ... Then one of the soldiers told the old man, 'Stay here, you're too old, it's fine.' Then another soldier came, looked at him, and spitefully gestured for him to get out. The old man had just started to explain that [the soldier's] colleague [had] told him not to when he received a blow to his head from the soldier's Kalashnikov ... yes, yes, an old man, I'm sure he was [not even] obliged to work at his age.

This account of the routine brutality of the security forces in their fight against terrorism singles out Lamia's narrative from those of the other women I interviewed. She is the only one who spoke of the abuses of the Algerian army in the same way as she did those of the Islamists:

> You see? I looked [hard] at that soldier—I was a witness—so he came to me, looked at me, and asked me brutally: 'Where are you going? Give me your ID card.' I was so scared. I thought he was going to arrest me, you know. He started asking: 'Where are you going? Why are you in this bus?' It was like an interrogation ... I didn't say anything. Any minute, he could shoot you. They weren't the terrorists, they were the army, but the way he beat that old man—unbelievable ... and they were the army, supposed to protect us, the people.

Acts such as this one that Lamia recounted were carried out by soldiers or the police under cover of the state of emergency introduced on 9 February 1992, the counter-terrorism decree of 30 September and the curfew imposed on 5 December that same year. These provisions allowed members of the security forces to abuse their power with impunity when searching for terrorists, and the use of violence against unarmed civilians reportedly took place at many other checkpoints, with women often paying the highest price. It was only in 1995, when Lamia had already left Algeria, that the army began to gain control of the areas the terrorists occupied, such as the one Lamia was travelling to that unfortunate day. These were areas in which the FIS had won a majority in the elections, and many of the inhabitants sympathized with the insurgent Islamists, partly because they were often their siblings, their children or members of their extended family. The security forces gained control over these areas only by means of brutal measures and extremely restrictive laws (Bedjaoui et al. 1999). According to Samraoui (2003), soldiers were authorized to kill any suspected Islamist, armed fighter or not, as they were regarded as potential recruiters of terrorists, at the very least providing them with logistical support. Between 1993 and 1995 dozens of people were killed on a daily basis, killings legitimized by one side as the 'fight against terrorism' and by the other as the 'fight for democracy'. Algerian people found themselves trapped between two conflagrations. Stories similar to Lamia's were very common at the time; many innocent people, including elderly and pregnant women, were violently beaten or raped. It is also important to point out, however, that some former members of the ALN, the former national liberation army, declared that they were not prepared to fight in an internal conflict, killing their own people or facing the possibility of being killed by friends, neighbours or members of their own family (Bedjaoui et al. 1999).

On the other hand, Wahiba Khiari (2009) recounts in *Nos Silences* (*Our Silence*), a novel framed by her own experience of the Black Decade, the experience of women and girls abducted, kidnapped and raped, often at false checkpoints set up by Islamist fighters dressed in army uniforms, graphically illustrating the high price women pay during times of conflict. Lamia herself invoked a popular joke of the time, 'Do you remember when we used to joke about it: "If they are [terrorist checkpoints], we will say: 'We are you', and if they are [security forces checkpoints] we will say: 'We are us'?"' The fact that she recalled this joke reveals that from the moment her bus was stopped she was in doubt as to whether it was the army or armed Islamists, and feared she would be kidnapped or even raped. This sense of apprehension can be traumatic in itself. It has indeed been reported by Habib Souaïdia (2006), a former security forces officer living in exile since 1995, that in 1993 soldiers were instructed to search and arrest women suspected of being associated with Islamist groups. This meant that all women living in or simply passing through 'Islamist areas' were considered potential suspects. The body searches allowed soldiers to take advantage of the situation, touching women inappropriately. Souaïdia reports that hundreds of rapes were committed by his former colleagues at such checkpoints between 1993 and 1995.

Terrorism and women's oppression

> Personally, I think it was much more difficult for women because, as a woman, you are not supposed to be outside, and terrorism was an opportunity to show more hatred and spite towards women. It was there already, you know, the need to control, the need to bully, the need to undermine women. And then there it was: the opportunity was there.

In Lamia's view, terrorism was an opportunity to exert more violence and hatred towards and control over women. It is generally recognized that the politicization of gender always occupies a key place in any national or international conflict, and women are often the first victims of political, economic and social repression. Agger (1994: 4) explains: 'Anything can happen if women leave their houses, move out into society and the public spaces, speak out and become visible, if they invade men's territory, bring[ing] disorder and impurity into society.'

Algeria is possibly one of the most androcentric societies in the North African region. The regime or '*le pouvoir*' that took over the country following its independence relegated women to the status of subordinate citizens, implementing a family law that categorizes women as minors throughout their entire lives (Lalami 2012). Nevertheless, this did not dissuade women from fighting to transgress these boundaries and access citizenship, despite the violence they often faced on the streets. Both the government and its political opponents, particularly the Islamists, also believed that women could be used as a ladder by their opponents to maintain or access power, and they became victims of the organized violence perpetrated by all sides during the Black Decade. Those women who were publicly visible, either because of their work or their political activism, were seen as a challenge to male political power. Lamia therefore interprets the escalation of violence during the Black Decade as another opportunity for men to try to force women to vacate the public sphere, to leave the streets.

Despite this, many Algerian women carried on working and studying during that time. In her speech at the 2014 International Women's Congress held in Algeria, sociologist Fatma Oussedik (2014) explained that in 1962, following independence, women only occupied 2% of the Algerian labour market, but that number had risen to 67% by 2014. Oussedik confirmed that the curve remained constant even during the Black Decade. Unfortunately, I could not access any statistics for that period despite two trips to Algiers, where I visited the Ministry of Higher Education, the offices of the UGTA (the main trade union) and the Algerian Research Centre of Economics and Development (CREAD). There is very little research or documentation on that particular period of Algerian history, and what is available invariably overlooks the experience of women.

Lamia continued her narrative by declaring that 'even if it was hard for men ... they killed more men than women perhaps ... women always had a raw deal when it came to violence'. Talking from exile, Lamia is trying to make sense of what happened twenty-five years ago. She knows that even previous to—and regardless of—the internal conflict at the time, women in Algeria have always had to face violence. Nevertheless, in Algeria at this juncture, the struggle to survive and to counteract terrorism appeared to take priority over the fight for women's rights (Lalami 2012). It was at this point that the Algerian feminist movement split into two main groups: those who continued to believe that the main enemy of women's rights was the Algerian authorities, and those who supported the cancellation of the electoral process because they feared the Islamists more. Djamila Belhouari-Musette (2006) gives an account of the feminists' clash during the Black Decade, claiming that Louisa Hanoun, one of the most respected feminist leaders in Algeria at the time and a role model for many women during the 1970s and 1980s, betrayed Algerian feminism. Hanoun was the only female political prisoner under the post-colonial regime of the 1970s, and as well as being the president of the women's rights organization the AEDHF (Association Egalité des Droits Entre Hommes et Femmes), she was also the only woman to lead a political party, the Worker's

Party (a Trotskyist organization). Following her declaration against the cancellation of the electoral process, Hanoun continued to play a prominent political role: she signed the Saint Egidio's Platform in 1995, at a time when terrorism was at its height and the GIA had much blood on its hands. The platform was seen by its organizers as an attempt to end the conflict. They called for the reinstatement of the democratic process and an independent investigation into human rights abuses against those FIS members who had been elected. However, the presence of Islamist leaders who publicly claimed responsibility for bomb attacks and the assassination of innocent citizens and intellectuals on the platform made it unacceptable to both the Algerian state and to many Algerian citizens. Hanoun lost her credibility as a feminist as many Algerians of the Islamist tendency claimed her as their own. This is only one small example of the struggle within the feminist movement.

However, to return to Lamia's account, it has become clear that perhaps her main reason for fleeing Algeria was to escape her father's control and the dictatorship of the politics of gender that discriminates so greatly against Algerian women:

> [W]hen I finished my studies, I never wanted to go back to the village. The idea of going back to the village was impossible. The village meant living under the same roof as my father: you go in and out under his watch.

Freedom is one of the most essential prerequisites for a human being's happiness, and Lamia seems to have led an unhappy life in Algeria, experiencing a very controlled childhood up until she left for university: 'There was no room for me to speak.' However, once she moved to the city, she was faced with other forms of fear and violence:

> When they killed my cousin, I told [my friend] Assia: 'I'm leaving. How, where, I don't know.' All I knew was that I had one goal: leaving the country. The UK was my destination. So I ended up getting my visa. I left. I confronted my father, and when I told him I was going, he lifted his hand to hit me—I think he was going to beat me [in a very low voice]—but anyway, he lifted his hand and he told me: 'How dare you?'

Lamia did not mention where or when the meeting with her father took place, but clearly it was after she received her visa for the UK. Her description suggests a confrontation in which her father was, at least physically, more powerful. Although she expressed a feeling of humiliation, Lamia also appeared to want to show that in reality it was she who was in the most powerful position, because she was holding a UK visa. This may have given her the strength to confront her father.

The migration process

Reaching the UK

> OK, I wanted to go to Leeds University to study, you know? But because I had no money when I arrived here, I worked as an au pair. It's when you arrive that you realize that it's not that easy, not as easy as you think, you see.

Although Lamia intended to continue her studies, on arrival she discovered yet 'another set of challenges'. At this point, I quickly took the opportunity to ask what type of visa she had been awarded on entry to the UK. 'Yes, of course, I came with a visitor's visa, and then I overstayed. The most important [thing] was for me to "put my feet here", as Fellag said, you know?' We both laughed. Interestingly Lamia mentioned here the Algerian playwright and comedian, Mohamed Fellag, a writer of satirical monologues. Lamia's quotation was taken from a play in which he recounts the difficulties that Algerian migrants face in trying to obtain legal status in Europe. Once Lamia overstayed her visa, she became 'illegal'. It is usually at this point that the disillusion begins for many people caught in a similar situation, without legal status, after they reach 'Fortress Europe'. Even more dangerous than the disillusionment are the practical and psychological implications for a woman who overstays her visa, not only because she lacks the status that will allow her access to employment, housing, health care and other services, but also because she runs the risk of being detained and deported. Lamia, however, stressed again what she endured in Algeria so that I could better understand why she chose to place herself in such a precarious situation—for example, the fact that in Algeria she was not even allowed to have a passport without her father's permission:

> Wait, wait, let me tell you first about how I got my passport. For me, it wasn't possible to get it '*au bled*'—in my village—because everyone who works for the local authority there knows my father. It's so small. My father

> never allowed us to travel to Tizi Bahbah and the big cities. He [always] used to drive us. So if I went to Tizi Bahbah on my own, someone could easily say to him: 'Aha, I've seen your daughter today', and then it's all over for me. So I made my passport [application] in [Algiers], although I wasn't a resident and my auntie couldn't [apply for] a residence paper for me because the house wasn't in her name.

As mentioned earlier, certain dominant social and religious paradigms in Algeria are used to justify the denial of full citizenship to women (Iamarene-Djerbal 2006). Despite the official post-colonial rhetoric of the Algerian constitution, which claims to follow a republican model, guaranteeing universal access to citizenship, there is an ambiguity that is clearly illustrated in the 1984 Family Code. 'Feroudja', another participant, who now lives in France, said that after the death of her husband, despite the fact that she had been known as a political activist, everyone in the city where she lived watched her every move and then reported back to her nineteen-year-old son on all the places she visited: 'The situation became unbearable, so I left.'

The Family Code was based on patrilineal rules, ignoring the changes that were happening in Algerian society, including the increase in women's employment in the public sector. Instead, it further consolidated the already oppressive laws against women: legislation banned women from leaving the country unless accompanied by a male guardian or holding written authorization signed by a male guardian (Lalami 2012). Although such authorization was not needed to apply for a passport, it was necessary to provide proof of address, which Lamia could only obtain from her father because she did not have a place of her own. Thus, she had to endure yet another stressful episode during her pre-departure period:

> I knew no one else … I was at the end of desperation, you know. I can't even describe the despair I was in … I was asking myself how many more obstacles will I have to face? … Every time I got something out of the way, there was something else.

Lamia expressed here the acute sense of isolation she was feeling at the time. She told me later that, out of her whole family, only one of her sisters knew about her project to leave, and no one apart from her father was able to give her the proof of address she needed in order to apply for a passport. Indeed, it is very common that houses are registered only in the name of the male members of a household: fathers, husbands or brothers. In any case, Lamia knew no one else in her family or village who could help her without having to confront her father.

Lamia did not want me to think that she was exaggerating her despair; however, she also wanted to stress her determination. She was also preparing me for what was coming next in her narrative: she wanted me to know why she had been forced to resort to 'abnormal' or 'immoral' means to obtain her passport:

> And so, I met someone [a man]. It was pure chance. I was going to … I can't remember where … It was very hot and I had no money, so I started hitchhiking … yes, I did, in the city! So, someone stopped [his car] and I went with him.

Lamia adopted a stronger, more assertive voice when recounting this situation, as if needing me to condone her transgression of what was culturally acceptable in Algerian society, and to convince me that it was vital for her to go with this man if she wanted to seize the opportunity to leave the country. It is interesting to see her use of the phrase 'went with him' rather than 'got in his car', which suggests that she may have met him again. In Algerian culture, the moment Lamia got into a car with an unknown man, she had crossed a patriarchal red line.

At this point in the story, knowing the insecurity of women living in Algiers and its environs at the time, facing the threat of kidnapping, abduction, rape or murder, I had to acknowledge Lamia's courage in hitchhiking. Indeed, according to *An Inquiry into the Algerian Massacres*, edited by Youcef Bedjaoui (1999), 3,700 women were killed between 1992 and 1998, although prior to November 1996 most of the news reports did not provide statistics of victims according to gender. Mokrane Ait Larbi (1999: 101), an Algerian lawyer, politician and advocate for human rights, together with other lawyers and human rights activists, published a report that recorded that at least 435 women were killed between November 1996 and December 1998 alone, of whom at least 149 were abducted and raped before being killed—in fact, in most cases, the kidnapped women were found to have been raped before they were murdered.

Lamia, meanwhile, continued her story, saying:

> But this was an old man. Anyway, I would have gone with anyone. He didn't have [pause] ... he wasn't [pause] ... so I told him my story. It was like God had sent him to me because, really, what's the worst that can happen to me? When you have no money, no support, no security, nothing, who cares? You really think I was worried about my security or being killed? If anything, the killing was there every day anyway.

For Lamia, as long as the man was 'old', he was to be trusted, in the same way that she trusted her former superior in the company where she experienced sexual harassment, with the difference being that this man helped her and did not betray her trust. Lamia justified her actions by emphasizing her desperation—she was not in a position to let the opportunity pass her by. Although she did not divulge any details about how this man helped her, by saying 'God sent him' Lamia made it clear to me that it was acceptable for her to take his offer of help. However, the silences between her sentences revealed her hesitation when describing both her own feelings and how she viewed the man: a man old enough to be her father. In any case, she felt she had no other choice.

In some areas of Algeria, if a woman goes out in public she needs to be shadowed by a man. If she has to sort out administrative papers, for example, a male guardian (father, husband, brother or son) will accompany her. As Feroudja explained:

> When my husband was alive, I was an activist both in my [local] association and political party. Everyone in the city used to look at me with respect. But once my husband died, I became [simply] his widow, because in Algeria you are always described as the wife of ... , the daughter of ... , the mother of ... . One day I called our regular plumber to fix my sink. He told me that he was sorry he could not come until my son got home. Then, you feel the humiliation.

Although Lamia's and Feroudja's circumstances were very different, they felt the same sense of humiliation, simply because of their gender. According to Lamia, this man appeared almost providentially at the moment she was feeling most humiliated, in despair, denied paternal support and with no other male in her life. Lamia did not describe how this man helped her but somehow he managed to get her a passport and visa. The worst that this man could have done, she says, was to kill her, but the worries about being killed were present every day anyway, and everyone was a target. This is illustrated by what follows in her narrative:

> I remember that we were told: if you receive a bullet, it will take ten seconds before you start feeling it, and then you die. This is what we were told. You see the fear they [instilled] in us? So when I was walking, I constantly told myself that I may have received a bullet [without realizing] and I was going to feel it in ten seconds, and then I would die. It was a bizarre sensation—the feeling was very bizarre. Because you tell yourself [pause] ... when you pass by 'dodgy' places sometimes, because you never know, it used to happen very suddenly: 'tatatata'.

Lamia's recurring imitation of the gun suggests a vivid memory of what the sounds represent: the fear induced by being in the vicinity of sudden death. I felt that much of what Lamia was describing here was similar to my own experience and to that of the other women I met during the course of my research. The interview, in this sense, was taking the form of an auto-ethnographic narrative of women who survived the atrocities of the Black Decade. However, despite the unbidden memories, I tried my best to remain detached and keep to my role as the researcher. As for Lamia, she was also reliving a very traumatic feeling, one outside the normal range of human experience: expecting to receive a bullet at every ten-second interval, the sense of being extremely close to death yet somehow continuing to survive.

Arrival in the UK

When Lamia grew calmer, she started speaking of her experience as a new arrival in the UK.

> Yes, when I arrived here, I worked as an au pair for six months ... euhhh, and I wasn't in touch with any other Algerians ... And then I made contact again with Louisa, who came from Algeria at the same time as me.

A brief glance at the work of Michael Collyer, one of the few scholars to research the Algerian community in the UK, goes some way to explaining Lamia's experience of relative isolation from her compatriots. Up to 2004, when Collyer's research was published, Algerians in the UK were mainly concentrated in London, particularly around Finsbury Park (known as a 'Little Algiers'); Walthamstow, the location of the former Algerian Refugee Council; and Waltham Forest, where the former Algerian Welfare Association (AWA) was based—both these organizations have since closed. These areas were far from where Lamia was living at that time. Overall, there were three waves of Algerian migration to the UK. The first comprised those who came to study in UK universities during the 1970s and 1980s, when the Algerian government offered scholarships to study abroad. Non-verifiable sources claim that 8,000 of these Algerians never went back and instead found work in the UK, becoming fully integrated into British society. The second wave was mainly composed of refugees such as Lamia, who fled following the rising violence of the 1990s. Collyer mainly speaks about members of the FIS, who, due to the repression of the party following the cancellation of the democratic process, automatically fell under Article 1 of the Geneva Convention and were granted refugee status. Finally, the third group, in the late 1990s, was that of the '*harragas*', those who risked everything to enter Europe illegally, often by boat. It is difficult to estimate the real number of *harragas* in the UK and how many of them are Algerian. From my observation, however, there is a considerable number of highly skilled women among those Algerians who have no immigration status and who prefer to remain invisible.

Lack of trust, even suspicion, among migrants from Algeria is also another factor that may have had an impact on Lamia's situation. A feeling of isolation is common among refugees who flee internal conflicts, but there is a deep-seated reason for the particularly high level of suspicion among Algerians in London who claimed asylum in the 1990s. According to Le Sueur (2010), there was a large division between the different groups of Algerians at the time. On the one hand, there were former members of the FIS, whose asylum claims were grounded on the fact that they had been persecuted by the Algerian security forces. According to the head of the London-based Algerian British Connection (ABC),[2] these former members of the FIS openly celebrated the assassinations of intellectuals in Algeria. On the other hand, there were secular intellectuals and highly educated migrants like Lamia who had fled in fear of

2. I conducted the interview with the head of the Algerian British Connection on 14 July 2015.

those very assassinations. Hence, it was common for Algerian women like Lamia to find themselves in a very isolated position. Lamia says that the contacts she made in Algeria and the information they gave her about finding a job in the UK were useful, but only temporarily. This experience was not necessarily specific to Lamia's case. According to the survey I conducted and observations I made during my fieldwork, as well as my personal experience, at the time of Lamia's arrival there were no professional networks among Algerians living in the UK to which newly arrived Algerians could turn for information about the sort of support systems available.

Lamia's following statement reflects her lack of such a support network:

> So I left that woman's house and went to live in Brixton, where I worked as an au pair again, this time for a Greek couple. First, I had a room, and then I lived for a few days with Louisa. She was the one who introduced me to the Greek couple. But one day the Greek lady told her: 'Can you please tell Lamia to leave; I don't want her here any more.' I had nowhere to go and no one to go to. I spent my nights crying again, as I was homeless, with no shelter and no right to work.

After climbing 'Kilimanjaro'—to use Lamia's own metaphor—in order to get to her much-anticipated European haven, Lamia was overwhelmed by disillusion. She was now back to spending her nights crying, reminding her of when she used to live with her aunt in Algiers. At that time, her tears were caused by the difficulties she encountered and the daily fear of terrorism, but at least in Algeria she'd had a roof over her head; now, she no longer had a job or accommodation, and was effectively homeless and destitute in London. In the very short time she had spent in the UK, she had already lost two jobs and—more troublingly—had become an undocumented or 'illegal' migrant. Although Lamia at this stage did not give any details about this period, it is likely that her visa had expired around the time she started working for the Greek family, which would explain why they decided they could no longer house or employ her.

When Lamia reached this point in her story, she lapsed into silence for a short time. I prompted her: 'You had no problems with the English language. Could you not find another job?' Lamia answered:

> No, I couldn't. Because I had no papers … it was hard. The funniest thing is, for me, before I came to this country, my written English was perfect,

> but I couldn't speak it, you see? So I took the Cambridge Proficiency in English exam. It was very easy for me. Then I worked in a restaurant, as everyone did, just to have something to eat … as a waitress and then as a chef. I was promoted.

So Lamia found herself an undocumented migrant, banned from working. She told me, however, that Louisa, the friend she mentioned above, provided her with somewhere to stay for a few days. She also spoke of another Algerian woman living in London, a former journalist, who gave shelter to many of her compatriots—an act of solidarity among Algerian women in exile, one that recalls the generosity of Lamia's aunt in Algeria.

At this point, Lamia was experiencing a situation she had never expected when she left Algeria. Nevertheless, she reminded me that because she held a degree in English literature, she had passed her English examination with ease, illustrating once again just how important being an educated woman was for her self-esteem. Once in the UK, although she held an English degree, Lamia had to go back to her studies, just as I did, but despite passing her Cambridge Proficiency examination, due to her lack of legal status she was forced to work in a restaurant. Although she found this demeaning, she recognized it as the route that many in her situation were forced to take. Lamia proudly pointed out that she was promoted to the position of chef as a result of her hard work and competence. By contrast, there was never any mention of promotion in Algeria. There, Lamia was offered no rewards of any kind; rather, she experienced sexual harassment and dismissal. Although the restaurant business was not her field of interest, the most significant element here is the sense of reward the work gave Lamia and its positive impact on her self-esteem. She may in fact have started rebuilding her fragile sense of self at precisely this point in her life.

Claiming asylum in the UK

Nevertheless, the question remains, given Lamia's experience of persecution and the abuse of women's rights in Algeria in general, why she did not claim asylum as soon as she entered the country. Lamia answered this by saying, after a pause, 'I did in the end. But it's not something I usually talk a lot about. Because, it's a bit … yeah, yeah … it was very hard. It was a very hard time for me.' Lamia seemed uncomfortable talking about her asylum claim, despite the fact that I had introduced myself as someone who also arrived in the UK as a refugee and who has possibly been through a similar experience. It is interesting to note that while she related her ordeals in Algeria in great depth, she chose to give very little detail about her experience of the asylum process. It is often the case that Algerians choose not to tell compatriots that they have claimed political asylum at all in order to avoid being stigmatized or labelled, although it appears from the way she responded to the questions that this was not necessarily the case for Lamia.

Jane Herlihy and Stuart Turner (2013) have investigated the ways in which refugees in general remember and construct their narratives, and how under the stress of forced migration, they tend to tell stories that are fragmented, leaving parts untold. There are several reasons for this, but one of the main ones for many women is the proven relationship between speaking openly about experiences of sexual harassment or, as in the case of Lamia, physical abuse by a close family member, and denying or hiding the truth in order to avoid exhibiting difficult emotions and feelings of shame. Thus, the reasons behind Lamia's reluctance to speak about her experience of seeking asylum may be related both to the events immediately before her departure and to the humiliations she undoubtedly suffered during the asylum process itself.

Papadopoulos's (2002) classic work on the impact of forced migration on individuals' mental well-being highlights two contrasting reasons why refugees choose to remain silent about their experiences: feelings either of resilience or of vulnerability. Papadopoulos explains that a person's exterior life can change very suddenly, but their ability to adjust their inner world to these events requires the sort of acceptance of reality that only flows from feeling emotionally stable and 'present'. This state of mind is out of reach for many refugees, who are often overwhelmed with feelings of loss, particularly loss of a 'sense of home' and locus of identity. When this is added to the difficulty of managing frequent, unexpected changes to asylum laws and procedures, it may be essential to them to remain silent about the migration process in order for the 'healing process' to begin. Forced migration leaves people temporarily disoriented, as though they were frozen in a type of hypothermia, and they need to 'defrost' in order to proceed again with normal life (Papadopoulos 2002). As Lamia said:

> In our community, political asylum is considered taboo, like [it is] something bad ... So they don't speak about it and don't give you information, because they never tell you they have been through this process. Or they don't want to be known only as [someone who has been] persecuted: the identity as a refugee fleeing persecution is not all that we are.

Many Algerians do not claim asylum at all, arguably due to a sense of pride that stems from the struggle against French colonial repression. According to Lamia, many of her fellow Algerians refuse the label of refugee. Indeed, many of the Algerians I met in London through my voluntary work with a migrant support centre were undocumented and showed no intention of claiming asylum, rendering difficult any research into the Algerian refugee experience in the UK. There is also another possibility, however, behind the fact that many of the other Algerians in this survey were also unwilling to tell me they have claimed asylum: they may have been particularly reticent as they did not want to admit that they had been refused or their claim had not been believed. Lamia too may have felt embarrassed at first to tell me about her humiliating experiences with the asylum process. In fact, the majority of the women who participated in this research, regardless of the country they currently live in, preferred not to say whether they had claimed asylum.

Albeit reluctantly, Lamia answered my question as to why it was so hard for her to claim asylum: 'It was because I lacked information and guidance ... And because I was a woman, I didn't think about claiming political asylum at all when I was looking for a way to get my papers here.' This remark suggests that Lamia, between the time her visa expired and her asylum claim, may have explored different paths to becoming a legal resident, or at least of extending her right to stay in the UK. During this time, her mental well-being certainly suffered as a consequence of the uncertainty and sense of exclusion from society. Her words also reveal the lack of support and information available for anyone seeking asylum in the UK. It is common for women, particularly those escaping war and conflict, to have little or no knowledge of or access to reliable sources of information about asylum procedures in the country they flee to; they may not even know they have a right to claim asylum, simply because women are rarely perceived as political refugees. Yet, as Forbes Martin (2003) and Moghadam (1994) argue, the countries at that time which produced the highest number of refugees generally lay within the 'patriarchal belt' (mentioned in Chapter Two), which runs from North Africa eastwards to Southeast Asia—although the majority tended to end up internally displaced within the region. Furthermore, Moghadam (1994), who studied the participation of Algerian women in public life after the country's War of Independence, points out that, despite their full participation in the armed liberation forces, women's social and administrative status had been rapidly reshaped by the Family Code, which denies women the ability to exercise citizenship rights. Transgressing both this legislation and traditional customs, as Lamia did, is therefore a de facto political act of resistance.

The 1951 Refugee Convention remains the key, internationally recognized source for the definition of a 'refugee', their rights and the legal obligations of states towards them. According to the Convention, a person is recognized as a refugee only if they have a 'well-founded fear of persecution' either by the state or by political groups operating outside state control. Persecution suffered in the private sphere of the family, as in Lamia's case, is not considered political but part of a 'private culture', and victims of this sort of persecution are for the most part not considered deserving of international protection. Many women refugees therefore do not fulfil the Convention's criteria. Nevertheless, if we look at the gender-specific problems Lamia faced, which included the threat of violence from her father and the general atmosphere of violence against women in Algeria at the time, she did in fact face persecution. Both the male-dominated culture and the presence of conflict contributed to her decision to leave the country.

There is controversy over whether gender-related persecution should be recognized as a basic violation of women's rights by an oppressive culture and/or religion. Heaven Crawley (2001) believes that an acceptance of cultural relativism is often used in an attempt to exonerate such oppression. What is crucial in such an argument is the idea that human rights are not universal; rather, it is thought that they need to be adapted to the cultural context. For example, the fact that Lamia's father beat her might be considered a violation of her human rights in a British or European context, but it seems this does not apply to a woman who bases her asylum claim on such an experience

(Guemar 2011). Indeed, Lamia's remarks suggest that her claim was refused and that her legal representative was not competent enough to defend a claim based on gender-based violence and discrimination. The main question is how to argue that such violence is persecution and to demonstrate that the state in the claimant's country of origin is unable or unwilling to protect her. This is extremely difficult, particularly if a lawyer is not already conversant with the specific problems women face. Women claiming asylum based on gender-based violence often find their applications are refused.

This situation undoubtedly added more stress to Lamia's life, but it was the ineffectiveness of her immigration solicitor that seems to have been her main concern:

> When I [got all the evidence for] my case and went to my solicitor, he told me: 'I have never seen anybody representing themselves like you do.' I was doing it like homework, you see; I was doing my research, all the expert [opinion] on what was going on in Algeria. The solicitor did nothing.

Luckily, Lamia is a highly educated woman with transferable skills and expertise, and she was fluent in English. This was of immense help to her when it came to finding evidence to support her asylum claim:

> My case was based on the abuse of women's human rights and, [because I am] a woman of strong opinions, on not being able to go back [to Algeria]. I got in touch with the organization SOS Femmes en Détresse [Women in Distress], because here they say: 'What will happen to you if you go back?' You know, the stuff about relocation: 'Why can't you move to another town [in Algeria]?' They have no idea that an Algerian woman cannot go to another town. They [will] find you and they [will] kill you, because, if you are a father and have a daughter living in another town, that is simply inconceivable, it doesn't make sense.

This was the first time that Lamia had mentioned a women's rights organization in Algeria, despite the fact that when she was living there she had need of their services. Lamia only got in touch with SOS Femmes en Détresse, which is based in Algiers, after her British solicitor had failed to argue her case adequately. SOS was formed in the early 1990s to tackle the urgent need of homeless women who had been evicted from their married home following divorce. The organization then expanded into other areas when it noted that divorced women were not the only victims of the Family Code; there were many other girls and women suffering from violence and oppression within the family, often forbidden to continue their studies, work or even leave the house—in other words, women who had been reduced to the position of domestic slaves. To defend her asylum claim, Lamia needed to prove that the harm she had experienced was sufficiently serious to be described as 'persecution' and could be measured against the spirit of the UN Declaration of Human Rights and the human rights entitlements recognized by the international community. Despite the difficulties involved in doing so, Lamia—spurred on by her dismay at her immigration solicitor's lack of understanding of her case—turned into a human rights activist in her bid to challenge UK asylum policy, realizing her agency in the process. She was not politicized in Algeria, or at least she does not portray herself as such; she never mentions involvement with any sort of activism in defence of women's rights there. It was only when she was confronted by the threat of deportation from the UK that Lamia became aware of how thin the barrier is between the personal and the political for any woman who dares to become visible.

It seems that Lamia had received the classic refusal letter from the Home Office, advising her to take steps to return to her country of origin where she could be relocated to another city of her choosing. When the British government decides to return women who have failed in their asylum claim to countries in which they have experienced violence and where internal conflict is ongoing, it is obliged to consider the routes and methods of their return, and the potential dangers facing women during this process. However, it is well documented that the Home Office rarely investigates these matters, and frequently disregards this obligation, wrongly deporting women or advising on their relocation within the country.

> When the barrister came to represent my case, she was a woman, and she was talking about how many restrictions [there are], and how an assertive, educated woman can get into trouble in Algeria ... I agreed with her—if a woman like that leaves [Algeria] and then comes back, she's not going to be trusted. They will say: 'She went around with Western people, and this and that.'

If women are lucky enough to be given a right of appeal against a negative decision, as Lamia was, the Home Office is required by law to consider the safety of their relocation. Whether it was realistic to expect Lamia to be returned to another, 'safer' part of Algeria was easily disputed at that time, and it seems that the barrister met with success; the rapidity with which she convinced the asylum adjudicator was no doubt due to her competence and her understanding of the Algerian situation.

It is interesting to note how Lamia highlighted the issues of mistrust and suspicion harboured towards women who have been living abroad once they return to Algeria. This helps explain why the majority of participants in this research declared their unwillingness to return home. The policy of 'relocation' therefore must be placed in the context of the politics of gender and the situation of women in the country as a whole. In Lamia's case, given the environment in Algeria at the time, the main problem would have been rejection by her father, which would have led to the whole extended family withholding any form of support, and all the social and cultural issues she would have to face as a consequence. The situation would have been worse because she was single, especially if she was returned to a rural area where women are expected to have male protection—which is in itself a paradox given the prevalence of domestic violence. Lamia would also face discrimination in terms of finding a job to support herself, a difficulty she had already encountered prior to her flight. Relocation was clearly not appropriate in her case, since it would have left her with no alternative but to seek her family's assistance, re-exposing her to a 'well-founded fear of persecution' and the risk of 'serious harm' that she had fled from in the first place.

The restriction of women's rights in a post-conflict context is not unusual, and post-1990s Algeria was no exception. For example, Article 7 of the Family Code requiring the presentation of a prenuptial medical certificate before registering a marriage was reinforced in 2006. Although not intended as such, most of Algerian society interpreted this article as requiring a certificate of virginity from future brides, and it is still widely implemented in this way. This practice was not new in itself, but the legislation made it 'official' and compulsory. This explains what Lamia meant when she mentioned the lack of trust towards women who return after living abroad, the most important aspect of which is related to women's sexuality. Against the backdrop of such discriminatory legislation it is not surprising that post-1990s Algeria saw violence against women on the streets increase to such a point that a draft bill outlawing such acts was presented to the senate more than once, although it was rejected each time, most recently in 2015.

The emotional impact of migration

Lamia appears to have found meaning in her plight and to have learned how to transform negative experiences into positive ones in a way that enabled her to deal with her day-to-day difficulties. According to Hajdukowski-Ahmed (2008), the adjustment to a new environment and a new life will differ with each woman. For example, Lamia intimated that she sees herself as a strong woman who successfully surmounted her own 'Kilimanjaro': 'It was very traumatic, but … I take a lesson from this: life has no meaning without certain struggles.' Papadopoulos (2006) explains that the negative meaning given to the word 'trauma' does not adequately cover its unique effect on people who experience oppression, ill-treatment and forced displacement. Lamia's narrative suggests that a person will react differently to the different stages of their migratory journey. This process of positive and negative reactions to trauma is well illustrated in Lamia's remark; in the end, she responded positively. As she explained in the interview, through experiencing painful events in Algeria she gradually became aware that she should look at the world in a different way and begin to appreciate life more. Such positive reactions to trauma often occur when people have experienced oppression or violence, or have been close to death (Papadopoulos 2006).

Incontestably, Lamia has exploited her inner strengths to discover self-reliance and find ways of relieving her trauma and overcoming the difficulties related to the migration process. As a professional woman, her determination to retrieve the kind of social status she had worked for back home seems to have motivated her to gain qualifications in a new field in her new country. She eventually found work as a project manager in a well-known organization, and although she mentioned at the beginning of the interview that she was about to be made redundant, she informed me a few weeks later that she had been offered a better position in another organization working in a similar field.

I asked Lamia what it meant for her to win her case at the High Court and to be recognized as a political refugee.

> For me, it was my father who was not for women's rights. For him, a woman is there to have kids and to nurture them, clean the house, and so on. I had no right to have friends, to have relationships, to go visit someone, to sleep over. Going to school was already something big.

Lamia's oblique response raises the whole question of refugee women's reconstruction of identity once they reach a safe place. As mentioned earlier, in Lamia's case, her reason for fleeing was strongly connected with the policing of women's conduct in Algeria and the harsh patriarchal rules she was forced to live under and which she transgressed, incurring her father's anger. It first forced her into internal displacement, as she left her village for the city, and then drove her across Algeria's borders to the UK. Here, Lamia reflects on the ambivalence of women's position within the so-called collectivity. It appears that she has constructed the whole of her narrative of exile around the question of the gender discrimination she has experienced. Thus, Lamia later asserted it was not primarily her cousin's assassination that had made her leave the country, nor the atmosphere of terror—it was also her experience of patriarchal restrictions. She refused to be reduced to the role of serving her brothers or to forgo her ambitions as a bright, educated woman in order to marry. Lamia, in this sense, agreed with the Home Office that she was not a political refugee as understood by the Geneva Convention. She distinguished herself instead as a woman who stood up for her rights against her father (a symbol of Algerian patriarchy) rather than as a political activist. As she explained to me during a previous conversation, she disregarded politics: she did not consider her struggle against the social conditions of being a woman in Algeria as political. She explained that she struggled against the role attributed to all females in her family, where a woman who works outside the house is seen as immoral or—at best—a rebel. It is interesting to note that Lamia portrays herself as non-political despite having been granted political asylum at the end of a long and complicated struggle.

The above remark confirms the conclusion drawn by some feminist scholars of gender and migration (Agger 1994; Moghadam 1994; Yuval-Davis 1997) that the majority of women become refugees within the context of relationship between gender, nation and nationalism. Furthermore, the mental well-being of refugee women is 'intimately connected with their gendered identities and both are influenced by the historical and the cultural context' of where they come from and the environment in the country of asylum (Hajdukowski-Ahmed et al. 2008: 211). In fact, Hajdukowski-Ahmed's (2008) research (see Chapter One) indicates there is a strong relationship between women's mental well-being and how they perceive their identity transformations during their journey into exile. She emphasizes that refugee women's identity and agency can be summarized in three essential points. Firstly, the terms 'refugee' or 'asylum seeker' are simply descriptions of a legal status in which people find themselves due to particular circumstances at a particular time in their lives. Secondly, refugees already possess 'multilayered' and 'multifaceted' identities even before they are forced to flee. Finally, while men's and women's identities are both impacted by the conflicts and human rights violations that are the initial cause of their displacement, women are the more vulnerable to violence.

The question of how such women negotiate new identities under new circumstances has unavoidably become a central issue of my study. Lamia is an excellent example of a migrant woman with a multilayered identity, revealing her capacity to be equally traumatized, angry, sad and, finally, resilient enough to even forgive her father.

Reconciliation and forgiveness

Personal reconciliation

> In fact, when I made peace with my father, yes, that is another story. I really had a hard time and [I] clashed with my father, because I am a bit stubborn, and I am not like 'because you are my father, I owe you this'.

The above quote from Lamia suggests that although she certainly does not regret having confronted her father, now that her life in the UK is more secure and in many respects better in terms of gender equality, she has retrieved a sense of self which has helped dissipate her resentment towards him. Here again, I discovered two different Lamias: the one who is happy and satisfied with her life in the UK, and the other who is still suffering from the trauma she endured before and during her journey, and who now expressed sadness when broaching the topic of her relationship with her father.

The process of making peace and seeking forgiveness from others depends on each individual's experiences and circumstances. Studies reveal that forgiveness involves moving beyond rage and restoring emotional cohesiveness (Zachar 2006: 68). Forgiveness, as demonstrated in Lamia's case, is also grounded in the traditions of Algerian Islamic culture. Being forgiven by a parent before they die is what every Algerian aspires to. Exile reinforces this desire, not only because it will be met with high social approbation, but also because it may help attenuate the guilt that is often associated with being forced to leave your homeland, family and friends. This appeared to be an important turning point in Lamia's narrative. After having portrayed her father as the main person responsible for her pain, she now, in retrospect, gave him credit for letting her go to university and encouraging her to study, particularly as it seems that her educational background helped ease her integration into British society.

> Because in the village, girls should stop at the baccalaureate. [They don't] even have the right to ask about going to university. So, many of them will be successful in their exams but will never dream [of stepping] into a university … This was in [my village], but it happened everywhere, you see. So the fact that my father let us to go to university was a big thing.

Lamia believes she could not have fought the asylum process if she had been illiterate or less well educated—and that was partly due to her father's attitude to girls' education. Other girls in her village did not have the right to even dream of going to university, despite examination successes: 'So I decided to be a bigger person … I didn't want him to die without forgiving me.'

Lamia repeated this statement many times, apparently wanting to take the opportunity of the interview to purge herself of remorse and relieve the pain she feels. Indeed, Agger (1994: 107) describes how 'it [is] sometimes possible for a healing process to develop alongside the actual research process'. Lamia was exteriorizing her pain by recounting the same facts again and again, a process which can be therapeutic in itself. Also, the fact that she is now content and secure in the UK has enabled her to transcend the pain as well as the anger she felt towards her father, particularly when he beat her, although she did appear somewhat confused, as her narrative shows, as to who should forgive whom. However, whatever the outcome, she did not want her father to die before they had the chance to mend their relationship:

> Because anger, it eats away at you, it's like a cancer. I had it for years ... but I let it go. I called a meeting with my father. I had to confront him again, but [ever] since, I swear to you Latefa, it's like someone took a burden from my shoulders ... I let him have his peace for the sake of reaching peace myself. And when I came back, I [had] never felt as good, so I said to my husband: 'Finally, in life, [I realize that] when you seek pardon from someone, you don't do it for them, you do it for yourself.'

Lamia was in full control of the process of reconciliation with her father (who has since passed away), but she was still tearful and emotional when evoking the meeting. It was her decision to bring an end to her resentment towards him after realizing she had been blaming him for all the horrors, humiliations, harassment and difficulties she had experienced in Algeria; in a sense, she had placed all the responsibility for the inequalities and oppression she had faced at her father's door. Having lived for some time in a country where respect for women's rights is enshrined in law, Lamia was mentally well equipped to call for forgiveness. She was not certain of the response she would receive, either from her father or from the rest of the family, but that was not the most important point. The motivation behind reaching out to her father was a personal one—her conscience would be clear. Moreover, the lack of a close relationship with family members back home can be particularly difficult to bear in the context of exile because they often represent the only concrete link a migrant has with what Cohen (2010) calls their 'imagined homeland'.

> And in fact this [oppression] wasn't personal ... No, it's not personal. This is a society in which my father was a victim [too], in which women have a second-class position or third-class, or God knows what, and me, I was fighting against that. So, in a way, it is not that he hated me or I hated him ... I had to admit that this was how girls struggle in the majority of Algerian families.

Lamia used the term second- or third-class (the literal translation is 'second-hand', with the allusion to merchandise) to describe women's position in Algerian society—a society in which, she came to realize, her father was also a victim to some extent.

Reconciliation in Algeria: Politics at home

But what about the other horrors Lamia experienced? Regardless of her father's behaviour, there were other situations in which Lamia suffered discrimination, harassment, persecution and, more importantly, witnessed terror attacks, during which she came close to being killed—as did so many others in Algeria at the time. What about reparations in terms of the country as a whole?

During the Black Decade, the Algerian army was accused by international human rights organizations of committing many of the massacres that took place (Chomsky 1999). Evidence to support these accusations came from victims similar to Lamia, who experienced the terror of those years at first hand. The National Popular Army, inheritors of the mantle of the Army of National Liberation (ALN), which was held in high esteem internationally for liberating the Algerian people from French colonial rule, lost its integrity as a result of such accusations, especially those made against a few of its generals who were believed to have been involved in the assassination of intellectuals and journalists. Hence, the army, after ending the bloody conflict, then had to face these accusations. As a result, the state considered the idea of a process of national reconciliation modelled on the Argentinean experience and the South African Truth and Reconciliation Commission.

In Argentina, a report by a 1983 commission opened the door to the subsequent trial of members of the army who stood accused of the ubiquitous use of torture. These trials were recognized as an important factor in appeasing political and social tensions after the end of the military dictatorship; however, they appeared to have had little impact on forgiveness and reconciliation at an individual, grassroots level (Balch & Lust2006). In the Algerian context, the restoration of security and peace following the horrors of the 1990s required answers to specific questions regarding the motives behind the generalization of violence, as well as the specific assassinations of intellectuals during that time. The main questions that follow are how such injuries can be compensated, and what should happen to those responsible for enacting them. In 1995, following a series of secret negotiations with leaders of the Islamic Salvation Army (GIA) (Belhimer 2014b), the Algerian army and the government attempted to respond to these two questions. President Liamine Zéroual, himself a major-general, proposed an amnesty law, which was known at first as the Charter for Peace and National Reconciliation (Arnould 2007).

According to Ammar Belhimer (2014b), Valerie Arnould (2007) and George Joffé (2008), the design of the charter was grounded in the historical Algerian cultural/religious concept of *rahma*, which can be translated as 'clemency'. It is also associated with two other religious concepts: *moukafa'a* (reward)—that is, a heavenly reward—and *taouba* (repentance), on condition that guilt is acknowledged and forgiveness sought (Belhimer 2014a). Arguably, however, the charter was also grounded in an aspiration among the majority of ordinary Algerians for a peaceful life. Thus, when in July 1999—three months after his election—President Bouteflika passed a law on 'civil harmony', it was widely approved in a referendum: 98% of Algerian citizens voted 'yes' in an 85% turnout (Belhimer 2014a). There was, however, little information on the main points of the law, which enacted special measures for the exemption from prosecution for members of terrorist organizations who had not committed assassinations, caused permanent disability, committed rape or used explosives in public places, and who promised to cease all terrorist activities. In September 2005, Algerians were called on to participate in a second referendum to decide on a general amnesty, in which they were simply asked to say 'yes' or 'no' to peace. Algerians again voted in favour: 97%, with 79% of citizens participating, only slightly less than the previous referendum (Belhimer 2014a). However, Moghadam (2010) points out that this amnesty was rejected by all Algerian feminist organizations and by many of those women who had been forced into exile, as confirmed by this research. Moghadam has further identified a new wave of Algerian feminists, including women psychologists focused on addressing post-conflict trauma, who opposed the amnesty and put forward an urgent demand to first end all violence against women in the country (Moghadam 2010: 180).

Drawing from this debate, and considering Lamia's personal experience of terror during the Black Decade, I was interested to hear her views on the *rahma*/reconciliation or amnesty, and whether she associated forgiving her father with the process of forgiving those who plunged Algeria into a climate of terror. My curiosity was particularly aroused by the fact that the violence perpetrated against women during these years has finally been recognized (Lloyd 2006), resulting in an urgent call on the Algerian authorities to respond with adequate policy measures. I asked Lamia: 'Have you heard about the vote on the amnesty in Algeria? What do you think of it, as a woman?'

> Ah yes, the amnesty law. Well, when it first came out I thought it was outrageous, I thought it was unfair because there is a difference: you put someone on trial [first] before you forgive them, and then you decide on an amnesty. For me, personally, the amnesty in Algeria would have been OK if families of the victims had been given the right support, or maybe if they had consulted them. You can't decide on behalf of somebody who was hurt [or had] a person close to them killed. For example, for my cousin's parents, there is no way they can forgive the killer.

In response to my question, Lamia quite straightforwardly suggested that she rejects the general amnesty, even finds it 'outrageous' and 'unfair'. She first talked in general about those who committed these crimes, and then moved on to give the example of her cousin's family. Without face-to-face confrontations or the trial of those who committed these acts of terror, Lamia believes there cannot be forgiveness. As for her cousin, she asserted that his parents will never forgive the murderer. Lamia now lives in London, and she witnessed how Algerians with FIS tendencies in exile in the UK condoned the assassinations that took place, and how, following the legislation of 28 February 2006, these same people were invited by the Algerian embassy to use the *rahma* law to benefit from the amnesty.

Lamia also addressed the question of healing as an important enabling device for reconciliation. According to David Brendel (2006), there is no miracle recipe for healing the traumas inflicted by war and conflict, and each society should find its own path, corresponding to its specific religious and cultural particularities. Consequently, understanding the pain of a traumatized community calls for attentive consideration of the individuals who have been personally affected. Indeed, collective healing is conditioned by the healing of these individuals; it is crucial that the two processes occur in parallel. Brendel (2006: 16) extends this argument further by saying that '[t]he two processes appear to stand in a dialectical relationship to one another'. Due to the complexity of individuals' reactions to trauma and their specific aptitudes for resilience, as well as the historical, political and cultural circumstances of the societies in which trauma has occurred, healing and reconciliation will not be an easy process, eliciting straightforward responses. This has been shown by the experience of South Africa's Truth and Reconciliation Commission, which allowed individuals to share stories, express their feelings, apologize and achieve some measure of forgiveness. Talking from exile, Lamia seems to be aware that no such process took place in Algeria, despite the high participation in the two referendums on the amnesty. Indeed, even if such a process had been initiated, women would have found it hard to participate due to the social barriers they face, particularly in the rural areas, and their difficulties in accessing mental health services.

I asked Lamia: 'Would you have been happy if you had been invited to the consultations that took place before the law of general amnesty?'

> Yes, of course, I would have loved having my say, at least as someone who has lost a close member of her family. No one can go and forgive on your behalf. You know, at least it would have been something if we had been consulted ... For God's sake, you see them [those who 'repented'] today, walking on the streets ... like nothing happened—those who killed Matoub, killed this [person] and killed that [person]. No, it's not right. But it has happened; maybe there is a positive side of this amnesty, I don't know. Is it because of the amnesty that Algeria has now regained its security? I don't know. All I know is that when you don't give any reason for what has happened—and it was not nothing, it was mass murder—it's not right.

Lamia clearly expressed the importance of having her say on the proposal for an amnesty; however, as Joffé (2008: 8) remarks, '[t]here was not to be any truth and justice commission as part of the process of reconciliation'. Instead, Bouteflika simply asked Algerians to forgive each other and live peacefully again, sharing public spaces, despite the fact that those spaces had witnessed a decade of assassinations, kidnappings and rapes. In fact, all the participants in this research without exception expressed dissent over the amnesty law. Lamia's voice betrayed her anger as she continued:

> You know what Bouteflika said to Matoub's mother when she questioned him once about her son? 'Where do you want me to bring your son's assassin from? From my pocket?' Do you think this is a way to speak to a mother who has lost her son—assassinated? And that was on TV for everyone to

hear. That's not a way of showing compassion. Yes, you may not know the killer [and] yes, you may not be able to do anything about it, but if you are the president of the country, you should be able to do something. It was not what she wanted to hear.

Lamia seemed to be very concerned with what is happening in Algeria, despite living far from the country. Matoub, whose mother Lamia mentioned above, was a famous singer and a symbol of rebellion for Algerian youth, especially in Kabylia, Lamia's home region. He was killed in June 1998. Lamia here expressed empathy towards a bereaved mother who was publicly humiliated by the same president who imposed the amnesty law on Algerians, a law supposedly grounded in the tenets of reconciliation and forgiveness. It has in fact been argued that one of the main reasons for the law's failure is the overall absence of respect for the rule of law in Algeria (Arnould 2007). As a result, there is a feeling of distrust, resentment and betrayal among the families of the victims of terror and the disappeared. During my observation of online discourse over the period of my research, and on my visits to Algeria, I noticed the sense of betrayal felt by the majority of Algerians, particularly women who experienced a dramatic increase in levels of domestic violence and sexual assaults on the street after the law's adoption. Although not officially recognized, it has been widely reported that several of those who 'repented' kept their weapons and have used them to commit so-called honour killings against female members of their families. International journalist Robert Fisk (2015) reported how sceptical highly educated Algerians were at the time about the real purpose of the amnesty law, which many considered as a way of whitewashing the crimes committed by both the Islamist armed groups and the Algerian army. The amnesty law was quickly renamed the 'Amnesia Law'.

It is also important to note that 'healing' as a prerequisite for 'reconciliation' is a notion policy-makers often use vaguely or ambiguously. They overlook its importance due to three assumptions: first, that the end of violence in itself brings individuals a form of healing; secondly, post-traumatic suffering will eventually disappear as time is the most effective healer; and finally, addressing post-traumatic pain is an unnecessary use of public money, particularly as it is more important to finance infrastructure rebuilding after the physical destruction of conflict. Consequently, the amnesty law does not mention post-traumatic stress disorder (PTSD) at all. During one of my several conversations with an

Algerian legislator who took part in a discussion on the amnesty, and who prefers to remain anonymous, I was told that the reasons behind this oversight lay for the most part in Algeria's 'lack of psychosocial expertise in post-conflict situations'; and even if there had been such expertise to hand, the regime was not ready to bear the expense. However, the fact that there are several female psychotherapists and artists living in Algeria who have been doing very important work with the victims of terrorism and/or rape during the Black Decade gives the lie to this statement. Added to which, the post-1990s coincided with a spectacular increase in the international price of oil, which represented 98% of Algerian exports and economic wealth—public expenditure rose to $800 million between 2004 and 2014, and the country was able to repay all its IMF debt.

Arguably, the regime has been unwilling to engage in the process of individual healing because it would need to establish some sort of truth commission and provide public spaces in which people would be able to give their testimonies. On the contrary, the presidential decree of 2006 made prosecution for human rights abuses impossible, and even muzzled open debate by criminalizing public discussion about the nation's decade-long conflict. This takes us to the question of who killed whom and why (see Chapter One), which continues to remain unanswered today because the government has 'for better or worse, prevented inquiries into such questions through its national reconciliation policies and its restrictions on foreign and domestic research' (Mundy 2010: 28). Lamia expressed pain when evoking such killings. According to Agger (1994), when a person suffers serious psychological trauma, as Lamia undoubtedly has, they will unconsciously try to develop the most appropriate way of healing. 'The healing process can be supported both by the conscious part of the "self" and by the structure of which the self is part or chooses to be a part' (Agger 1994: 111). Lamia appears to have placed herself in two different contexts: the personal, private one, in which she has developed a coping mechanism through which she was able to heal the pain inflicted by her father, and the public one, where she cannot reconcile herself to the memories of the terror she witnessed.

The 'myth of return'

Finally, I asked Lamia: 'Are you planning to return to live in Algeria one day?' She replied: 'No, I will never go back to Algeria. I will go maybe for a visit, of course. We do have ties over there, but I have never thought to go back. I never imagined living there again after all that.' This response accords with some interesting data revealed by the survey I conducted for this research: out of 180 women who responded, up to 80% said they miss Algeria but only 30% had any intention of returning; 39% were not sure about it, while 78% said there were barriers to their return. These barriers, my survey revealed, are mainly social and political. Three out of the fifteen women I interviewed not only said that they have no intention of going back, but also that they do not miss Algeria at all. These figures show that Lamia is not an exception.

To clarify this point, it is necessary to explore a little more deeply the barriers other participants thought they would face if they decided to return. All those I interviewed mentioned their disagreement with the amnesty, considering it an act of betrayal towards women who stood up to terrorism, suffered harassment and violence, lost family members and often ended up in exile. However, participants have shown a great deal of resilience in rebuilding their lives within the societies in which they now live. To illustrate, 83% of respondents are working in highly skilled positions, including academia, and up to 28% have now obtained a postgraduate degree in a different area to their former subject of expertise (due mainly to the lack of equivalence between their Algerian diplomas and those in their new countries). One participant, who lives in France, summarized the situation by saying: 'I won't go back, because the main reason why I left Algeria is the lack of women's rights. A woman's life over there is daily social suffering.' Another participant from London gave more personal, tangible reasons:

> Algeria [has become] a country hard to live in. I get frustrated with almost everything when I go on holiday [there]. Horrible staff at every public administrative [office], mountains of stupid paperwork, no facilities for children, no libraries, no parks, no grass, no safety, a poor education system, no sense of health and safety, not to mention the hospitals. And the Islamization of the society, with a very poor understanding of religion, focusing only on women's outfits and [on] beards.

The agency and resilience of these women is demonstrated by their ability to rebuild their lives, and most importantly, reconstruct their identities as highly skilled women. In fact, I would argue that all the participants revealed some symptoms of trauma alongside their success in fully participating in the life of their adopted country. For these women, adaptation to a new environment was a process requiring coping abilities and emotional resources (Hayward et al. 2008). However, returning to today's Algeria, if only for holidays, involves frustration and stress, and—at least in Lamia's case—fear:

> I've been here [more than] twenty years. I now feel [at] home here. And believe me, every time I leave Heathrow for Algeria, there is a fear that never leaves me. When I go on holiday anywhere else, I'm fine. But [travelling to Algeria] I stress, I can't even drink my coffee before going to the airport, because something comes back [to me] and suddenly I feel vulnerable. Yes, vulnerable, that's the word.

What makes Lamia's narrative so compelling is her capacity for articulating her emotions, and the way she discerns between the private and the public when speaking of her experiences in Algeria and the UK, including her decision not to return to Algeria. Her feeling of vulnerability once in Algeria is no doubt due to her status as a woman. Lamia has described her fear, despair and sadness, together with her hopes and her exceptional courage in surviving the horrors of that time and surmounting so many obstacles during her journey to safety. It took her twenty years to feel at home in the UK, but she has now created another Lamia. This Lamia has full rights to the city and enjoys gender equality; she holds a British passport and can travel freely on holiday anywhere, yet going back to Algeria still provokes stress and fear. Another Lamia may have been born, but feelings of fear and vulnerability recur when she revisits the place where she lived through terror and violence. It is important to note that it was only following 9/11 that the idea of post-terrorism mental health care was raised. Since then, PTSD has even been redefined as a 'post-disaster mental health problem' (Yuval et al. 2006: 239), and it has been agreed that those who witness such an event can never fully recover.

Resilience: Negotiating a new identity

Lamia next moved on to speak about her new life in the UK:

> I should have come here much earlier, and I am certain that the best thing I have ever done in my life was to come to London. You know, here, I feel

> I fit in, like it was meant for me to live here. Yes, there are some problems, but very minor compared to what I have experienced in my life—and there is no fear.

Lamia stressed the fact that she is happy with the woman she has now become. She has reinvented her identity, successfully completed the process of 're-selving', and has reconnected with her inner self, the one that fought her father's repression from the time she was a very young girl (Hajdukowski-Ahmed 2008: 41). Here again, Lamia repeated herself in order to stress that she has retrieved the woman she always wanted to be, the one who has now freed herself from the patriarchal restrictions in Algeria, and who is very aware of the socially constructed values of her new society where, she believes, ideas of gender equality and women's freedom are taken for granted (Forbes Martin 2003). She is finally a woman who works and participates freely in the day-to-day life of the city, with no need to seek the permission of a male relation. Although recognizing that problems and issues do occur, she explained they could not be compared to the horror and fear she previously experienced:

> In Algeria, I used to fear everything ... When you see a policeman, you start worrying, especially if you are a woman: '*haggarin*', you know. As soon as I see a policeman talking into his walkie-talkie, I start shaking. There's something about it I can't figure out. But I do go [back] at least every two years.

Lamia spoke about fearing everything in Algeria, recalling her fear of terrorism, physical assaults on the street, her father, her boss and the police, whom she describes as '*haggarin*'. This insult derives from the Algerian word '*hogra*'. According to Algerian sociologist Abdelmadjid Merdaci (2004), the term holds a very specific political meaning, which includes the idea of oppression, bullying and contempt. The fact that several incidents of arrests of unmarried couples on the streets have been reported on social media, particularly on Facebook, vindicates Lamia's attitude.[3] In such cases, the woman will invariably be subject to intrusive questioning and humiliation if she cannot prove that the man she is with is a legitimate chaperone, as prescribed by the Family Code—that is, a male relative. There is no law preventing a woman

3. Accessed 22/04 2023140 couples agressés en quelques mois, Entre le marteau de la police et l'enclume des malfaiteurs - Algerie360

from walking on the street with a man she is not married to, but as Lamia has shown, the implementation of the amnesty legislation in a highly corrupt society, in which judicial power is not separated from legislative power and is influenced by patriarchal attitudes, has given the state the right to arbitrarily control women's 'conduct'. The police, as the frontline representatives of the regime, frequently abuse their power and humiliate women. Added to this, a picture of police beating a woman activist during a demonstration denouncing Bouteflika's fourth term in office went viral in February 2014, and was picked up by the international press, provoking an online conversation on Facebook and on blogs, in which Algerian women living abroad demonstrated their solidarity with their compatriots in Algeria. This solidarity is inevitably accompanied by a feeling of guilt at having left behind relatives, friends and colleagues who are still suffering from this kind of archaic behaviour.

Despite this, Lamia still continues to visit Algeria. Many exiles develop long-lasting transnational ties to their homeland, which become important both in reality and in their imagination. Lamia mentioned she is returning to attend a wedding in her home village soon, and this seemed to make her happy, calling to mind the work of Papadopoulos (2005) which points out that the loss of 'home' remains the main trauma for people who have been forced into exile. Papadopoulos explains that 'home' is the metaphor used by refugees in general to describe the loss of three important things: the geographical space, including its culture, history, language and religion; the emotions related to that geographical space, including family experiences and memories; and the locus of identity it provides—that is, the positive validation of an individual's sense of identity by others who know and value them for what they are. Lamia was looking forward to attending the wedding in her village, which she explained has kept its traditional way of celebrating cultural events in defiance of the introduction of new practices conforming to radical Islam and new behaviours imposed by the market and globalization. Lamia, from outside Algeria, has constructed a somewhat idealized vision of the way things are in her village (Cohen's 'imaginary homeland'), which is immediately contradicted by the recurrence of the fearful memories that plague her each time she does return:

> Over there now, everyone is getting on with their lives, all is normal like before the terrorism ... [pause] But for me, nooo, it's still there, somewhere

> in my mind: who is going to be killed today? This question, oh my God, can't leave my mind every time I think about Algeria. You'll be amazed to hear that when I go to Algeria, I always expect the worst.

Conclusion: Coming to terms with the past

Lamia, in telling her story, gives us an insight into her traumatic experiences in Algeria during the Black Decade, her later struggles with a 'gender-blind' asylum process, and her determination to establish herself within a new environment, negotiate a new identity and reconstruct her damaged 'sense of self'. She also expresses her desire to come to terms with her past, using her new, more politicized understanding of the circumstances in her homeland. As such, her narrative has also allowed us to explore the impact of political, state-driven 'reconciliation' in Algeria itself. I would argue that it was important to dwell at length on Lamia's experiences because, although necessarily unique, they nevertheless encapsulate in many crucial ways the experiences of many of the highly skilled and educated Algerian women this book investigates. I present some of these other testimonies in the following chapter.

4 Fragmented Narratives of the Black Decade: Identity, Transnational Space and Belonging

Introduction: Algerian women in exile

As mentioned in the last chapter, Lamia's narrative appears to capture the experience of many educated and highly skilled women who lived through the horror of Algeria's Black Decade and who consequently decided to flee. Her case study clearly reflects the complex, often interrelated reasons behind such decisions, as well as their gendered basis: it shows that she was driven to seek asylum in another country as much by the harsh patriarchal restrictions, discrimination and harassment she experienced as by the indiscriminate terror, which nevertheless left her with traumatic memories of violence. This chapter uses an analysis of my survey data, supported by selected quotations from the interviews I conducted with other highly skilled Algerian women migrants, to confirm the insights revealed by Lamia's interview and enlarge on the subjects it raised.

The analysis is broken down into different sections. The first explores the circumstances under which the participants were forced to leave Algeria and looks at the international community's reaction to the situation there in the 1990s, particularly the persecution and assassination of intellectuals and members of the professional class. The second investigates the participants' life experiences outside Algeria and raises key issues relating to the way they have attempted to negotiate new identities in the countries to which they fled. The third section looks at the barriers participants believe they would face if they returned to live in Algeria. Finally, the last section investigates the professional and cultural networks to which these women belong; it explores their use of online resources and the role these play in enabling them to maintain their relationship with Algeria and engage in political discussions over the position of women's rights in the country, as well as their perceptions of belonging to a female Algerian diaspora.

Persecution and the decision to leave

The women who participated in my research took the decision to migrate during the Black Decade and its aftermath due to a variety of circumstances, and this meant that not all of them could be considered 'refugees' as understood by the 1951 Refugee Convention and its protocols. Here, I would like to point out that the majority of participants left Algeria by air, even those who fled under coercion. In relating their pre-departure conditions, they spoke of a variety of reasons that led them to leave Algeria—from terrorism and political persecution due to their engagement in the public sphere, to social discrimination and gender-related persecution. Evidently, as in Lamia's case, these different factors often overlapped, as 'Maya's' quotation illustrates:

> Let me make it clear to you: when I left Algeria in June 1994, I was in a bad relationship with [my husband]. At a party attended by family and friends a few months earlier, he [had suddenly] announced that he wanted to repudiate [divorce] me. It was such a humiliation. I went to seek help everywhere, visited all our friends and his family, but they all took his side. We [then] received a death threat in a letter from the GIA, and because I am half-Algerian, half-French, I went to the French consulate to organize our departure. He refused to leave with us. I took my children [to France] and left him in Algiers; he was assassinated five months later.

Maya had worked as a sub-editor for the same newspaper as her murdered husband. She explicitly stated that her decision to leave was based primarily on the shock and humiliation she had felt when her husband declared publicly that he wanted to divorce her, without even informing her first. Under Algeria's Family Code, Maya would have had to stay in the family home until the divorce process had ended, anywhere between three months and two years (Ait Zai 2011), but in any case, as for many Algerian women in her situation, Maya had nowhere else to go. In Algerian culture, it is very common for the family house to be registered in the name of the husband, even if both husband

and wife have contributed towards buying it. Maya explained that when she went to SOS Femmes en Détresse to seek help, she was told that as she was half-French it would be better for her if she left the country, especially as terrorism was reaching its peak at the time. At this point, Maya was seeking some form of solidarity as a woman suffering discrimination as a result of the Family Code (a piece of legislation that both SOS and the left-wing milieu she and her husband frequented strongly condemned). She was disappointed by the response, believing that the apparent lack of support was due to the fact that she was seen not as a woman but as a 'foreigner' who could take advantage of her French passport to leave the country. Yet despite all that had occurred, when the GIA sent its death threat, Maya expressed her solidarity with her husband and offered him the chance to leave the country with her. During the interview, she expressed sadness that her husband had considered her act of solidarity an offence to his male pride. After repudiating their marriage, it appears he was too proud to accept her offer; he was assassinated five months after she and the children had left Algeria. In tears, she explained, 'We never got divorced, but he is not here anymore.'

The following quotation, taken from an interview conducted with 'Louisa', who now lives in the USA, further highlights the links between discrimination and violence towards women and the climate of terror at the time:

> For us, it was going or dying. You go, you don't know where. You meet other people, different people, and at some point, you lose yourself, you don't know where you are any more. It is a symbolic death because you are out of your realm. Call it heaven or hell, but for me, it was an after-death.

Louisa and her husband were both journalists in Algeria. She explained how difficult it was to obtain a visa from a Western country; Algeria appeared isolated in its war against terrorism. However, when an opportunity to leave the country in the form of a job offer for her husband in the UAE arrived, they discovered that not even their combined salary was enough to pay for the flights. Louisa sold all her jewellery to buy her husband a ticket and enable him 'to find a decent place to stay', while she remained in Algeria with her baby for a further few months. In the meantime, she continued to work and provide for herself and her child, despite the persecution she was forced to endure as a female journalist.

As Lamia commented earlier, terrorism in Algeria appeared to provide a further opportunity for certain elements of the male population to violently express hatred towards and exert more control over women. This is corroborated by the testimony of another participant:

> I left in September 1994. I would have been killed, so I had to leave Algeria within twenty-four hours. The reason was that I had appeared on French TV strongly criticizing the GIA. Well, I must admit that, as the director of an institute of higher education, I had already been threatened by the GIA, which was threatening to destroy all Algerian universities. They knew that the director was a woman. They came during the night [as] they assumed that I was living in the institute's accommodation, [and] set [it on] fire. The whole institute was completely destroyed.

'Nadia', a left-wing political activist, faced persecution due to her academic position. She was the first woman in Algeria to be appointed as the head of an institute of higher education specializing in medical sciences. She held a PhD in chemistry from France, and on completing her doctoral research had been offered a job at the CNRS-Paris (the French National Centre for Scientific Research), an offer she had declined in order to return to Algeria. Her subsequent nomination as the head of a medical school occurred at a time when the Algerian government was engaged in a programme of political and economic reform.

Nadia went on to recount that on two occasions she had excluded students because they were wearing what she termed 'inappropriate clothes': the young woman was wearing a *niqab* (covering her entire body) and the young man an 'Afghani kind of '*nisf-sake*' [Islamic clothing]'. The incident became a hot topic of discussion amongst the students and staff, and one day a student came to her office and warned her that it was about time she observed 'Islamic rules'. Nadia explained that this incident finally persuaded her to consider fleeing—to France in particular, as she had studied there and even previously been offered a research position at a prestigious institute. Despite this, it was not easy for her to obtain a visa:

> So, I applied for a French visa. They told me that I could leave, but without my children, who were three and six at the time. I asked if there was a law that says a mother can leave her kids in such a situation, and if 'yes', I reject

> this law and say 'no' to it, especially [given] that my husband was already in France for a conference ... A few days later, a high-ranking military officer (I cannot tell you his name) contacted my family to say: 'OK, she can leave with the children now; we have enough deaths on our [hands].' They contacted [a minister at the French Foreign Office] who sent a fax to Algiers advising the consulate to give me permission to leave with my children. I don't know what had been discussed, I just went to pick up our visas, took my children, and left the country the following day. I cried so much on the plane that the passengers thought I had lost someone very close.

This quotation illustrates the contradiction between Nadia's private and public life, as a mother and as a professional. She explained that the immigration officer at the French consulate considered the persecution against her as political and serious enough to grant her permission to leave Algeria for France; however, her position as the mother of two young children was not taken into account. This decision was an example of the general lack of understanding of the specific needs of women who seek international protection, as detailed by Crawley (2001). Added to this was the fact that, as Pierre Bourdieu and Jean Leca (1995) state, there had been a sharp drop in the number of Algerian citizens granted French visas: whereas 800,000 visas of various kinds were granted in 1989, by 1994, when Nadia applied and terrorism was at its height, this number had fallen to 100,000. This fall was undoubtedly linked to the fact that the right to asylum was increasingly 'less respected in France and in Europe in general', and French politicians on both the right and the left had begun to vie with each other as to who could appear the most hardline on immigration (Derrida 2001: 9).

Nadia's experience of leaving the country was rare; it had certainly been facilitated by her family's privileged connections with high-ranking military officers, as well as her position within the Algerian Ministry of Higher Education. Having said that, the threat to her life was real: between 1992 and 1994, around the time Nadia's institution was attacked and she was receiving personal threats, several Algerian professionals and intellectuals were assassinated, were kidnapped or disappeared in sinister circumstances. During that time, in 1993, a group of internationally renowned academics and scholars, including Pierre Bourdieu and Jacques Derrida, founded the Comité International de Soutien aux Intellectuels Algériens (International Committee for the Support of

Persecuted Algerian Intellectuals, CISIA).[1] CISIA, as part of the International Parliament of Writers, called on the international community to open its borders to persecuted intellectuals and form a network of 'city refuges'. These cities would be ruled by the 'law of hospitality', giving an unconditional right of asylum to any intellectual or writer fleeing Algeria (Derrida 2001). Although the CISIA initiative was commendable, it has been accused of being selective, only condemning the persecution of those intellectuals who had supported the cancellation of the democratic process in a bid to prevent the FIS from gaining power (Sidhoum 2003). It is interesting to note that none of the participants in my study mentioned the existence of CISIA, and neither Maya nor Nadia appear to have benefited from its support. In fact, it seems they only heard about the organization a few years after they had arrived in France. Nadia's story of her departure was mainly shaped by her feelings of sadness and insecurity, and her anger at the attitude of the French authorities.

By contrast, 'Feroudja' stressed the oppressive social norms encapsulated in the Family Code, and the harassment and discrimination against women as the main reasons behind her decision to leave her country:

> I left at the end of the Black Decade, in early 2000, just after I became a widow. I could not live in peace from the time I was widowed. A single woman cannot live in peace in Algeria, especially if she is divorced or widowed. You always need to have your husband, father, brother or son with you in order to be [left] in peace. I rejected that life. So, it's the laws and the harassment of women in my country that scares me, rather than the terrorism.

A former university lecturer, Feroudja lived and worked in one of those Kabyle cities that were little affected by terrorism, at least until 1997. She was an active member of the Berber Cultural Movement (MCB), until she left, citing its increasingly separatist ideology which she blamed on 'foreign and imperialist influence'. Feroudja also mentioned her involvement with the RCD (Rassemblement pour la Culture et la Démocratie), known for its secular ideology, but she also left this political group, this time because of what she described as

1. CISIA, a solidarity network of intellectuals, academics and writers, was established in Paris in June 1993 following the assassination of several, mainly French-speaking, secular Algerian intellectuals. Bourdieu was elected as its president.

its gender discrimination: 'They pretend to be democrats, but when it comes to women, they are all the same.'

Feroudja explained that when her husband was alive, she was respected by everyone in her area and in her workplace, but his death changed this irrevocably:

> I used to go to meetings late in the evening without any harassment on the streets, but after I lost my husband, even though they knew who I was, merely because I had become single, I lost my rights. I wasn't even supposed to be out after certain hours.

This statement shows the cultural, psychological and social barriers Feroudja suddenly faced after her husband's death. These barriers were mainly due to the generally accepted stereotype, particularly prevalent in rural Algeria, of divorced or widowed women as intrinsically promiscuous and a threat to social stability. Moreover, it appears entrenched in the Algerian mentality and the dominant social discourse that if a woman wishes to exert her full citizenship rights beyond the private sphere, she needs to be accompanied by a male guardian. In this case, exile is seen as an existential condition for those women who decide to leave the 'silent and invisible lives' imposed on them by patriarchal norms (Agger 1994). Added to her grief over the loss of her husband, Feroudja explained that becoming a widow reduced her status from a political activist to a silenced mother, only allowed to leave the house to work and provide for her children. She felt that she was reduced to invisibility and this, to her, was much more violent and distressing than radical Islam, terrorism and the upsurge of physical violence. It is important to add that Feroudja was extremely active on social media during the Hirak, proudly sharing pictures and videos of women protesting in Algiers and other parts of Algeria.

Feroudja's account contrasts in some ways with that of 'Sonia', who, following her graduation in the late 1980s from a regional university in Algeria, moved to Algiers to work for an international NGO:

> In Algiers, life was much better for me as a single woman. [This was] before the rise of Islamism; it wasn't a place of blind terrorist attacks everywhere. I had rented a small flat on my own and never had any problems. My neighbours used to respect me, including the young men in the area. When I was offered a position in West Africa I took the opportunity and left; it

was there that I met my husband. In the meantime, back home, things were getting worse. When our child was born, it was not possible to stay in West Africa, so we started to think of moving to a place where we could live in peace, where schools and other services are of a good standard. We ended up in Canada.

In understanding the circumstances in which the decision to migrate is made, it is often crucial to mention the role of the neighbourhoods in which women live. In contrast to the city Sonia came from and in which she graduated, her new surroundings in Algiers seemed more tolerant towards single women. The quotation above suggests that one of the key factors behind her departure was her ambition to widen her experience in her chosen field of international human rights law. However, once she became a mother, other factors influenced her decision not to return to Algeria; she was determined to find a place to live where she and her family could find peace. 'Peace', in contrast to war, terrorism and the harassment of women, is a theme mentioned in several participants' narratives.

Women's decision to leave their homeland in times of conflict can take years to implement, as a result of factors mainly determined by the fact that men and women experience conflict differently. Women often lack the resources and have little control over their movement—particularly in the Algerian case, where they must always be accompanied by a male guardian, regardless of their age. For example, when 'Khadija' explained why she delayed making the decision to flee, she cited her fear of losing her career, but it could also have been because her male guardian (her father or brother) disagreed. As soon as she married, however, the couple decided to leave:

> My idea to leave Algeria arose years before I left, when the violence was at its peak between 1994 and 1999, after completing my studies. The living conditions were bad but I decided to carry on with my career. I mainly worked as a journalist and was happy with that, but everything else was going wrong. [When] I got married in 2003, my husband and I agreed on the gravity of the situation and decided to leave the country as soon as an opportunity arose. He went to the Canary Islands on a business trip [and] I joined him two months later. A few months [after that], we left for mainland Spain.

The fact remains that the increase in the feminization of Algerian migration only began in 2000. Although the Algerian army declared a final victory against the Islamist armed forces in that year, random terror acts, assassinations of journalists and kidnappings continued. At a press conference broadcast on Algerian TV in July 2002, the Algerian military's chief of staff declared an end to the war against terrorism, but insisted that fundamentalism and radical ideology remained an issue against which the civilian government would continue to struggle. To quote his words: 'Terrorism is over, but watch TV programmes, listen to sermons in mosques, and look at what is taught in schools today; you will see that radical Islam is still there, blooming' (Algeria-Watch 2002). Although it was incontestably true that the decade of terror was over, it was arguably the case that Algerians had also witnessed the premature death of their dream of democracy at the hands of the army.

When President Abdelaziz Bouteflika came to power in 1999, he promised a return to peace and security. Knowing Algerians' deep attachment to Islamic values, the statement made by the chief of staff did not pass him by unnoticed. What followed was the implementation of an extensive government agenda aimed at curbing the Algerians' renowned rebellious characteristics—a kind of 'psychological disciplining' of the population, mainly by means of the school curricula and the mainstream media, but also through the influence of the *zawiya* (the Islamic Sufi order) (Roberts 2003). Bouteflika and his government were aided in their programme by the substantial increase in the price of oil between 1999 and 2008, which helped them purchase social peace.

Bouteflika may have used his own acquaintances among and affiliations with the Sufi *zawiyas* in Algeria to influence the Algerian people, who had previously inclined towards support of religious extremism. He presented radical political Islam as a disguised heresy, a threat, and disseminated the message that 'true Islam' in North Africa is rooted in Sufism. This policy, however, risked politicizing the *zawiya*, and ultimately may have damaged them. Nevertheless, Bouteflika's instrumentalization of the *zawiya* is one explanation as to why there was limited popular opposition when he altered the Algerian constitution to enable him to remain in power for a fourth term. He was also no doubt aided by the fatigue of the general population and their desperate desire for peace after the long conflict of the Black Decade. The few activists who did oppose the fourth term were met with criticism, and

Bouteflika, despite the fact that he was by then suffering from very poor health, was re-elected. The Algerian ruling class had successfully played on popular fears of radical Islam to suit their political purposes.

However, in 2019, when Bouteflika's entourage announced his candidacy for a fifth term in office, the deterioration in his health was too evident to hide. Hence, his decision to stand violated the Algerian constitution on two fronts: not only had the constitution been revised in 2016 to limit presidential mandates to two terms, but also Article 102 states that, in the case of incapacity, the president must hand over power to the head of the senate for ninety days. When, in April 2018, he was taken to inaugurate a renovation of an important mosque in Algiers, Bouteflika looked extremely ill and totally absent. Many Algerians, including those living in exile, felt a deep sense of shame, which they expressed in an outpouring on social media. The population's dissatisfaction with the corruption and poor state of governance was also manifest in a series of strikes. These actions had been increasing throughout Bouteflika's last term in office, and they finally led to the huge wave of protests that began in February 2019. The Hirak spelled the end of Bouteflika's reign.

One important point to draw attention to here is the appointment, during the presidency of Bouteflika, of female imams known as *mourshidates* ('Islamic guides') by the Algerian Minister of Religious Affairs, in order to combat Islamic radicalization. Amal Belalloufi (2015) reports that *mourshidates* are required to hold a degree in Islamic studies, which entails a certain level of psychosocial knowledge. These imams work with the women and girls in the mosques, and visit prisons, hospitals and schools, their role being to spread a tolerant form of Islam and prevent the radicalization of young girls by steering them away from radical preachers. At least 300 *mourshidates* have been appointed in the country during the last decade (Belalloufi 2015); however, unlike their male counterparts, they are not allowed to preach or lead the prayers in mosques. Despite the seemingly 'progressive' nature of the decision to appoint female imams, albeit with little real authority, one of the consequences of the authorities' use of Islam was the reinforcement of a patriarchal ideology. This provoked a rise in violence against women, which was often tacitly supported by the media and the police, and which found its extreme reflection in political Islam.

Khadija continued, relating her experiences of the aftermath of the Black Decade:

> I was feeling threatened, first as a woman and second as a journalist. At that time, my work and my political affiliations were clearly both anti-system and against terrorism, so I was fighting both sides, which was very hard. It was a fascinating job; however, it was difficult to achieve anything in the security and sociopolitical situation Algeria was plunged into during those years. There was an opportunity for us to leave, so we did.

I recall here one of the first conferences called by Bouteflika following his election, when he compared journalists to '*tayebat al hammam*' (a pejorative term meaning 'women gossipmongers'); the underlying message was: 'You will get what's coming to you.' After that public statement, the repression and violence against journalists began to rise. For Khadija, working as a journalist was challenging but enjoyable, but by 2003 she and her husband felt compelled to leave the country. During the summer of the previous year, at least four journalists had been killed in Algeria, adding to the huge losses suffered by the media during the Black Decade. One of them, Abdelhak Belriadouh, a regional correspondent of *El Watan*, committed suicide in the most appalling circumstances: after being kept in isolation and tortured for three days, he was dragged into the streets of the city where he worked and left there; shortly afterwards, he took his own life (IREX 2005). Following this incident, Transparency International published a press release on 16 September 2003 calling on the Algerian government to provide journalists, particularly those working in small cities, with more protection. However, the noose tightened, particularly around those journalists (and others) who dared to denounce the rising tide of corruption. Many were forced into silence or exile, while others sank into depression and some, like Belriadouh, committed suicide.

Khadija and her husband were working in a small city in western Algeria where there was little available protection, so once an opportunity to leave the country arose, they took it. She explained how she found herself on the Canary Islands—by chance rather than by choice. She did not give me any details about this particular part of her journey, but told me that she could only join her husband a few months after he had left. They spent two years there before they could leave for mainland Spain. During this time, the Canary Islands was one of the routes taken by many undocumented migrants from the African continent in their bid to reach Europe—very few were deported but they were usually held in detention centres before being sent to Spain and released. Once in Spain, however, many ended up in limbo, unable to obtain a work permit—until 2005, when the Spanish government granted an amnesty to 700,000 irregular migrants (Tremlett 2005). Khadija briefly mentioned the amnesty, so I assumed that she and her family may have benefited from it to regularize their administrative status.

On a different note, it is important to mention that a considerable number of participants who left between 2000 and 2010 received scholarships from the Ministry of Higher Education to study abroad, or self-funded a postgraduate degree. Those who succeeded in their studies, perhaps the majority, prolonged their stay and then exchanged their student visas for work visas. As 'Wahiba', who holds a master's degree in science from a UK university and who now works in banking, explained: 'I wanted to go back but the situation over there discouraged me. I applied for a job and was hired, so I stayed.'

Some participants, however, did not say what their immigration status was. This was mainly the case with those who left in the post-Black Decade period, which coincided with the imposition of harsher restrictions on migration to 'Fortress Europe'. Here again, it is likely that the 'most immediate cause of this new displacement is the devastation wrought by more than 30 years of neoliberal policies in the whole region' (Cetti 2015: 53), including the dismantling of public services and the aggravating factor of gender discrimination in the workplace in Algeria, rather than the immediate fear of terrorism. The narratives of the majority of participants also make clear the role of professional positions, levels of educational attainment and various kinds of financial and social support, such as scholarships or professional transnational networks, in shaping the decision to leave. However, my in-depth interviews with these women also revealed a certain degree of post-traumatic stress due to the context in which their departure occurred, which first and foremost involved the loss of a sense of 'home'. Papadopoulos (2002) suggests that the loss of 'home' is a metaphor that not only refers to the loss of a physical space but also the loss of continuity in an individual's relationship with the external world. 'My journey to Spain was a mixture of feelings,' explained Khadija. 'It was a kind of relief, yet it was also painful. Leaving behind my whole life, my job, my family and friends was hard.' As outlined earlier in the book, loss of home also involves the loss of an external locus of identity that could enable the individual to value themselves in exile.

The different stories I have mentioned here show that it is difficult to distinguish voluntary migration from forced migration in times of war and armed conflict. This is especially so in the case of the women here, whose experiences of departure are unique in content but similar in context: that is, their struggles in both the private and the public sphere in Algeria at the time. The following sections illustrate how the process of regaining a sense of 'home' through the reconstruction of new identities is also gendered, and how the recovery of a complex sense of self 'open[s] up a space for developing agency' from which 'transforming opportunities [can] emerge' (Hajdukowski-Ahmed 2008: 41). These sections will also show the very concrete ways in which access to resources, levels of education and the circumstances under which participants arrived in their new countries shaped their desire to either join or ignore existing Algerian networks, including professional ones, and create new meanings of solidarity.

Rebuilding lives and a sense of self

This section explores different phases of the participants' experiences of exile, from arrival to adjustment to living in a new society. Many of them faced difficulties in rebuilding their lives and professional careers, although more than two-thirds (78.5%) said they had now entered the labour market. In many countries, however, their lack of secure legal status delayed their access to higher education and work opportunities. The women I interviewed offered detailed accounts of the difficulties they faced on their arrival. Many had to surmount the classic barriers which confront all migrant women, such as lack of native-language skills and knowledge of the system, problems with childcare and the immigration authorities, as well as lack of money. In this section, I have chosen to quote some of these stories, each shaped by the particularities resulting from their different contexts. 'Nadia', for example, described her initial reaction on arrival in France thus:

> I spent the first year crying and hoping to go back every day ... Meanwhile, I joined groups and organized debates on the situation in Algeria, seeking

> help from French intellectuals and politicians. I was not here to stay and, above all, I was not looking for a comfortable life here. We were only here for peace: '*ehrabna*' ['we ran away']. One year passed, and I was still hoping to go back to my job in Algeria, but things were getting worse over there. At some point you tell yourself: you can't stay like this, you need a job.

Sayad (2004) calls this feeling of entertaining the hope to return any day, the 'double absence'. Nadia's story of fleeing Algeria was very specific: as seen above, her departure involved the intervention of high-ranking members of the Algerian and French governments. She recounted that when she arrived in France she seized the opportunity to organize meetings and to speak out about the horrors she had witnessed in Algeria. It is very common for forced migrants to develop a feeling of guilt for having left friends and family members behind to face the situation they themselves have fled, and to want to contribute towards helping them in some way. For Nadia, speaking out was also a way to ventilate her feelings and affirm her role as a political activist. Several times during the interview she pointed out the importance of challenging the dominant discourse in France about the situation in Algeria at the time of the Black Decade, especially on the question of 'who killed whom'. Nadia refused to fall into the trap of being stereotyped as a passive victim or oppressed woman when she was in fact a political activist, persecuted because of her professional position and left-wing views.

Although engaging in political activities is very common behaviour for most political exiles, it can be difficult for women to exert their agency on arrival in another country, even for the highly skilled among them. This is due to many factors, the most common being barriers of language and culture. Nadia's almost immediate involvement in political activities, however, was not only facilitated by her knowledge of the French language and culture, but also by the network of French left-wing politicians and academics working in her field. Nevertheless, the attitude of the authorities was one of alarm:

> France saw all of us arriving in one go [and] the French authorities panicked … newcomers every day. My husband and I had a small flat in France. There was [always] a queue in front of it and there was solidarity amongst us, but the French politicians, especially the French left wing, broke our networks of solidarity.

As Nadia's remarks show, although France, due to its involvement in Algeria, had seen the crisis coming for years, it was not prepared to receive such large numbers of exiles in such a short space of time (Aggoun and Rivoire 2005). Looking at the current Syrian refugee crisis, it appears that history is repeating itself; those Western countries who implement foreign policies that create chaos in other countries often forget that such chaos inevitably results in high numbers of refugees at their borders. Already having accommodation in France made it easier for Nadia and her husband to act in solidarity with other comrades and colleagues arriving from Algeria. However, these acts of solidarity did not last, because French politicians were determined to control the situation, expressing concern that the Algerian conflict could be transported to France with those fleeing into exile.

It was of little surprise to me that Nadia was among those women I interviewed who have been most involved in the recent Hirak. As she said, when I spoke to her later during the Hirak, 'I don't do anything on my weekends now. Every Sunday, I make my way to the [Place de la] République; it's part of my routine.' Despite having achieved a certain degree of integration into French society, Nadia still dreams of an Algeria free from Salafism and religious fundamentalism:

> The majority of those in [the square] are remnants of the FIS who found refuge here in France. [But] I go there every Sunday to show my solidarity with my sisters back home in the fight for their eventual return to political life, with the support of French politicians.

According to historian Bernard Ravenel (1998), French politicians and intellectuals, including many on the left, held divergent views on the cancellation of the Algerian electoral process in 1992. The Socialist Party (PS) began to distance itself from the Algerian government, while the Communist Party (PCF) continued to support even its harshest military actions against the Algerian people—as Ravenel reveals, the PCF had always supported the Algerian army and its military coups even prior to the Black Decade (Ravenel 1998). The political differences around the cancellation of the elections had repercussions on French migration policies, particularly in relation to the Algerians arriving during that period. Nadia describes a situation of panic, particularly as expressions of solidarity among political exiles tend to lead to political activism and debates, which the French state was not prepared to tolerate in the case of Algerians. In the UK, the government also implemented similarly divisive policies, such as 'dispersing' refugees fleeing conflicts in the Global South outside London, often to isolated and deprived areas of the country.

Nadia spent a year publicizing the horrors taking place in Algeria, all the while nurturing the idea of returning to the country (her reasons for not returning are explained later in the chapter). She then realized that she had to find work, and naturally she thought of going back to the Paris laboratory in which she had worked while studying for her PhD:

> They told me I was welcome but to get [a salary] would depend on the paid positions decided by the central government. In other words, there was nothing for me. But I rejoined the lab anyway and worked ... as a 'volunteer'. [But] when a paid position was released, it was given to a French man, much younger than me.

Nadia had just experienced the multifaceted discrimination of race, age and gender. She was forty years old when she arrived in France, and by now she had come to realize that she was in a much weaker position than when she had left the laboratory eight years earlier. Added to which, according to a report on the politics of gender in France, French employers still perceive children as a barrier to employing women; neither can the presence of racial discrimination against Maghrebi North African women in French academia and other professions be discounted (Lepinard and Lieber 2015). My survey showed that up to a third of participants were refused a first job in their countries of migration because of their Algerian nationality. However, for the specific case of Algerians who had fled during the Black Decade, another factor has to be taken into consideration, as Nadia explained:

> Then I realized that we were all considered terrorists. So either they do not respond, or they tell you: '[T]his is not Algeria.' They don't even invite you for an interview. One day, the School of Medicine called me; it was through a friend who intervened for me. But then, guess what? I couldn't take the job because we realized that my papers did not allow me to work.

In reference to Nadia's first comment that all Algerians were considered terrorists, it is important to point out that during the Black Decade, the GIA organized several attacks in France and murdered many French nationals living in Algeria, principally because it was believed that France supported the Algerian regime in its war against the FIS and radical Islam. The most spectacular GIA terrorist act occurred on 24 December 1994, when the GIA diverted an Air France flight between Algiers and Paris, threatening to crash it in Paris. In another example, on 25 July 1995, a bomb exploded in an underground station in Paris, killing four people and leaving seventy-six injured (Dejevsky 1995).

The irony was, as she explained above, that when Nadia was finally invited to take a job in a university medical school after three years of job hunting, she realized that her immigration status did not allow her to work, dealing her morale a severe blow:

> I cracked under that pressure. One day I went to the prefecture [local authority] and told them I was not leaving the office without a work permit; I made a scene. Then, surprisingly, someone came to see me, took all the information about my background, and provided me with a work permit, renewable every year. I remember … a social worker [calling] at [my] home. I had to explain why I made that scandal at the prefecture.

For Nadia, employment was crucial for her feeling of integration into French society, as well as being key to regaining her independence and, most importantly, her mental and emotional well-being and sense of self. The psychological impact of exile on women such as Nadia is examined in a study by Lynda Hayward et al. (2008: 201), which defines the circumstances in which women try to adjust to their new environment as a time of 'temporariness and precariousness [due to] their refugee situation'. Nadia told me with regret that she never worked in academia again, but what she laments most is the fact that she has never had the opportunity to carry on with her research or publish her work. Like Nadia, many other participants felt it was necessary to re-establish their academic or professional careers in order to regain some of their lost identity.

In countries other than France, various other factors obstructed women from resuming their original professions, as Khadija, who now lives in Spain, explained:

> I have never been able to work as a journalist. There are so many reasons for that, but one of the most significant is because we have two children. Also, during the past decade, we moved a lot around Spanish territory, and

> this instability, [without] a permanent location, was not conducive … to rebuilding my professional career. We finally settled down in 2010, but the economic crisis in Spain, [which began in] 2008, did not help us at all.

For the majority of participants, the fact that their Algerian qualifications were not recognized and a lack of knowledge of the language of their new countries were the main barriers they faced to resuming their profession. As for Khadija, her remark suggests there were other factors related to childcare responsibilities that prevented her returning to work after her complex and traumatizing journey of migration. Mothers who are new to a city tend to have very little knowledge about the types of support available to them; this becomes even worse if they are new mothers like Khadija, who described the isolation she felt after giving birth to her first daughter. After receiving work permits, Khadija and her husband moved around the country to wherever they could find jobs. Travelling from one place to another made it difficult for her to build any local connections with other Algerians who could have supported her.

Eventually, after a few years on the move, the family settled down in 2010. Although Spain had enjoyed rapid economic growth during the early 2000s, attracting many African migrants, the global economic crisis in 2008 affected the country badly, and the rate of unemployment increased until it was one of the highest in Europe. The high level of unemployment impacted migrants first, and within migrant communities, it was the women who were the most affected. Khadija, however, never gave up writing. At the time of our interview, she was writing a novel based on the true story of a young Algerian woman from a rural village who dares to defy the patriarchal norms by pursuing a career in the theatre, and as a consequence, is burned alive by her brother. Khadija had heard of the story in Algeria but had never been able to write about what happened and thus grant the victim some justice. The woman's family and the authorities described the murder as an act of terrorism and endeavoured to cover it up, along with many other acts of violence against women, including similar 'honour killings', in rural Algeria. By the time I was finalizing this research, Khadija had published her novel in France and was able to speak out at last about the violence meted out to women in Algeria.

Other participants in this study experienced easier arrivals and adjusted more smoothly to life in the countries to which they migrated. Louisa, who first fled to the UAE before moving to the USA, spoke of what she termed a 'good experience' compared with others who went elsewhere:

> Because, you see, it depends on the country to where they have gone. After living in terror of being killed, I went to a country known for its security. The manner in which they speak to women over there was a big difference to what I was accustomed to from Algerian men.

Louisa seems to have been agreeably surprised at first to discover, as she put it, that the stories of violence against women in Arab countries were partly due to widely diffused stereotypes. She also mentioned the amount of resources allocated to women-only facilities in every aspect of daily life in the UAE. She had to perfect her academic Arabic, as well as learning to adapt to a new working environment, but explained that there were resources and support available to help with her professional readjustment, and within only six months she started working as a journalist again. She and her family spent twelve years in the UAE, which she described as happy and financially comfortable, but 'when our daughter was growing, we started thinking about her future, her access to universities, etc.'. The Gulf countries, particularly the UAE, are known for not granting permanent residence or citizenship to migrants, regardless of the length of time they spend in their territories. This discriminatory law was a constant reminder to Louisa of her temporary status and created a sense of living in limbo that was, perhaps, similar to Nadia's, despite the two living in different countries under very different circumstances. Also, after having lived in the country for many years, Louisa had begun to realize there was in fact a great deal of discrimination against women, and all the attention displayed towards women that had impressed her on arrival was precisely part of this culture of gender discrimination. When an opportunity presented itself, the family moved to the USA.

However, for the majority of participants in my survey, the lack of recognition of their Algerian qualifications meant they had to retrain or return to their studies. Some said the main reason they resumed their education was to improve their job prospects, others wanted to perfect their knowledge, change careers or gain entry into the networks of professional bodies in their new countries, and one participant added, 'I wanted to deepen my knowledge, not only to work, but also for my personal development.' Many of these women had to start their higher education again from zero, or qualify in a different field. This was particularly the case for medical doctors. Indeed, this study revealed that several doctors who migrated to countries other than France faced difficulties in pursuing their medical careers. As one participant, who now works as a counter assistant in a pharmacy in the UK, said: 'Algeria spent so much money on educating us up to this level, but lost us. Unfortunately, with the non-recognition of our diplomas, our host countries will also lose us, and God knows they need doctors here.' In London, I met a few Algerian women doctors who had migrated during the 1990s and were now working as consultants in teaching hospitals or as general practitioners in local surgeries, despite the stressful and expensive process of requalification. In the UK, the General Medical Council (GMC) requires that all non-EU doctors attain a very high score in the IELTS English examination,[2] before they are allowed to sit the Professional and Linguistic Assessments Board (PLAB) examination.[3] All this often takes more than three years. A similar process was reported by participants living in Canada and the USA.

However, there were occasionally other reasons for re-entering or pursuing higher education. One participant revealed:

> My degree was insufficient to find a good job with a good salary, so it was necessary to enrol for a master's when I arrived. However, regarding my PhD, I found it unnecessary, and would not advise any woman to go for it if she does not intend to work in academia again. It was a five-year waste of my life, but it was imposed by my family and I had to obey, unfortunately.

This quotation intimates that undertaking further studies may have been a condition imposed by this participant's parents before she was allowed to prolong her stay abroad. In some cases, Algerian parents are held accountable by other members of their extended family for their daughter's 'conduct', and it is often considered unacceptable for a young woman to travel or stay abroad if not for the purpose of further education or marriage. Other participants

2. Accessed on 22/04/2023 https://www.ielts.org/for-organisations/why-accept-ielts-scores
3. Accessed on 22/04/2023 https://www.gmc-uk.org/registration-and-licensing/join-the-register/plab

explained that the only motive for undertaking further education was to obtain an extension to their visa.

This section concludes with some telling statistics garnered from the survey: around one-third (31.33%) of participants declared they had been discriminated against because of their Algerian nationality, but only 7% said they experienced gender discrimination when applying for jobs or training. Meanwhile, 10% said that their immigration status at arrival was often a barrier to accessing education, funding and the labour market, but it depended upon the country to which they migrated. Lack of space, however, means that this summary cannot do full justice to the participants' various routes to finally achieving a successful professional life. Given the general discourse on migrant women, particularly those who flee war zones, it is highly likely that organizations and policy-makers overlook their aptitudes and fail to recognize their resilience and the positive ways in which they have overcome traumatic experiences. Yet my study revealed these women's agency and their ability to cope with adversity, showing that, if given the right support, they comprise a positive resource for the countries in which they settle.

Integration, language and identity

The question is, how did these women negotiate their new identities and adapt to their new environments? Their narratives illustrate just how essential it was for them to resume their work and retrieve their lost social positions, a process that involved reinventing a self and negotiating a new identity in a dialogical way (for more on this, see Chapter One). Studies on 'identity' necessarily have to consider the role of language, a tool that is vital to accessing social networks. Indeed, the complex and intertwined issues of language and identity appeared to play a formative role in creating a sense of belonging (or otherwise) in these women's new social and professional environments.

To the question in the survey regarding what languages respondents use to communicate with their family and their Algerian friends, more than a third (81%) replied that they used French, followed by Algerian Derdja (69%) and English (43%), with Amazigh and Arabic at 18% and 17% respectively. Respondents were allowed to choose as many options as they wished, which meant that many of them were likely to be alternating between more than one language, mainly mixing French with Derdja. French was also the language they tended to use online, followed by English. Very few comments or articles were posted in literary Arabic. During at least two conferences at which I presented some of the findings of this study, I was confronted with two particular questions: why was French the dominant language used by the participants in your research and why was the Arabic version of your survey unpopular? These questions demanded an explanation. Although Algeria is a member of the Arab League and Arabic is its official language, nearly all the inhabitants of North Africa, including Algerians, are assumed to be of Amazigh ethnicity. This contradiction reveals that language is often subject to a geopolitical logic. Louisa, for example, related her experience of exile thus:

> I am deeply Algerian but I am imbued with French culture; I am particularly open to modernity and knowledge. French is my 'war booty', and I am proud to call myself a Francophone secular Algerian woman who rejects obscurantist Arabism, which only brought us Salafism and terrorism.

Like Louisa, the majority of participants were educated in French, at least up to high-school level, and also belong to the post-colonial generation of educated women who took part in the passionate political debates about socialism, Marxism, Amazighism, Islamism and secularism that took place in universities and workplaces during the 1970s and 1980s. Like Louisa, the majority of participants also described themselves as secular. Secularism or *laïcité* is related to the French cultural touchstone of 'liberty, equality, fraternity', which was introduced into Algeria during the colonial period through the imposition of the French language and culture. In the process, the colonizers impressed on the minds of Algerians that French was the language of 'civilization', representative of a 'white culture' far 'superior' to that of the 'black, barbaric, indigenous peoples' (Fanon 1968). The use of the French language was enforced in the education system, state administration and many other fundamental aspects of Algerian life. Any Algerian who did not adhere to the colonial culture and the principle of *laïcité* was portrayed as backward and uncultivated, lacking in scientific knowledge and rationality, a mindset that also regarded Algerian women as oppressed by their Muslim/Arabic culture. According to Malika Rebai Maamri (2009: 1), this was a policy of brutal acculturation, alienating Algerians from their cultural heritage by means of the imposition of French as the dominant language, 'ousting' indigenous languages such as Arabic and Amazigh.

Algerian society was left deeply fractured as a result of this policy, and although the French language never had official status, it remained widely used in the majority of university and academic faculties, governmental organizations and NGOs, making it 'de facto co-official' (Rebai Maamri 2009: 2). Its use also persisted because most of the teachers, administrative personnel, public health workers and university lecturers were exclusively trained in French. As a result, the Francophones (French-speakers), who regarded themselves as modern, rational and secular, clashed with Arabophones (Arabic-speakers), who saw French-speakers as Westernized and therefore a threat to the drive to reassert an 'authentic' Algerian identity based on Arabism and Islam.

The clash deepened during the rise of radical Islam in the 1990s, when many Francophones became the target of terrorist attacks. There is now a large body of opinion that argues that religion served as the grounds for the violence that followed the cancellation of the election, but Amin Maalouf (1998) is a dissenting voice: he asserts that the violence was more rooted in the conflicting linguistic conditions in which Arabophones, Francophones and Berberophones found themselves in post-colonial Algeria. For example, following the assassination by the GIA of acclaimed poet, journalist and author Tahar Djaout in 1993, a declaration by Arabophone writer Tahar Ouattar deepened the conflict. Benrabah Mohamed (2013) recounts in his work *Language Conflict in Algeria: From Colonialism to Post-Independence* that when asked if he thought the death of Djaout was a loss for Algeria, Ouattar answered that 'It was firstly a loss for his family, and secondly for France. Of course, this is not to say that all Algerian Arabophones are religious fundamentalists or adhere to radical Islam; the best counter-example to this is Arabophone feminist writer Ahlem Mosteghanemi (2003), who strongly criticized the failure of post-colonial politics to address the fraught subject of cultural identity, belonging and language.

My research appeared to confirm Maalouf's argument. For Louisa, for example, language played a key role in introducing the notion of violence into Algerian society. Indeed, the first observation she made when she arrived in the UAE was that the Arabic language taught and spoken in Algeria failed to transmit the beauty of Arabic language and culture, which she only discovered once she was there:

> When I first arrived in the UAE, I received a linguistic shock to hear some beautiful Arabic expressions which I couldn't answer: '*habibty*' ['my love'] and '*habibat albi*' ['the love of my heart']. I had never heard these expressions in my Algerian-Arabic language. I didn't even know how to respond to them. Algerians are wordless people when it comes to expressing love, not only due to a reserve but to a real lack of vocabulary. We don't know how to speak about peace ... because all our references are about the *moujahidins* [the former combatants in the War of Independence] and their exploits against France, and already in the semantics of the word '*moujahidin*' we find '*moujahid*' and '*jihad*'—all that you hear is war and violence.

Louisa believes that the post-colonial regime confiscated people's independence and their historical consciousness and replaced it with a new political consciousness, using nationalism as a tool of social conditioning, translated through a language that always refers to violence and war. Apart from the fact that she needed to fit into her new environment, Louisa had also suffered from radical Islam in Algeria, and this no doubt predisposed her to absorbing the influence of the global media. In most parts of the world, the bipolar political debate has been transformed from left versus right to secular versus religious, giving birth to the new lexicon of *jihad*, *jihadism*, *moujahids* and *moujahidins*, with all its terrorist connotations. While Arabic was the language of resistance against the French occupation, French in turn became the language of resistance against an obscurantist radical Islam during the Black Decade and afterwards. After explaining that many French-speaking intellectuals and French teachers, including women, were persecuted and assassinated by the GIA or driven into exile during the conflict, Nadia commented that during her last trip to Algeria, she discovered the spread of a new language she did not own:

> You'll read written large on the facades of their houses and businesses, '*koulou hada bi idniallah*' ['all this is with permission from God']. And you hear [the term] '*mashallah*' ['thankfulness'] everywhere. Those '*oumi*' and '*abbi*' instead of '*baba*' ['dad' in Algerian] and '*yemma*' ['mum']—this language is not ours.

According to Martin Stone (1997: 193), the radical Islamists who appeared in the late 1980s 'used strategies and tactics identical to those of the wartime *moujahidin* who had defeated the French'. However, unlike the resistance struggle, supposedly influenced by anti-colonial philosophers such as Frantz Fanon, Jean-Paul Sartre and Simone de Beauvoir, the new ideological force that drove the anti-intellectual violence during the Black Decade was influenced by a radical form of Islam that portrayed secular Francophones as enemies of their political project—that is, the institution of an Islamic state in Algeria. This may explain not only why the participants in this study are mainly Francophones, but also their ability to adjust and adapt to their new Western environments; they consider themselves as speaking a Western language, with all its related cultural, social and political implications, and this facilitates their adaptation.

Narratives of regaining selfhood

Many of the participants in my research seemed not to have experienced too many difficulties in finally achieving a sense of belonging to their new societies, despite the various forms of discrimination they faced. Those who migrated to France, in particular, felt no sense of 'otherness' since they considered themselves culturally French and well equipped to merge into the French environment. As one interviewee said: 'For me, when I left Algiers for Paris, it made no difference at all. Coming to Paris was like moving house within Algeria; I couldn't consider myself as an "immigrant", I had simply moved.' Another, who also lives in France, pointed out: 'Being a Francophone, French culture was not alien to me. I think I was already "integrated" before I came here.'

The process of integration or adaptation cannot be dissociated from women's sense of self and the reconstruction of self in exile. This involves a dialogical process, with the feeling of belonging 'here' and 'there' at the same time. This two-way process is not only based on the migrants' acceptance by their receiving societies but also on their ability to 'let go' of their differences. Exile is a process that involves learning new customs, cultures and values without which it would be difficult to achieve a sense of belonging:

> Integration for me is to understand the British culture, live the best of both cultures [Algerian and British], and respect British rules and customs. It is both ways, to give and to receive, to be open to other cultures and faiths, and to regard them as equal.

This quotation also suggests that the migrant experience is an opportunity to place the self within a larger context. As stated above, and seen via various examples in this book, participants appear to exhibit certain universal values that they have learned in their day-to-day lives, although it has become common when speaking of a sense of 'transnational belonging' to associate this with the movements of the elite or the highly skilled. As one of the participants pointed out: 'Integration is to show that the Earth belongs to all despite the controlling borders; competences [and skills] have no frontiers.'

Khadija explained that although having children was at first a cause of isolation, it later became a key factor in making her feel that she now belonged in her new environment:

> I belong to Spain in several ways: my two daughters were born here, their school [and] their friends [are here], and the mark of the family is on this [place]. I also have a linguistic link with Spain that makes me feel closer to the society. It does not mean a loss of my identity, but the gaining of a new one.

It is often the case that solidarity between women is built around parenting and childcare. Placing their gender above other identity markers, such as religion or nationality, mothers often share the task of babysitting when childcare provisions are not available. Khadija described how she had made many friends in the locality through picking up and dropping off one another's children at school. She stated that she has never missed a parents' evening and has attended birthday parties, school trips and other events. Khadija, who speaks good Spanish, seems to have taken all the opportunities she could to establish friendships with the parents of her children's classmates.

Khadija's knowledge of Spanish was an important factor in her integration and eventual sense of belonging, particularly as it is more common that migrant mothers are pushed into socializing with one another when their children are in the same schools. A Swansea University project on 'Parenting in a Multi-cultural European City', which I helped coordinate in 2008, showed that schools in Europe sometimes provide migrant parents with lessons in the country's language. In the UK, for example, basic English and other literacy skills were taught in nearly all state schools, alongside other community projects aimed at empowering migrant parents, although this provision has since been compromised by funding cuts and the closure of free ESOL (English for

Speakers of Other Languages) classes. The loss of such projects is particularly unfortunate, as it is now generally recognized that mothers who are involved in their children's schooling benefit from such programmes of empowerment. The men tend to be excluded from this process, and as a result, women become more aware of cultural differences and start to challenge their own cultural norms, often rejecting patriarchal rules transposed from the culture of origin. Khadija went on to explain that she has now reinvented herself, adopting a new identity without losing her original one; her identity is composed of both her old and her new self.

The survey also revealed that half (53%) of the participants considered themselves to belong to an Algerian network, although for two-thirds of them it meant little more than meeting with other Algerian women and sharing experiences. Among other things, participants mentioned lack of time as one reason for not networking or attending gatherings. As noted earlier, often isolated from family and friends, mothers—particularly single mothers—struggle with childcare costs. Added to which, rebuilding professional lives in a new environment is time-consuming and demanding. Interviewees gave their answers greater depth by mentioning other perceived barriers to networking:

> Those [Algerians] who came to the USA with green cards ... spend their time in Pakistani or Saudi Arabian mosques ... They have nothing to do with our Maghrebi sense of Islam. The wives wear the *hijab* ... I'm sorry but I don't feel any [sense of] belonging to this hypocrisy. I don't trust an Islamist whatever [their] level of education. I don't get together with anyone. I have so many friends in the grave today and [undertook] that entire, cruel journey into exile because of 'them'. So I prefer to keep away from 'them'.

Louisa's quotation reminds us again of the current debate on political Islam and its effects on Muslim communities in the West, particularly when terrorist acts are committed in the name of Islam. Although Louisa was one of the few who mentioned this issue, members of the 'Algerian Women Diaspora' Facebook network have discussed it on a daily basis. We will see in Chapter Five how Louisa explains that her withdrawal from the protests during the Hirak was mainly due to her feeling that it had been hijacked by former members of the FIS. Also, following the terrorist attacks in Paris in 2015, Algerian women living abroad and particularly in France, at least those who considered themselves to be secular, were frequently urged to dissociate themselves from their communities, members of whom were often wrongly stereotyped as radical Muslims. The subjectivity of this process can make it problematic to negotiate belonging to a society that does not see any difference between secular and non-secular Muslims, and which considers all Muslims to be a threat to its national identity and internal security.

Several studies highlight that one particularly important point to explore in relation to highly skilled migrants is the development of their professional identity and the construction of new professional careers, and the direct influence this has on their level of integration and contentment. For example, Jacqueline Taylor (2008: 3), who has researched the implications of the term 'professional identity' or 'occupational identity', stresses the 'important relationship between the occupations that people engage in and the construction, maintenance and rebuilding of a coherent and satisfactory identity'. Thus, career and life satisfaction are interlinked and can provide a good tool for measuring happiness. In the case of the participants in the survey, the creation of a strong vocational identity often acted as an important mediator—several declared that they needed to first develop their professional identity in order to feel a sense of belonging to their new societies. One of the respondents commented that she had wished to further her knowledge and build a career in the field of philosophy because she had always dreamed of eventually becoming an academic researcher: 'I used to dream of Kant, Plato and the Agora square. In Algerian universities, I found myself trapped in poorly transcribed theories.' After completing her PhD, she found work as a lecturer and researcher at a university in Belgium, where she feels fully integrated. This participant also pointed out in the survey that she had no intention of returning to Algeria, a question discussed in the next section of this chapter.

It is necessary to emphasize here that Algerian academia has never been open to debates on current social and political issues. For many Algerians of my generation and that of the participants in this study, there was (and still is) a stigma against the humanities, including philosophy, literature and the social sciences, which are considered unsophisticated subjects in comparison with the hard sciences and medicine. The selection of candidates to study science and medicine was made fully two years before entering the last year in secondary school to sit the baccalaureate, and it was mainly based on the marks a student achieved rather than their aspiration to study a particular topic—so anyone who obtained average or below-average marks was oriented towards literature, social sciences and law. Also, during the 1980s, these subjects began to be taught in Arabic, which made them more susceptible to being linked to radical Islam, while hard sciences and medicine were mainly taught in French, with all the related associations with French culture and secularism. This not only helped to feed the conflict between Francophones and Arabophones mentioned above but also encouraged a politics of social exclusion based on academic pathways and subjects.

Karim Khaled (2014) even goes so far as to exclude violence as a factor in pushing academics and intellectuals to leave the country during the Black Decade, an argument that my research—as previous chapters have shown when documenting the trauma of life in Algeria during and in the aftermath of the Black Decade—does not uphold. However, the reasons he puts forward for the mass exodus of the highly skilled during the 1990s, regardless of gender and particularly for those who migrated to France, have some validity. The first is that migration expressed sociopolitical opposition to the government and its dominant policies, characterized by the ideology of a single-party state. The second is that migration was also a protest against the exclusion of academics and experts from the management of the country's affairs. Generations of academics had had to endure bureaucratic and centralized oversight of their research projects and publications, and of the attribution of funding to attend conferences and other scholarly events. As a result, the main vocation of the university was distorted: no longer an open environment for research and academic debate, it turned into a heavily censored space.

Khaled (2014) argues that, for a long time after independence, the remuneration of Algerian university lecturers and researchers was similar to that of civil servants, and they were only required to teach and reproduce the ideology of the ruling party (the FLN). In addition, despite changes in governance since independence, patriarchy arguably remains the focal culture in many Algerian institutions, including academic institutions. One quotation taken from the survey provides a particularly good illustration of this: 'I came here because in Algeria I couldn't study photography. Researchers are forbidden to study [the work of] photographers such as Hamilton, and other "erotic" topics.' According to the second volume of the *Oxford Encyclopedia of Women*

(Smith 2008: 190–92), 'the western meaning of the word "eroticism" often refers to some of the most complex existential, political, artistic and literary dilemmas, as well as to a few of the most problematic debates of western philosophy'; furthermore, 'eroticism is very often associated with the empowerment and liberation of women'. Thus, given the influence that radical Islam, grounded in an extreme version of patriarchy, holds in Algerian society today, it would be vain to hope for the introduction of such a sensitive and complex topic into the academic, let alone public, debate. The respondent cited above is the one participant who declared her sexuality as lesbian, a further factor behind her decision to leave her homeland. I was not able to interview her but had the opportunity to converse with her via the Facebook chat room, where she confirmed that her reason for leaving Algeria was both to further her studies and to have the chance to be open about her sexuality.

Participants also mentioned discovering new subjects of study once they had arrived in their host countries, including topics about which they already had some knowledge but were not taught in Algeria simply because of the lack of human resources and relevant infrastructure. For example:

> To work as a doctor [in France], you need continual updates, so I undertook complementary training [in] such [areas] as homeopathy, and facial and corporal mesotherapy. I studied for a master's in obstetrics, and my PhD [was] on nutrition and obesity. I've attended several international congresses and seminars. My training as a doctor in Algeria was very good but here I've widened my knowledge, learned lots more, because [this country] has all the means needed to update knowledge in … fields that have not yet been introduced in Algeria.

This quotation refers, in passing, to how the ability to gain professional recognition in another country relies on self-motivation and often self-funding. Indeed, attending conferences and training, as this participant did, can be very costly. One point of interest here is the difference between participants who answered the survey in French and those who did so in English, regarding the question of the barriers they faced in accessing courses, training and the job market in their new environment. Only 8% of those who responded in French mentioned lack of funding as a problem, as opposed to 18% of those who answered the survey in English. It is impossible to draw a rigorous conclusion from this observation, but it could be posited that these numbers are a reflection of the high fees both international and home students are required to pay to access higher education in the USA and UK. It is beyond the scope of this research to look at particular cases, but from my own experience in the UK, undocumented highly skilled migrants, including those who have claimed asylum and are waiting for a decision on their claims, are required to pay international fees if they want to take a higher education degree. This has excluded many women from undertaking postgraduate courses, despite their obvious academic ability.

The participant quoted above seems to have taken the opportunity to use all available resources in order to update and widen her knowledge. For many others, however, the highest barrier they have had to surmount is that their Algerian qualifications are simply not recognized: 'Diplomas obtained in Algeria are not recognized in the country where I live or any of the European countries'; 'Do not deceive yourself, our diplomas are not accepted.' This lack of recognition, whether in relation to their academic qualifications or their previous professional experience, was mentioned by almost all the participants in this research. The amount of frustration this subject appeared to provoke suggests that the reconstruction of the self in exile generally takes time and effort, and also requires such markers of 'recognition'.

The 'myth of return': Missing home but where is home?

The participation of many of these women in the Hirak in 2019 and 2020 may be seen, to some degree, as a way of venting the frustrations described above that had accumulated for more than two decades. Indeed, the research in the following section was undertaken before the Hirak erupted in Algeria, bringing with it hope of radical change. The narratives and comments of these women about their experiences of visits to Algeria, before the Hirak, is testimony to their belief in the need for such change.

The 'myth of return' is arguably the strongest defining aspect of a diasporic community (Clifford 1994; Safran 1999). The way members of a diaspora hold on to this myth is complex, and it mainly serves to maintain traditions built on solidarities. However, members of diasporic communities also realize that they are not and will never be unified in the old sense, as they are irrevocably the product of several interlocking histories and cultures, belonging to one but at the same time several homes. This is confirmed by Sonia, who admitted that she finds whenever she returns on holiday that 'Algeria [has become] a country that is hard to live in now'. Many other participants agreed with her on the fact that public services, for example, have dramatically deteriorated in the post-Black Decade era. In relation to the state of Algerian hospitals today, four participants evoked chronic illness as the main barrier to their return.

Thus, although nearly all the participants in this study (82%) declared that they miss Algeria, only a third considered eventually returning, while two-thirds said there were too many barriers in place—social, political, economic and domestic. More than two-thirds (78.16%) said that of all the barriers they faced to returning, the first concerned the social environment and private life. The amendments to the Family Code in 2005 were supposed to have given women greater freedom; however, participants expressed concern about the lack of information and communication from Algerian consulates concerning the amendments and their impact on women's rights, particularly regarding women married to non-Algerians. In practice, many of the Algerian civil servants working in embassies and consulates remain deeply influenced by patriarchal ideology and do not implement this new legislation in a way that enhances the position of Algerian women living abroad. As a result, women may be reluctant to return to Algeria, as consulates are the first point of contact between a country and its expatriate community, as Louisa illustrates:

> We are scared to approach the Algerian embassy and consulate here in Washington because of their negative language. So you tell yourself: 'Oh, OK, let's keep away from this, we don't want to reopen any pain or be reminded of the reality of what Algerian society has become today.'

In addition, participants frequently mentioned the 2005 amnesty legislation (see Chapter Three), which is often held responsible for driving Algerian society into the arms of a more radical kind of fundamentalism, as a barrier to their return. As one participant remarked:

> We [women] have not been consulted about the reconciliation. I am of course against impunity. That's why we have learned to be discreet over there, to look left and right and behind before walking anywhere. Now it's a bit safer, or at least there is no danger of death, I think.

In general, participants showed an attachment to an 'imagined Algeria', which they identified with the sort of Algeria that women of their generation fought for and dreamed of: pluralistic, tolerant, just and economically prosperous. It is this 'imagined Algeria' that they carried into exile and to which many of the women I met (and I myself) dream of returning. This is set against the Algeria some of the participants, such as Nadia, experience when they return on visits to the country:

> And you know what? This summer I was there and got out in Algiers. I was walking and suddenly felt a hypoglycaemia: I'm diabetic. It was Ramadhan and everything was closed, everything, everything. I wanted a glass of water and it wasn't possible. They will never see me in Algeria during Ramadhan again. While in our religion, you don't fast if you are ill, no restaurants are open [there], and if they see you take a glass of water or eat ... I feel that even the democrats play the game [of the reconciliation law]. You should see how my family is watching me when I go there now! My sisters and I used to be left-wing activists; they all pray and fast now. They have forbidden too much now, too much.

Nadia deplored the fact that, as she described it, radical Islam has now gained a hold over nearly everyone in the country, placing greater restrictions on daily life. She expressed her disappointment that even close family members, who continue to claim adherence to democracy and secularism, now practise a particularly strict form of Islam.

As well as actual visits to the country on vacation or business trips, cyber facilities and online social networks allow frequent virtual returns to Algeria, sometimes several times a day, and this has made it obvious to many of the participants that the Algeria they dreamed of does not exist. Louisa commented: 'We can't return to Algeria any more because we have adopted another way to approach life, and I don't want to disadvantage my daughter.' According to these participants, and many observers, a sort of mutant Algerian society has emerged, one that faces great challenges in the reconstruction of its economy and identity, particularly given the current geopolitical climate in the region. It appears to remain a country that is now 'alien' to those women who do not live there any more, as Nadia demonstrated:

> One day, I went to order cakes and the baker told me: 'Come back tomorrow after the Maghreb prayer.' I said to him: 'My watch does not indicate the

> time in prayers but in hours and minutes.' I insisted and showed him my watch: 'Look, sir, it does not indicate prayers [laughs], give me a proper time please.' He simply couldn't answer, because you see, he didn't even know what time the prayer was because I'm sure he doesn't pray himself. But everything has become linked to religion over there. What they want is to transform the language of Algerians, all you hear is '*Inshalla*', '*Bi-idni Allah*' ['God's will']. They have the laundered money from terrorism and they have [built] shops and big villas now, [and] you'll read written large on their facades, '*Koulou hada biidniallah*' ['All this is with permission from God'].

Here, Nadia gives concrete examples of how she sees changes in today's Algeria, both in relation to the implementation of the amnesty law, which allowed terrorists and wrongdoers to escape accountability, and to the rise of what she sees as 'backward' behaviour and a 'strange' religious language introduced in the name of Islam. Not only Nadia but many Algerian women I met during the course of this study think that there is a loss of spirituality in favour of a series of prohibitions that are alien to the version of Islam formerly known in Algeria. Participants almost all grew up in families who practised Islam but have now adopted secularism, rejecting the radical practices that have mainly emerged from a version of Islam known as Salafism, believed to have been imported from Saudi Arabia. This may not of course be representative of all Algerian women living abroad, but it is arguably the case for many of those highly skilled women who fled the country during the Black Decade.

Algerian public opinion appears to hold two views on returning migrants. The first is materialistic in that it considers mobility as a marker of a high status; migrants are assumed to be rich, coming back to show off their wealth. The second is more concerned with social behaviour and presents migrants, particularly women, as adopting arrogant attitudes towards their country's indigenous culture and habits. It seems that Nadia experienced both views. However, despite her strong criticisms of Algeria today, she is one of the very few who voiced the idea of returning:

> I agree that we should think about our future; we can't stay here for ever. However, we can still perceive [over there] the high cost of the Black Decade. Have you been to mental health hospitals in Algiers? All the kids who witnessed their parents' beheadings and other violence are now traumatized adults ... This is only what is visible. Whether by murder or by exile, Algeria

> has lost the majority of its intellectuals, those who [wish] for the good [of Algeria], those who love the country.

Nadia's desire to return, however, is undermined by concrete facts. Among these is the lack of mental health care provisions for those who witnessed the horrors inflicted on their parents during the Black Decade. They are now aged between twenty-five and thirty-five, and are a part of the age group that constitutes the majority in Algerian society. Nadia went to visit mental health hospitals because she plans to set up a company specializing in providing care and support to women with complex health needs, including mental illness and learning disabilities, on her return home. However, she denounced the bad governance, corruption and favouritism that are now affecting every section of Algerian public administration and higher education institutions, including access to medical schools and academic departments formerly known for their integrity. It may be that she was referring to these scourges of good governance when expressing the belief that only a small part of the problem is 'visible'.

According to Nadia, those Algerians with honesty and competence were either killed or persecuted and forced to flee during the Black Decade. From her point of view, those who now govern Algeria do not want the best for the country. As mentioned earlier, Nadia holds a doctorate in chemistry and was formerly head of a school of medicine in Algeria; she now works as a secondary school teacher in France. 'Also, I haven't published any work in my field for so long, so the Ministry of Higher Education will never hire me again there.' Nadia realizes that she has not been able to rebuild her academic career and this would prevent her from assuming the same position she had before she left the country. As mentioned earlier, there are no official statistics on how many academics left during and after the Black Decade. However, Nadia also revealed:

> We've heard of a circular from the Minister of Higher Education that all those who left during the Black Decade will be [reinstated] ... if they so wish; those who were forced to abandon their positions. Me, I left within twenty-four hours, they knew it. I was the director of an important institution. In 1994, when I was there, I received a call from the [man] who later replaced me to tell me: 'Listen, I cannot cover you any further, you must resign from the post.' It was a special situation where everyone was leaving ... We all resigned, as you know; we were forced to do so.

Nadia was not able to verify if the person who replaced her was competent or not. She expressed sadness over her loss of professional identity, which she was unable to replicate in France, and showed an awareness that even if she returned to Algeria, she would never be able to work in the same position.

According to the survey, more than two-thirds (84%) of respondents paid short visits to Algeria between 2013 and 2014, but the definitive return is 'the myth that doesn't always happen'; However, it is this myth that facilitates the development of generational diasporic consciousness over time. (Abdelhady 2011). The following quotation from my survey provides an apt illustration:

> It seems to me that women have to be twice as strong and aggressive to live in Algeria. It's also not easy when you are a single woman. A married woman is more acceptable, socially speaking. Being a woman in Algeria is a daily combat. After four months there I realized I wasn't ready for that, so I came back.

Maalouf (1998) contends that many of us would reject our inherited conceptions of identity, to which we adhere through habit, if only we examined them more closely. Participants in this study know that the future of any society now depends on accepting each other's identities while also accepting the need to be recognized in turn as an individual. They also appear to be aware that their identities comprise a rich mixture of different senses of belonging: some are linked to the particularity of Algerian history, the country's struggle for independence and the different post-colonial stages of consolidating new national values, and others correlate it to their religious as well as their Amazigh and Arab heritages. An Algerian is composed of all of these influences. Maalouf explains that from the moment we begin to acknowledge that we are made from these rich components, we can approach others with values based not on nationality and religion or race but on other, intrinsically human ones. As a consequence, a more serene relationship with others is created. We find that amongst 'us' there are people with whom we do not share any values, while amongst 'others' there are individuals with whom we can feel very close. Maalouf also argues that migrants who are aware of this are now in their millions worldwide, and their numbers are growing. Together they are creating a 'cultural melting pot' and a new conception of what identity ought to be, which enables them to embrace the cultures in their new societies without friction. Being on the edge of two or more different communities, often with contradictory values, they can play a key role in building bridges between these communities and become the 'cement' of the societies in which they live.

This argument is made concrete in the following quotation from Louisa, who previously said that she would not return to Algeria but nonetheless holds strong ideas on how to fix some of the country's social problems:

> I have absolutely no pretentions to say 'I know better.' The person who challenges me always teaches me a lot, and so I've learned a lot. I always try to project the best image—it's not even the best image, it's my image. But [Algeria], where to start from? In post-colonial Algeria, the notion of love was destroyed. We do not love each other, we haven't learned how to love each other; very few Algerians are conscious of that. I only want us to learn not to keep our heads down. We can become … valued like all other societies, because reconciliation starts with loving yourself, and so the image you are offering to others is beautiful. It's a way to say to others: 'I love you, and that's why I'm offering you my best image.' … It's a process of learning, you see … and when you start talking with serenity, then contact with others becomes easy, it's not a confrontation any more.

It is salutary to recall that Louisa fled persecution in Algeria, where she was on a 'death list'. At the beginning of the interview, she described exile as either heaven or hell. She also confessed that it was only when she read about my research and when I asked her about returning to Algeria, that she realized that during her twenty years of exile she had gained better communication skills and more openness towards other Algerians. The counterpart of this, she believes, is a process of learning how to value yourself, to reach the serenity that enables you to share the best of yourself. She wants to transfer this understanding back home, a place where memories seem to have remained frozen in turmoil, conflict and hate.

As Maalouf (1998) explains, those who lack the ability to assume their own diverse identity markers find themselves excluded or isolated and discriminated against in the societies where they live. They will try to avenge themselves against those who practise discrimination, and will harbour thoughts of self-hatred and hate towards others, leaving them open to extremist ideas—a hatred of which history has given us too many examples (Maalouf 1998: 46). It would be too easy to conclude that Louisa's exile is a paradise, particularly in comparison to nearly all the literature on exile, which presents it as a time of misery (Sayad 2004). Nevertheless, no one has the right to deny Louisa her happiness and her resilience in learning how to overcome the harsh side of being forced into exile, to work on herself and extract the best out of herself, and then to offer it to others.

In this regard, I would like to add that many of the participants in this research, and other women survivors of the Black Decade whom I have met during the last several years, support the idea of the urgent need to inculcate a transnational character, based on universal human values, regardless of religion and discriminatory immigration policies. It does not matter to them whether this vision is shared with Algerians or with others, as long as the positive benefits are shared by all in their new communities, which in turn need to show recognition of their contribution. As one survey participant remarked: 'To integrate is to make friends, to contribute to the host community with the new things [we] can offer, and to be recognized for that.' Needless to say, the ways in which migrants contribute to all aspects of the daily life of the societies in which they now live are countless, despite the overwhelmingly negative media representations. For this participant, her ability to integrate and make new friends, despite the hostility she has encountered, rests on receiving recognition and acknowledgement of her contribution to society. The various examples cited above show that integration or adaptation is thus a dual and dialogical experience. Media owners and policy-makers have powerful tools at their disposal that could, if used positively, represent migrant women's success in a way that benefits both their new societies and their countries of origin.

In terms of seeking to establish ties with other Algerians, it is interesting to note that the type of gatherings the respondents seem to prefer are mostly cultural, private and familial (88%), and in equal number, academic talks, conferences and seminars (59%). Participants do not aspire to only meet Algerians of the same gender but prefer those sharing their political views. As Feroudja explained:

> We [secular feminists] have not fallen, because we fought, although we failed, unfortunately. But I'm convinced that our struggle will [continue] in the future. I'm deeply committed to secularism because, as you know, in Algeria

> we need to bring reason into religion; we must read and listen to such people as Mohammed Arkoun. The Maghrebi feminist movement has conducted a great battle over this. I refer to Latifa Lakhdar … although we declare ourselves to be secular, we all need to help bring reason into religion.

Feroudja hopes to see reason return to religion in a future Algeria. She appears to believe that it is the only way to oppose organized violence perpetrated in the name of Islam, and suggests that a better interpretation of Islam can be found in the work of renowned Algerian scholar, Mohammed Arkoun (2002), and one of his followers, Tunisian feminist Latifa Lakhdar (2002, 2007), who, according to Wassyla Tamzali (2014),[4] dominates the contemporary debate on Islamic thought.

Tamzali reinforces Feroudja's argument; both insist that secularism is the only way for the Algerian people to live together in peace again. Yet many of the participants in this study appear to have come to believe that patriarchy is the main issue that impedes the implementation of gender equality in Algeria. Although patriarchy is alive and well all over the world, not all patriarchies are alike, and the Algerian version is particularly harsh (Knauss 1987). On the one hand, equality is guaranteed by the Algerian constitution, but on the other it is jeopardized by an article in the same constitution stating that Islam is the religion of the state. Indeed, as we saw in Chapter Two, the Algerian reservation on CEDAW, particularly Article 2, suggests that it places Islamic law above any UN instruments of international human rights. As Feroudja explained: 'Equality is a basic principle of human rights, which cannot be spewed [out]. It is the minimum requirement if one has to take the decision to go back home.' Meanwhile, Wahiba added a comment to the question on why she cannot think of returning: 'Because of the "*hogra*"—a word that you can't translate into any other language because it only exists in Algeria.' The word '*hogra*' not only refers to the perceived contempt of the authorities but also describes the social and institutional injustice and discrimination that hampers women from fully participating in public life. Participants sometimes compared Algeria in this respect with its neighbour, Tunisia. As one participant

4. Wassyla Tamzali is an Algerian writer, lawyer and feminist. I recorded her speaking at a seminar organized in Oran on 27/10/2014, prior to the Congrès International Féminin pour une Culture de Paix Parole aux Femmes, Oran, 28–30 October 2014.

remarked: 'After living in Tunisia for more than three years, I realized the impact of Islamism on my society.' Regarding return, she pointed out:

> I signed a contract with the Algerian Ministry of Higher Education to return after my PhD, but I would like to add this comment. Today, women are judged according to the values Islamists oblige them to conform to rather than to what the real Algerian culture is. When I [go there] and walk outside at 7pm in [my city], many men ask me to go in their cars to give them pleasure … so my ideas [about] return are mixed.

This participant wears the *hijab* but still experiences sexual harassment if she happens to be on the street at a certain time of day and in certain areas of Algeria, as if she were trespassing in a space owned exclusively by men. During my last two visits to universities situated outside Algiers, I asked if female students can stay late in the library whenever they need to, something we used to do before the Black Decade. The answer was 'definitely, no' because of the harassment, which takes place regardless of whether women are veiled or not, whether they are students or not. Marnia Lazreg (2009) argues that the conception of the veil as a means of preventing sexual harassment is a myth, with its roots in the same argument that blames rape on the way women dress.

The opening of a democratic window of opportunity with the Arab Spring, triggered by the 'Jasmine Revolution' in Tunisia, revealed the extent of the patriarchal norms that were prevalent in Tunisian society. I learned later from the Facebook account of another participant, an Algerian feminist, who as a union activist in Tunisia had fought to force the government there to lift its CEDAW reservation, that she had decided to return to Algeria after experiencing what she believes was the successful Tunisian transition to democracy. She now works as a university lecturer on a topic related to gender studies. Indeed, transferring skills on gender equality learned abroad to Algerian academia—and to society as a whole—remains an imperative. The following statement from Wahiba is very explicit about this particular challenge:

> Returning back [home]? I feel times have changed in Algeria, women are [fighting] for change and claiming their rights, even if it's very hard … You know, it's a struggle. I also don't want to impose my feminism onto other

> Algerian women, but just to show them that freedom does exist, you don't have to take off your veil or go out every night, you can just be free within your mind for a start, because freedom is first of all a state of mind.

Wahiba hesitates about returning 'home' and nurtures conflicting ideas on to what extent Algerian women have achieved their rights and the freedom to make use of them. I have argued elsewhere that Algerian women have recently been able to make their mark within the professional and academic spheres (Guemar 2011) despite an increase in wearing the veil, a condition they are forced to comply with if they are to enter the public arena. Wahiba, meanwhile, expressed sympathy with her compatriots in Algeria, telling them that it is necessary to achieve internal freedom in order to break free of the obstacles to external freedom. There is now a growing body of opinion among women's rights advocates that argues that freedom for women should not be defined from a purely Western feminist viewpoint, which demands that women should refuse to wear the veil and should socialize in public. Wahiba similarly believes that women's rights may be hard to attain in Algeria but the struggle should continue and should be supported from outside, but only insofar as this is not perceived by women in Algeria as an intrusion into their internal freedom to feel secure and content in the context in which they live.

The subject of the 'myth of return' is therefore often difficult to concretize. Returns, real or virtual, and projects that engage with 'home' depend on the establishment of a diaspora. The following section is an investigation into the network of highly skilled women that I discovered during the course of my research, in order to ascertain whether its members consider themselves as belonging to a diaspora.

Perspectives on an Algerian women's diaspora

My survey revealed that 57% of the respondents considered themselves to be part of an Algerian network, and among these, three-quarters (75%) declared that belonging to a network meant being part of a community and 87% said they used this network to meet other Algerian women to share experiences. During my fieldwork, I also asked my interviewees about their perception of the existence of a diaspora of Algerian women. The majority of participants, although they said they believed such a diaspora does not exist, agreed there is an urgent need to establish one. What follows is an interesting comment from Feroudja, who now lives in France:

> No, there is none. However, there is a will to establish a diaspora, there is a will to do something for Algeria, but there is always something there to obstruct the transmission of solidarity mechanisms between women. The Algerian regime manages this division wherever Algerians are through [its] consulates, embassies, fake diasporic organizations, etc.

This suggests that the Algerian regime may consider diasporic networks a threat. Feroudja explained that, after all, the idea of an independent Algerian nation was born in France within a network of anti-colonial Algerian migrants, and that is possibly why, whenever an initiative has been taken to establish another such network, it has been regarded with suspicion by the Algerian authorities as a potential threat to the established order. She also denounced the lack of solidarity between Algerian women, whether in Algeria or abroad: 'There are constant rivalries to gain the empathy of a "male" in order to survive, and that's how jealousies are [created]. It destroys the sisterhood [and] solidarity.' Feroudja described herself not only as an Algerian academic but also an activist and feminist, who, despite being retired, in a mixed marriage and living in a small city in France, continues to be very knowledgeable on current women's rights issues in Algeria and elsewhere.

Wahiba, who lives in the UK, writes a blog dedicated to Algerian issues. She explained how pleased she is to see that her blog is mainly visited by women, although there are men who have also voiced their admiration of her outspoken style and provocative topics. Wahiba recounted:

> I started [the blog] maybe because I was like you, hunting for a diaspora. Are there any Algerian women out there? And it turned out that, yes, there were many ... They started to pop up like mushrooms, saying: 'Oh my God! There are Algerian women who can write well!'

Wahiba assumed that, in contrast to other countries, the Algerian women in the UK were not connected to each other: 'Generally speaking, there is ... no solidarity, which is the main issue.' She explained that the women she knows are 'all very highly qualified, or they are still students, or have finished [their studies] and are now working'. Like Feroudja, she mentioned 'the sense of mistrust among us Algerians'. She explained that women do not want to see each other because they are afraid of the 'evil eye'—that is, the jealousy their successful lives might provoke. The other interesting point she made, which I have myself verified, is that some Algerian women prefer not to meet with their compatriots because of the judgemental positions they tend to hold on each other's behaviour:

> Many have now started drinking [alcohol] or doing things that normally an Algerian woman shouldn't be doing ... Oh yes, another point, Algerian women don't trust Algerian men here, so [one of] the problems for creating a community is this: some women have been transgressing Algerian norms and have become rebellious.

Similarly, for Khadija, it came as a shock to discover that although Spain was one of the preferred destinations of highly skilled Algerian women who left after the Black Decade (Labdelaoui 2012), no network of solidarity has yet been established there:

> To my knowledge, there is no support network between Algerian women to facilitate their integration or in order to [help] find a job or other specific help. It's a real shame! I wish there was a meeting point or a support network for us; maybe it's the right time to create one.

Another participant returned to the point of the divisions among Algerians: 'It saddens and angers me. Everyone is suspicious of everyone. It's draining. We are the new Greeks, a people that thrive on drama.' For 'Fatiha', a secondary-school teacher in the UK, suspicion and lack of trust are the main obstacles to establishing a network of solidarity between Algerian women in her local area. She also claimed that in the UK 'most of the other Algerians are not highly educated and tend to be "radical Islamists"'—this last point was also referred to in Lamia's narrative in Chapter Three. Meanwhile, other participants stressed the hard work they had to put in to rebuild their professional lives in exile, implying that establishing networks and attending meetings can be too time-consuming. Louisa, the journalist living in the USA, described the many barriers she faces in meeting other Algerian women:

> We live in an exploitative society [and] it wants you to be involved only in American affairs. For example, when I wanted to establish a community organization, I was told to only participate in local politics ... So if you

> want to be involved in Algerian politics, it can only be done during your spare time, and here, life is fast and hectic. You'll have to work very hard to afford this spare time. And then, you must find a good, solid group of Algerians who are very committed to a specific cause.

Louisa added later, 'I also tried to set up an Algerian women's reading group, but believe me, it didn't work.' Once again, this suggests that the experience of migration results in a greater awareness of the universality of many issues. Louisa's desire to establish an Algerian organization that could engage in and cooperate with the local community's events, issues and welfare was undermined by the lack of help and support. She was told such an undertaking would only be possible if she could manage to find some spare time, which seemed an impossible task given the pressures of work and the hectic pace of life. Louisa appears to criticize the exploitation of workers as well as the capitalist work culture in the USA, in which working hours range from forty per week to sixty or more if the individual, regardless of gender, aspires to promotion (Saad 2014). In the same way as the other participants, if more pragmatically, Louisa denounced the lack of an existing 'solid network', and she deplored the attitude and lack of support from Algerian embassies.

Maya, living in France, appeared more concerned about the way the phenomenon of regionalism creates a further barrier to establishing a network:

> I am connected to a group of Algerian women intellectuals who fled here. We meet sometimes but regionalism remains the main issue, as it was in Algeria. I remember once I invited the group for afternoon coffee. The discussion was around whose cake tastes better—the usual Blida versus Algiers [contest]—then whose dresses are the most beautiful, whose accent is classier, etc. The discussion quickly turned to [the question of] which region's women participated most during the war [against France], and suddenly it all became political, [revolving] around the Black Decade. In the end, no one agreed on anything. I became sickened [by it] and I just do my own work [now].

Regionalism is both a well-established way of networking and a scourge in Algeria, and is grounded in the country's system of post-liberation governance (Merolla 1995). The particular network an individual belongs to is believed to be the main criterion for nomination to a high-ranking position in the government, and this attitude is then transferred to Algerians' social and domestic lives. The quotation above suggests that regionalism even continues to affect the establishment of networks of solidarity among Algerian women abroad, at least in the French context.

On the other hand, in the UK alone, at least four networks have been created with the aim of transcending such divisions and promoting collaboration between transnational groups of Algerians, including those still in Algeria. These networks include, at a national level, the International Federation of the Algerian Diaspora (FIDA) and the Algerian International Diaspora Association (AIDA), and other more local groups such as the Algerian British Connection (ABC), chaired by a woman; the National Algerian Centre (NAC), also with a woman chair; and the Algerian Solidarity Campaign (ASC). However, although these initiatives are commendable, in practice none can claim to have mobilized the energies and active participation of highly skilled Algerian women.

Another point of view was expressed by Wahiba, who described herself as a British-Algerian feminist. During the interview she praised the courage of Algerian women in general: 'Algerian women are fighters and I have great respect for them; that's why I never criticize them. They have enough stick … Yes, I think there is an Algerian diaspora amongst women, at least in the UK.' To prove her point, Wahiba asked: 'Was the "network bomb" of the FLN not set up by a group of four young women during the Battle of Algiers?' This episode of the Algerian War of Independence was made known to the international community through the 1966 film of the same name (Gillo Pontecorvo's *The Battle of Algiers*). The attacks of 9/11 and the invasion of Iraq revived the popularity of this film in Western countries. Wahiba believes that resistance is part of the historical consciousness of Algerian women, and that those women living in transnational spaces will overcome the barriers that obstruct their mobilization and will create a diaspora. Unlike other participants, although she voiced some hesitation, she believes that an Algerian women's diaspora does exist in the UK.

Nevertheless, when in February 2016 the Algerian government introduced discriminatory amendments to the constitution, there was less reaction than might have been expected. There had been no consultation with those living abroad before its adoption; even worse, Articles 51 and 73 exclude binationals from occupying senior positions in the state and civil services. Arguably, its adoption was mainly a pretext to exclude those highly skilled Algerians who had been driven to leave the country from participating in a future administration. Although some Algerians living in Paris, Washington, Montreal and even Algiers expressed dissent over these exclusionary articles, the introduction of the constitution failed to mobilize the thousands of Algerians, including Algerian women, who now live abroad.

In the final analysis, my research revealed the existence of a wide transnational network of highly skilled Algerian women who left the country following the violence of the Black Decade. However, it is clear that a diasporic consciousness and solidarity between migrants do not develop spontaneously on arrival in the receiving country (Cohen 2010). However, the fact that participants responded so widely to my survey, and agreed to share their experiences, is a welcome sign that there appears to be a will to establish solidarity between women. The seeds for an Algerian women's diaspora have been planted.

Cohen (2010) argues that similar experiences, including the most traumatic one of departure, shape the formation of diasporic identity, and as the fieldwork for this book suggests, many participants maintain solidarities that encompass transnational ties. In terms of their agency, they have for the most part been highly successful in their education and careers, and their participation in this research demonstrates that their network is specifically and de facto 'intellectual'. Many of the participants, because of their experiences of migration, believe they are now more mature and more capable of bridging the interests of their new societies and those of their home country; hence, they are prompted to advocate for better working conditions, less corruption, greater justice and, most importantly, gender equality in Algeria. It appears that most of them have no wish to return to living there, but they do desire to see political, social and economic change in the country. The following chapter documents how they responded to the sudden emergence of the Hirak movement and the massive demonstrations demanding just such changes.

5 Women of the Black Decade and the Hirak

Introduction: The power of history

This chapter relates the ways in which Algerian women mobilized around questions of dignity, democracy and justice during the revolutionary period of the Hirak that began in February 2019, and how the women who participated in my research engaged with this movement for change. Throughout Algeria, women in their thousands joined the Hirak to challenge the regime and its government, which they believed had made a mockery of democracy, and confronted the corrupt elites who profited while so many ordinary Algerians, including women and children, drowned at sea in desperate attempts to reach 'Fortress Europe' and a better life. The collective memory of the struggles of the Black Decade was reappropriated by those partaking in the protests, and this history became a powerful (though painful) symbol of an Algerian common heritage, allowing women who fled the country during this period to recapture their historical legitimacy, both as activists and as part of civil society—although, as many of these women point out, the legacy of the unresolved conflicts of the 1990s later became a cause of division, serving to destabilize the Hirak.

Drawing on interviews with these exiled women, some of whom returned to Algeria to take part in the Hirak, I explore their role in, and connection and engagement with, contemporary politics in Algeria. This raises in a new context the questions of an 'imagined homeland' and the development of a diasporic consciousness that is fashioned by historical and personal circumstances, as well as by gender and other social constructs. The chapter finishes with the testimonies of these women, relating their activism, the disillusionment of some with the course of the Hirak, their differing assessments of the situation, and their hopes or fears for the future.

The course of the Hirak

Over the past few years in Algeria, and most intensely during the last months of 2018 and early 2019, an online campaign led by activists, social media influencers and respected politicians, and echoed in the chants of football-stadium audiences, was mobilized to prevent President Abdelaziz Bouteflika from standing yet again as a candidate in the presidential elections. Although he was a sick and aged president—he later died on 17 September 2021—whom Algerians had neither heard nor seen for years, his supporters (including his brother, who many believed to be the real powerbroker in the country) were pushing for a fifth term in office in clear violation of the Algerian constitution.

The Hirak truly began on Friday 15 February 2019 in Kherata, a city in north-east Algeria, when hundreds of citizens took to the streets to voice their rejection of a fifth term for Bouteflika. Historically, Kherata is renowned for its defiant resistance to colonialism, especially evident in the demonstration of 8 May 1945, which was brutally suppressed by the French. It was not surprising, then, that this was the city that in 2019 saw the first in a wave of demonstrations that swept Algeria in protest at a political decision that many saw as a humiliation for a country of 1.5 million 'martyrs', a people that had sacrificed so much for its freedom in the past. The peaceful but determined character of the demonstration gave many Algerians, including those living abroad, the courage to break free of the worry that had held them back from political protest for so long, fearful that the country could be plunged back into the horrors of the Black Decade. During that internal conflict, it is reported that nearly 200,000 were killed, around 20,000 disappeared, and thousands took the route of exile. The trauma of these years still lies buried within Algerian society and its diaspora.

Following the peaceful protest in Kherata, leaflets and messages were widely circulated, both physically and via Facebook, calling on all Algerians to join the demonstrations on the streets planned for the following Friday (which was 22 February), with instructions to observe peaceful methods, chant anti-fifth term in office slogans and call for a radical change in Algeria's system of governance. On that Friday, and on each Friday for several months afterwards, the country experienced one of the most impressive social movements for democracy the world has seen. In the capital, Algiers, the protest began somewhat timidly in the morning—demonstrations had been forbidden in the city—but after Friday prayers in the afternoon, millions of people poured onto the streets, creating what has since been called the 'Blessed Hirak'.

As on all occasions when Algeria's citizens have perceived an overwhelming need for change, women were present at the protests, and their involvement remains crucial in the struggle to build a modern, fully democratic Algeria, in which the rights of all are respected. In Algiers, women marched to emphasize the importance of regaining their 'right to the city' (see Chapter Three)—reclaiming the public space and their ability to exercise their citizenship in full. Many Algerian women, including large numbers of young women, also protested in Paris, Marseilles, Montreal, London and Washington in support of the struggle of their peers back home to oust the '*issaba*' ('gang')—a term used during the protests for any member of the government who worked with Bouteflika. In different capitals across the world, Algerians showed their solidarity with their compatriots by organizing sit-ins in front of their embassies or in the main squares, chanting similar slogans to those heard on the streets in Algeria. On Saturday 23 February 2019, a group of Algerians living in the UK also gathered in front of the Algerian embassy in London's Riding House Street in support of the movement for democracy and freedom in Algeria. I joined with my daughter and another woman, accompanied by her two toddlers. We were among the first to arrive that afternoon, but within a few hours, the square was full—although mainly with young Algerian men. It must be noted here that London differs somewhat from the other centres of Algerian exile in that it is a city that offered sanctuary not only to liberal intellectuals but also to members of the Islamist Salvation Front (FIS) and its armed wing (the GIA) after the cancellation of the elections in the Black Decade. This was reflected in the initial make-up of the demonstrations in support of the Hirak there.

Meanwhile, in Algeria, in the following week, cities across the country witnessed their second Friday of a peaceful Hirak. This time, many thousands of women, particularly young women, took the lead. The slogan '*Djeich chaab khawa khawa*' ('The army and the people are brothers') was chanted by everyone in a sense of (imagined) unity. Those of us living abroad viewed the inspiring images of these demonstrations, widely shared on Facebook, with emotion;

they awakened in us the feeling of dwelling in exile and evoked a longing to return. An ardent desire to support our peers in Algeria pushed many more Algerians living in different parts of the UK to travel to London to gather in front of the embassy once again on Saturday 2 March. Although more women and families than the previous week attended, the crowd was still predominantly male, and the demonstration was joined by well-known former figures from the FIS and was broadcast by El Magharibia a Media, a radio station (based in London at the time) owned by the son of Abbassi Madani, a leading figure in the Islamist movement. For many Algerian women living abroad, however, it felt imperative that they show their support. Wahiba told me her reasons for joining the solidarity protests in London:

> I am here to show support for the women protesting back home, because their huge presence in the Hirak, as protectors of our brothers, sons and husbands, is extremely important. Without us women, the police and army will not hesitate to shoot protestors.

I met Wahiba at the protest in front of the Algerian embassy on Saturday 2 March 2019—her continuous engagement in Algerian affairs has been referred to earlier. She explained, smiling, that in 2014 she was 'here in this place to [also] say no to [an extension of] Bouteflika's fourth term in office ... I'm glad that people are now waking up'. Wahiba's words reflect the assumption that, at the beginning of the Hirak, women's participation in the protests was motivated primarily by their determination to protect the male protestors from police brutality and military repression. In contrast, other participants in this study reported that their commitment to the Hirak arose from their resolve to refuse the humiliation that would be inflicted on the country if Bouteflika was elected for a fifth term, or—even worse—if his brother continued to govern the country along with his '*issaba*'.

The following week, on 8 March, the third Friday of the Hirak, millions were reported to be marching in Algeria, linking the celebration of International Women's Day with the Hirak. Men, women and children chanted songs of freedom, including 'La Liberté, adopted as the hymn of the Hirak, making the day particularly memorable for everyone present. Images of a young ballerina dancing in Didouche Mourad Street, and another of a woman offering a rose to a policeman, went viral. Everywhere the Hirak took place, banners with photos of heroes of the anti-colonial war of liberation against France formed part of the backdrop, including in the Western capitals and especially in Paris. Many women held up portraits of the *mudjahidate* (the women who fought against colonization). The presence of iconic female figures who had participated in the Algerian war of national liberation, such as Djamila Bouhired, or the Black Decade of the 1990s, such as famous human rights activist Fadela Chitour, marching alongside young protestors, showed the world that all Algerians that day were united for the same cause: refusing Bouteflika a fifth term in office and calling for a radical change in governance, the eradication of corruption and the institution of the rule of law.

If it was to be successful, the Hirak had to remain united, regardless of political ideologies, gender, age or any other identity markers. Nevertheless, while women and the youth played a key role in maintaining its peaceful character over the coming weeks, the question of the extent to which the Hirak was to be a movement for social justice and gender equality began to arise as early as the fourth week of protests. The mantra of '*machiwaktism*' ('It's not the time for this') was the answer that many leading figures of the Hirak gave to the feminists who organized '*les carrés des féministes*' (the 'feminist squares') on the edge of the protests in Algiers, Oran, Paris and London. A confrontation between a few of the demonstrators and women standing in these squares was quickly dispersed, but the feminist agenda was postponed on the pretext that Algeria as a nation should be placed before any other demand, including the need to address social inequalities, particularly gender inequality. Trade unions and other economic forums were also sidelined. Over the next two years, many in the movement repeated that the priority was to overcome the power of the military and establish a civil government, in the belief that this would automatically lead to the establishment of social rights.

Nevertheless, the community of Algerian women living abroad were proud of the achievements of the Algerian people since 22 February 2019 and admired the peaceful demonstrations across Algeria calling for democracy and respect for the constitution; they offered their complete support to the Hirak, commending its non-violent, civic and inspirational nature. As early as April 2019, a group of women from the crowd took over the organization of the Hirak in London. For us women, it was a question of asserting ourselves within a community that had marginalized us for so long, reoccupying public space and celebrating our transnational activism and the longed-for success of an Algeria reconnected with its diaspora. Many noted the significant progress for women that had been made in Algeria in recent decades, including the reform of the nationality code which also benefited the children of Algerian women married to non-Algerians living abroad (see Chapter Two), and they stressed the importance of maintaining and strengthening these rights. There was also an urgent desire to challenge any expression of unjust contempt or *hogra* from the authorities, which young Algerians consider to be the long-standing attitude of those in power towards their citizens. In London, the presence of undocumented migrants, known as *harragas*, was significant. Their desire to express support for the Hirak overcame their fear of visibility and deportation.

Those women living abroad who were able to travel flew to Algeria for the chance of experiencing at least one Friday of this historic movement. 'It was just magical,' H.N., a woman who lives and works in France, told me, while K.C. added, 'I took unpaid leave from work to come and march in Algeria, to be there physically with my brothers and sisters'. On Friday 19 April 2019, I encountered women friends from Paris and Montreal amongst the huge crowd in Algiers, and together we chanted slogans in rising hope of a free and more democratic Algeria.

For months, despite the resignation of Bouteflika on 2 April 2019, the protests continued, the demonstrators refusing all the government's offers of dialogue or an alternative electoral process. The relationship between the government (and its institutions) and the Algerian population was broken, and it seemed that trust was no longer possible. In response to the stubbornness of the Hirak, the authorities then decided to employ repressive methods. To date, nearly 300 Algerians have been detained for their political opinions, many of them women: never in the history of contemporary Algeria have there been so many women political prisoners. Pictures of detainees were widely spread in cyberspace; they were shared on social media in support of international campaigns calling for the prisoners' release. Members of international and national trade union bodies, myself included, joined the Hirak Women's Collective, comprising women trade unionists and feminist activists, to engage in a campaign of solidarity with two of the female trade union activists who had been imprisoned, Dalila Touat and Namia Abdelkader.

They were both released in March 2021, a testimony to the strength of this international campaign.

Bouteflika's resignation marked the Hirak's first victory. Many observers believe that the numbers joining the demonstrations began to diminish from that point, and call the demonstrations that followed 'Hirak 2'. This second iteration called for radical changes in the Algerian system of governance. Slogans against the army appeared, such as '[Throw] the generals in the trash' and '*Doula madania, machi askaria*' ('A civilian state, not a military state'), in direct contrast to the chant of 'The army and people are brothers' heard at the beginning of the Hirak.

On 12 December 2019, despite the fact the demonstrations were still ongoing and no agreements had been reached between the Hirak and the regime, which was still holding hundreds of political prisoners, a presidential election was announced, to be overseen by the National Independent Authority of Elections (ANIE). ANIE was meant to be completely independent of the administration, which stood accused of fraudulent behaviour in all previous elections. Its members were chosen from civil society, with more than seventy recruited from the diaspora (Algerians living abroad were only granted the right to vote in the country's elections in 1997), but—perhaps unsurprisingly—less than 10% of these were women.

On 15 March 2020, the protestors had to take the difficult but necessary decision to stop all physical marches because of the high number of deaths related to the Covid-19 pandemic. What happened next was an incredible switch from marching on the streets to cultivating a large online presence, ensuring that the word could travel quickly at a global level. There followed a series of talks, conferences and debates via Zoom and other platforms, mainly initiated by Algerians living abroad. The online platforms not only helped to sustain the movement but also gave many women living outside Algeria the opportunity to participate and engage in transnational political activism for their homeland. With the memory of the bitterly divisive Black Decade in mind, these women were key to sustaining the solidarity created during the Hirak. They maintained strong ties with women activists in Algeria, organizing online debates, showing support to Algerians facing the pandemic by collecting and sending money, and continuing to cultivate the inspiring idea of the Hirak, all online.

Finally, on 13 June 2021, a new parliament was elected. The percentage of women parliamentary representatives fell from 30% in 2013 to just 8%, as ANIE disregarded the promised quota. The majority of Algerians considered this a non-event; they questioned the independence of ANIE and the legitimacy of the new government. Nevertheless, whatever the future of the Hirak—and, as we shall see in Chapter Six, some of the participants in my research were pessimistic about the outcome—the shadow of fear that the Black Decade cast for so long appears to have been dispersed, and the existence and importance of Algerian women's diasporic networks vindicated.

Women in the diaspora during the Hirak

As we have seen in the previous chapters, the dynamics and hierarchies of gender (as a complex social construct) are not abandoned on arrival in a new country but can continue to operate within diasporic groups. Traditional patriarchal rules and customs are often reaffirmed in exile. In many cases, these social dynamics can restrict women's participation or opportunities for leadership in a variety of areas, particularly in certain social settings. Nevertheless, as Zohra T. Sullivan (2001) explains, while a diaspora can emerge as a space that controls women's behaviour, it can also in certain circumstances represent a space of female empowerment, solidarity and mutual support, which facilitates forms of self-organization. This was evidenced most vividly at the height of the Hirak, when the patriarchal norms began to appear fragile.

For example, in Algeria, on Fridays (the traditional day of rest and prayer in a country that is 90% Muslim) the streets are usually empty of women. Indeed, before the Hirak, the participants in this research who had travelled back to Algeria on frequent vacations over the last two decades often mentioned this issue in their interviews; they found it difficult, as women, to go out walking or shopping on Fridays, particularly if they did not wear the *hijab*. When the Hirak brought women out onto the streets in their thousands every Friday, it gave real hope to Algerian women living abroad that fundamental changes were taking place. It seemed as though feminisms of a new kind were coming to the fore in Algeria, although for some women, such as Wahiba, who supported the protests from their adopted countries, their role was first to support the male protestors and only then to raise the demand for equality.

As a female Hirakist in London explained to me, despite holding a banner with the photos of political detainees that depicted many women as well as men, 'We must first help our men to free themselves from the authoritarian regime before we can ask for equality.'

Most of the women I interviewed during the course of this study had lived in their countries of exile for at least two decades. As such, they appeared to find in the Hirak not only a physical space in which they could show their support for their peers back home, but also an opportunity to give voice in their online networks to the unresolved traumas of the Black Decade, their plight as professional women forced to flee their homeland, and the difficulties they had encountered in the countries they fled to. As the demonstrations continued, however, their support for the Hirak and their belief in its potential to deliver change began to be undermined. On the one hand, the countries in which they now lived (generally considered to be governed by the rule of law) seem to regard themselves as legitimate exporters of Western democratic values to countries caught up in internal conflicts, such as Algeria. This meant that in Algeria itself, as soon as Bouteflika withdrew from the electoral race and the Hirakists' discourse began to radicalize, the regime was able to start accusing *'ayadi kharijiya'* ('foreign hands') of attempting to destabilize the country. These 'foreign influences' were said to be located in those Western capitals in which Algerians were the most vocal in their support of the Hirak. On the other hand, the increasingly patriarchal and sometimes violent discourse of many of the Hirak's online influencers appeared to push many of these women away from the protest movement. The complex emotions these different forces elicited in many of the women supporters of the Hirak are exemplified by Louisa's explanation as to why she decided to stop attending the protests in Washington DC's Dupont Circle:

> I am a feminist and a secular, apolitical, Muslim, Berber, Algerian-American. I have lived and worked in the Gulf [as well as the USA] but never have I been manipulated [into working] against my country or been in the pay of anyone in any of these geographical places. Never forget that Algeria is not an island apart, [and] geopolitics is mega-important. I love my country of origin and will do everything to support it internationally [but] without going so far as to sign a blank cheque to all these self-proclaimed chiefs of the Hirak, who do not take into consideration the international situation.

In general, the motivations behind the mobilization and participation of Algerian women abroad in the Hirak are not well understood. These women showed great support for the Hirak, sometimes even taking over the logistical organization of the solidarity demonstrations, as happened in London, Paris and Montreal. I would argue that for many of those women who had fled the Black Decade, the Hirak represented an opportunity to accomplish a 're-selving' process (see Chapter One for an analysis of the concepts of 'de-selving' and 're-selving'). Struggling to find their voice for home while far from home, the participants in this research have shown an extraordinary adherence to the idea of the Hirak, often taking leave from work to travel to Algeria to attend the weekly protests alongside their compatriots.

For most (myself included), activism in their new countries, communities or neighbourhoods was already part of their daily lives, and this was extended into supporting their compatriots both during the Hirak and when the Covid-19 pandemic struck. During recent research conducted by myself and other colleagues (Guemar et al. 2022), we discovered that Algerian women in London were heavily involved in fundraising, preparing food and collecting goods to meet the needs of those in their city communities and in their home country who were struggling during the pandemic. These acts of solidarity revealed the existence of a network that could be rapidly mobilized at times of crisis. My online observations uncovered the same scenario in France and Canada. In Canada, especially in Montreal, highly skilled professional Algerian women, including former journalists who migrated during the Black Decade, were facilitating online debates every Sunday, disseminating the same slogans as their compatriots in Algeria and elsewhere. As soon as the pandemic began and the physical demonstrations halted, the networks created during these weekly solidarity protests switched to organizing debates online, as well as supporting those Algerians in Montreal who suddenly found themselves in need—particularly students, undocumented migrants and visitors who could not return to Algeria following the decision of the Algerian government to close its borders in an attempt to limit the spread of the virus.

In June 2019, when Bouteflika's resignation did not appear to satisfy the demonstrators, the authorities decided to demobilize the Hirak by force. The following month, I met a few of the women who had previously participated in my research in the Place de la République in Paris—all were there to support the Hirak that still persisted in Algeria despite the diminishing numbers on the protests as a result of the mounting arrests. However, at this stage, although most supporters were there to denounce the detention of political activists, some were beginning to question their involvement in a movement that they believed lacked leadership and realistic goals. One of these women, harking back to the years of the Black Decade, told me:

> It's hard for me to believe that [members of] a society who were killing each other no more than two decades ago can now protest together in unity and with the same objective. Are we united? Let me doubt this. Although, of course, we all want change and better governance.

With Bouteflika's resignation, demonstrators acquired a taste for victory and radicalized their demands, moving from slogans such as '*Djeich chaab khawa khawa*' ('The army and the people are brothers') to '*Daoula madania, machi aaskaria*' ('A civilian state, not a military state'). Fridays and Tuesdays (the day for student protests) continued to witness euphoric demonstrations, demanding '*yetnahaou gaa*' ('they will all go'), in defiance of the increasing repression. As with the Arab Spring, Facebook and YouTube played an important role in instantaneously transporting these slogans from the Algerian streets to those living outside the country, and vice versa. Any suggestion—whether put forward by the government or by supporters of the movement—of a personality who could become a spokesperson for the Hirak was automatically rejected and fiercely discouraged by a hostile discourse, also emanating primarily from cyberspace.

When the date of a new presidential election, 12 December 2019, was announced by the army, a call for a boycott was launched from Paris, London and Montreal via YouTube influencers. The election boycott was well supported and the new president, Abdelmadjid Tebboune, is still regarded as illegitimate by the majority of the population. However, both the election and the call for a boycott caused a deepening of divisions within the movement itself. In London, on the day of the election, a group of people stood outside the Algerian consulate chanting and often insulting anyone who entered the building to vote. Following a physical attack on the consulate, the police were called to intervene and protect both the building and the voters. This scenario was repeated outside other consulates in those countries where Algerians were invited to vote. Hirakists used the terms '*Khain-Khaouana-Harkis*' (traitors)—epithets used during the Algerian war of liberation to mark those who collaborated with the French army and administration—and even threatened to 'name and shame' anyone who attended a polling station abroad or in Algeria. The rifts in the Hirak were beginning to show, and this appeared to shake many of those women I spoke to for my research who had lived through the Black Decade. One participant I met at the Algerian consulate in London during the referendum explained to me in tears:

> I left Algeria in the nineties following the cancellation of an electoral process for a parliament. I was looking for freedom and democracy. How can [it be that] the people who were frustrated in their victory at that time, and whom I have supported, are now standing outside this building shouting at me because I came to vote? I exiled myself for so many years precisely because I was looking for democracy. I refuse today to be told not to vote, here in the UK, a place of freedom and democracy.

As mentioned earlier, the spirit of the 1990s and the Black Decade appeared to shadow the Hirak in both beneficial and detrimental ways. When the regime looked around for how best to maintain itself, for example, it began by impeaching a few of the generals involved in the cancellation of the electoral process in the 1990s. But when it presented its roadmap for the future, proposing a return to the (postponed) electoral process, including organizing a referendum for a new constitution and the election of a new parliament, followed by local elections, the Hirak overwhelmingly rejected it. The problem was, however, that no alternative roadmap appeared to be on offer, and many Algerians, including those living abroad, began to leave the protests and abandoned the task of mobilizing opposition, often with deep regret.

Women as political actors: Hopes and fears for the Hirak

The crucial role that women have played in agitating for political and social change in Algeria can be witnessed throughout the country's history. Women have been a forceful presence in all Algerian movements for freedom and democracy, even before independence from French colonial rule in 1962. Their participation in these wide popular movements challenges the stereotypical representation of women in the region as oppressed victims of a patriarchal culture, with little agency. During the Hirak, women not only took part in the protests but also volunteered to organize protests, and most importantly, shared comments and information on social media. In Algiers, but also abroad, in places such as London, women reclaimed the public space in a multitude of ways—from participating in the protests to providing meals for the protestors, cleaning up local areas after the demonstrations, and through artistic creation and expression.

However, one participant in my research sounded a warning note by recalling not only the historical role of women in Algerian struggles, but also the way in which public knowledge or recognition of this role was often suppressed after these struggles were over:

> Women fought within the FLN for independence. They were very important participants in the liberation struggle, but we rarely talk about them. I discovered that, in the history of immigration, we rarely hear about what women did [in Paris] on 20 October 1961, after [the massacre of possibly hundreds of peaceful Algerian protestors by the police in Paris on] 17 October 1961, when Maurice Papon [head of the Paris police] threw Algerians into the Seine, [unleashing] police repression against people who were simply demonstrating for freedom in Algeria. Unlike 17 October, we forget 20 October, we never commemorate it. [But on] that day, in the Paris suburbs and across France, immigrant Algerian women marched, demanding the release of their men who had been imprisoned. They demanded the truth about Papon's police repression and about those thrown into the Seine. So, in the Hirak of today, it's no surprise that Algerian women are present in the fight, but those who fought for liberation transmitted a message to us: they fought for their emancipation, but the day after the liberation, they were told to go back to their kitchens.

Another of my research participants also sounded a note of caution, albeit from a different perspective, expressing her doubts about the course of the Hirak, which she believed was falling prey to the growing influence of fundamentalist Islam:

> Revolutions are obsolete now, at least in our region: the '*moukawama*' ['resistance'] ended when Wahabism and Salafism invaded people's minds. This explains the failure of the Arab Spring, and of course you will see that the Hirak will not go far.

Now well established in France as a lecturer in the field she studied in Algeria, she explained how hard it was to finally gain a CDI (a permanent contract)—but now that she has one she believes she can influence policy without having to protest alongside those espousing political Islam, whom she can never trust due to her experiences in the Black Decade. Like this interviewee, some of the other participants in this research found protesting alongside those who had participated in the horrors of the Black Decade to be simply inconceivable.

An earlier incident in Algeria on 29 March 2019 seemed an unwelcome harbinger of the divisions in the movement to which these women alluded. Participants in the feminist square set up at the central faculty of the University of Algiers found themselves under verbal and physical attack: their banners were torn from their hands by demonstrators who shouted 'This is not the time!' and accused them of dividing the movement, with some even claiming that women's equality is against Islam. The assault tarnished the image of a protest movement that up until then had been lauded for its pacifism and for the participation of women in exceptionally large numbers. Nedjib Sidi Moussa, a witness to the attack, wrote in *The Brooklyn Rail* (2019) that the aggression was clearly misogynistic and demonstrated the difficulty of taking up a position for gender equality when some in the Hirak seemed to be falling under the influence of political Islam.

Other women, however, transcended their misgivings by continuing to join in the protests, declaring that freedom from a coercive regime and the implementation of the rule of law were their primary concerns, because only then could transitional justice begin to shed light on what happened during the bloody decade of the 1990s. Yet another interviewee, Maya, a secular left-wing feminist of the Black Decade generation, who had become one of the most loyal and assiduous supporters of the Hirak in Paris, although still believing in the idea of 'a beautiful revolution', did not hesitate to express her disappointment concerning the later divisions in the movement that were manifested in the Place de la République. Nevertheless, she still attended the protests:

> At the beginning it was good, but then came political opportunists who destroyed our union, our peaceful revolution … But I still come because I believe that it's important to continue, if only out of loyalty to the prisoners of conscience who believed in the idea of the Hirak … Do you know how many detained women there are at the moment?

Even as I heard a feeling of political fatigue in her voice, she confirmed that the continuation of the fight for the release of all political prisoners in Algeria remained a priority for her.

We have to look a little deeper into the social make-up of Algeria today and into its past to attempt to understand why these divisions began to appear in the Hirak. However, as Andrew Farrand (2021) explains: 'In the English-speaking world, little has been written about Algeria since the war of independence ended 60 years earlier, and its recent history [is] even more impenetrable.' Thus Algeria, a country the size of a continent, is largely unknown to the outside world, particularly the English-speaking countries. There is a need for a more nuanced understanding of the country's history and current sociopolitical situation, which I can only touch on briefly here.

It goes without saying that colonization, as well as the decolonization process, including the revolutionary struggles, internal conflicts, forced migrations and establishment of diasporas abroad, have long destabilized the idea of a unified identity and nation (Sullivan 2001). The stubborn persistence of the Hirak in Algeria in its attempt to maintain unity evokes the post-colonial rules of nation-state building, which deliberately ignored any social differences or conflicts that could threaten to disintegrate civil society. However, post-territorial and post-national changes have complicated what Benedict Anderson (1998) famously termed an 'imagined community', reopening ethnic, religious, class and gender differences that were often repressed by the ideology of post-colonial nation-state building. In France, the former colonizer and hence the country that witnessed the arrival of the largest number of Algerian exiles in the 1990s, these differences appeared to emerge again during the Hirak and were clearly visible in the Place de la République.

Having said that, to be faithful to history, it is also important to note that the Hirak in Algeria itself was mainly initiated and organized by the young, both men and women, all born during or after the Black Decade and thus less influenced by historical enmities. For them, the problems they experience on a daily basis, such as unemployment, lack of housing and a corrupt bureaucracy, are not related to the Black Decade but to corruption, *hogra* (contempt for the people) and poor management of the oil revenues by those who first took power in 1962 when Algeria gained its independence from France. Long before they took to the streets on 19 February, young Algerians were already expressing their dissent through football chants, artworks and university debates, as well as by volunteering for activities that substituted for the lack of local services across the country. Nass Elkheir (a grassroots organization committed to social action and environmental protection), NABNI (a citizen think tank) and RAJ (another grassroots organization focused on cultural activities, human rights and citizens' rights) are just a few examples of associations and forums that have had a significant impact on the awareness of young people, opening their eyes to the importance of protesting against injustice, mismanagement and corruption.

Political parties, on the other hand, appear to have lost all credibility among the young. An initiative called NIDAA 22 was created at the beginning of the Hirak, but despite the inclusion of many prominent figures, it did not last, partly because of the state's repression and partly because of divisions amongst its members. Bridges appear to have broken down between this important demographic of Algerian society (young, sharp, open to the world via social networks, aspiring to a better future and a more transparent and democratic Algeria) and the generations of their parents and grandparents, who were either involved in the mismanagement of the country since its independence or, even if they were actively opposed to the regime, seem to remain held back by past traumas.

Meanwhile, there are still gender barriers to participation in protest movements in Algeria, which affect even younger women:

> For me, [participation in] the Hirak was a matter of geographical location. I have to say that because where I live at the moment, it's not OK, it's not acceptable, for women here to go and protest against the government, or anything else. So I could only take part in the Hirak when I was away from my hometown. I contributed in that [sometimes] I could take part in it, but I could never do it in my own town. I always had to do it with my family, and I couldn't really control the times in which I was [present].

This interviewee completed her PhD at a Tunisian university, where she witnessed the 'Jasmine Revolution' of 2011. I first interviewed her in 2013, before she returned to Algeria in 2015, where she now lectures on English literature, gender and post-colonial feminist studies. She drives about two hours a day to her university, as she continues to live in a very conservative rural town (it is known for having sheltered Islamists during the Black Decade).

> This was the case for many women in rural areas in Algeria. Yes, as I said, if you're in a big city it's OK, but in small cities or in rural areas it's not OK for a woman to do such things. It was OK on 8 March 2019, [as it was] a very, very big march in the main cities, perhaps the biggest protest during the Hirak. After that day, the media were talking about the Hirak, about what happened on that day. They kept repeating that because of women and thanks to women it was peaceful, and that we were not attacked by the army because women [were present] … But did this have a strong influence and impact on the direction of the Hirak? No, I don't think so.

She explained how she stays in touch with former colleagues and peers who also travelled with scholarships to study post-colonial feminism abroad but, unlike her, had never returned to Algeria. She keeps in touch through social media or by attending conferences in other countries, the latest being in Berlin during the Hirak, and has been able to see how the Hirak is viewed from the outside. She recalled: 'Once in Berlin, I felt very proud as everyone was praising the peaceful character of the Algerian Hirak.'

Can the spirit of the Hirak be sustained?

It seems that the transnational mobilization of and loyalty to the Hirak, especially during the pandemic, as well as a commitment to the liberation of detainees, represented an important step towards building trust between old and young, and between women in Algeria and their compatriots in other countries. For example, 'Samira' declared on 8 March 2020:

> We thank the diaspora for its support. It is thanks to you that we hold [onto] and keep [up] our morale … Thank you for the debates that women from the diaspora organize online and for inviting us to participate. It gives us the courage to stand against this system.

Samira is an academic and radical Hirakist who returned to Algeria a few years ago after receiving her doctorate from an Italian university. A mother of two, she was among those women who, despite being left-wing feminists, continued to protest every Friday. When she was arrested and had her phone confiscated, hundreds of Algerian women across the world partook in an online display of solidarity. Despite the setback, after her release, Samira carried on attending Friday protests in the city in which she lives and works. She was very active on her Facebook page, which went viral on 4 January 2021 when she commented on the three-year sentence handed down to a young protestor for posting memes in which he mocked the new president, Tebboune. The video had 51,000 views within a few hours. She wrote:

> All these young people were taken to detention only because they dared to ask for freedom and justice. This can happen to my son, to yours, to all our young people. I teach in a university and see first-hand how the youth are suffering from our [biased] judicial system, which is under the control of this corrupt regime. [Yet] the only thing you all want is to leave the country? Leaving is not a solution, we don't change a country like we change a [pair of] shoes: a country is in our genes, our blood and our history.

A year later, on 5 January 2022, and following what many described as the end of the Hirak, Samira posted the following comment:

> Many have given up and plan to leave the country. The promises by the elected president of a 'new Algeria' have proved illusory and misleading. The only concrete thing I experience on a daily basis is the reduction of my purchasing power. Prisoners of conscience are still in prison. The Mediterranean continues to reject the corpses of our *harragas*. And my phone, confiscated so abusively, is still with the police, to whom I am not wishing a happy new year.

In both of these Facebook comments, Samira mentions migration. Her first comment suggests that she is addressing her colleagues, as well as other academics and intellectuals, who have been part of the Hirak and continue to believe in its relevance but who are now thinking of leaving the country. She urges them to think again. Next, she mentions the economic crisis—the product of twenty years of corruption, the fall in oil and gas prices, and the Covid-19 pandemic—that is seriously harming the country. Indeed, the latest World Bank report on Algeria (2021) raises the alarm about a possible economic crisis to come. The situation resembles that which preceded the riots of October 1988 and which led to the rise of political Islam, provoking the violence of the Black Decade. Samira also mentions the *harragas*, people who continue to risk their lives crossing the Mediterranean in an attempt to reach Europe. The last sentence in her comment then reminds her Facebook audience that her confiscated phone is still with the police, suggesting that police repression and the silencing of the Hirak still continues, and by implication, that the struggle must also continue.

However, the following quotations, taken from 'Malia', whom I maintained contact with after interviewing her for my initial research, provide a contrast to Samira's opinion. In 2019, Malia organized a conference in her university to which she invited me as a guest speaker on the subject of 'gender and asylum'. I took the opportunity to ask her about her views on the direction of the Hirak:

> I share with friends and colleagues from inside and outside Algeria the same views about the Hirak. One of my master's students, who is now studying for her PhD in the UK, was interviewed by a British journalist about the Hirak. I heard her interview and we [seem to] hold the same opinion that the Hirak is a beautiful idea but it will not bring any changes for women.

Malia believes that what discouraged the majority of young women from sustaining their mobilization around the Hirak was a reminder of the many occasions their mothers or grandmothers were pushed to the fore during the war of liberation and the struggles of the Black Decade, only to be later 'sent back to the kitchen', as another participant commented earlier.

> People were happy to invite women to join the marches [to provide] protection against police violence, but the moment feminists started talking about their rights, things changed very quickly and the [discourse of] '*machiwaktism*' ['It is not the time for this'] took hold. In cities outside Algiers, even in other big cities, I would say women didn't even dare to speak about their rights, didn't dare to reveal themselves as feminists.

Whatever their views now, arguably the Hirak was an opportunity for women exiles and their peers in Algeria to attempt to negotiate new ways to remember the past, and build a common future in which trust and solidarity would prevail. Despite the intergenerational traumas—the legacy of the Black Decade—the Hirak provided that diasporic space so desired by the victims of those troubled years, a space in which everyone was able to express and share their pain, and look towards a better future. Malia agrees but claims that when women's demands became more radical, it caused splits among participants in the Hirak, due to the deeply ingrained conservativism of Algerian society:

> In a way, I can understand, as feminist groups in Algiers were using very provocative language, knowing that the things they were saying were against general Algerian values: for instance, they didn't simply call for women's rights but also for the right to abortion.

These splits weakened the Hirak. In London, the two women who volunteered to take charge of the logistics of the Hirak only lasted in the role for a few months. They were forced to withdraw from the task of organizing and supervising the protests by attacks against them on Facebook pages administrated by Algerians living in the UK.

Another participant in my research during the Hirak, a university lecturer in Algeria, offered a different perspective on why women's support for the Hirak began to diminish. She mentioned the concrete issues of the pandemic and the subsequent lockdown, as well as the repression the state meted out to the demonstrators, which had very specific consequences for young women, as she explained:

> A lot of my male colleagues had acknowledged the strength of women during the Hirak in the city in which I teach—they were thankful, they respected the women because it was thanks to them that all that happened. We women gave them the courage to speak [out]. Now, women have left the Hirak; we're not going [to the protests] as we used to in the beginning, especially with the pandemic. Women respect health protocols more than men here in Algeria. Also, the majority of young women [have] kind of lost interest [in the movement], probably because of the series of arrests of many young women students in the Hirak. It had an impact when some young women from my university, for example, were detained, even if only for a day. It shocked their families because, in our society, a woman's reputation is still a subject of family honour. Many of those who were detained have been abandoned by their fiancés or threatened with divorce.

The regime knows this is a weak point in Algeria's patriarchal society and has exploited it in order to intimidate young women protestors, no doubt because it recognized the importance of women's participation to the success of the Hirak. Unfortunately, many Hirakist social-media influencers have also played the patriarchal card against women in the movement, trying to force them to follow certain groups or chant certain slogans.

Nevertheless, despite the repression and the patriarchal leanings of some in the Hirak, many women continued to protest. They were only stopped by the pandemic, although when the Hirak went online, it gave even more women the opportunity to take part and share their views on how to make societal changes. However, my interviewee stressed her view that 'the Hirak was really killed by the new government's repression and the pandemic, even if there are some people who are still resisting'. To my question of what she thinks the outcome of the Hirak can be now, she replied:

> I think [the Tuesday student] protests have failed because people didn't really know what they want, they only knew what they didn't want. And then ... people even started insulting each other on social media, sometimes [using] hurtful names. When [young] women heard these things about other [participants], they didn't know what was meant, so they started [to organize] a number of debates—between urban areas and between secular and non-secular [Hirakists]. Some of them wanted an Islamic state, others wanted a secular government. None of them truly knew what either side meant; they had simply heard things about [them] online and thought, 'Yes, that suits me, so I'm going to follow that.'

This university lecturer preferred to limit her remarks to the Hirak that was taking place on Tuesdays, the protest day for students, which she and many other academics joined. She expressed her concern about the fact that young people know very well what is harming them, but lack leadership and the experience to know how to make positive changes and prepare for a better future. She appears to blame online activists and their influence on the youth in the Hirak:

> It has become taboo to introduce oneself either as a feminist or as secular in Algeria nowadays. So, for me, the Hirak is a failure. People didn't truly know enough about how to make a successful government, [they] no longer believed in democracy ... Now I see this: they were married to social media ... [and when someone] came and lectured them, they would just follow them.

> That's why it felt as if there's no kind of intellectual substance, no guidance or leadership.

She emphasized that she believed the lack of leadership and the competing, often antagonist, discourses had led to a weakening of solidarity among her student supporters of the Hirak:

> In the beginning, RAJ[1] was organizing forums, where they talked about a new Algeria. They wanted a second republic. Then [this discourse] disappeared, because basically some of them have been arrested, but also because of the different discourses that have been spread by the media. Many people were later [labelled] as 'evil' ... and that's how they lost their solidarity. RAJ has now been dissolved.

In the eyes of my interviewee, concepts like political Islam or secularism were not well understood by those students who claimed to be adherents. She also deplored the spread of online hate speech, particularly when directed against women, which she believes contributed to the failure to sustain the Tuesday Hirak.

This negative vision of the development of the Hirak was shared by many women living in rural areas of Algeria. In some cities known for their religious conservatism, women were discouraged from protesting. If they did, either the police arrested them, detaining them for a few hours, or men in the streets—even Hirakists—harassed them and prevented them from participating in the marches. 'Lynda', who now lives in Scotland but originally came from a small city in the south-east of Algeria, known for its harsh patriarchal code of conduct, commented:

> Women's rights were abandoned in the Hirak. We cannot call this a revolution any more because you cannot make a revolution without [involving] every single part of Algeria and every single part of Algerian society ... A movement cannot succeed if it only involves two or three main cities and excludes women's rights from its aims.

In a completely different setting, in Paris, Nadia also expressed her disappointment with what she saw as religious conservatism taking hold of the

1. The RAJ (Rassemblement Actions Jeunesse) was a youth forum which became known for its local grassroots mobilization of young people.

Hirak, revealing as she did so the way in which the enmities of the Black Decade, left unresolved by Bouteflika's amnesty law, began to be reawakened amongst Algerians abroad as the Hirak lost its unity of purpose:

> In Paris, I saw some of my former Algerian women comrades from [the socialist party in Algeria] the PAGS. They continue to march at the Place de la République every Sunday, despite the hijacking of the Hirak by the Islamists. They do not even wear the *hijab* but they massively support Rachad.[2] Can you believe that some of the founding members of Rachad justified the assassinations of left-wing intellectuals during the Black Decade?

Many women, nevertheless, continued to call for unity. One young woman, speaking at one of the later protests in London, declared:

> I am not here to see divisions among us. I recognize myself both in the Amazigh [Berber] and national flags. I do not know what Rachad is nor the MAK.[3] I am Algerian, Muslim, Berber and British, and I'm here to support people of my age in Algeria who are protesting for a better life, more justice and more opportunities for the youth.

Many other young Algerian women were present at the protest that day, alongside their mothers, and all applauded the young speaker. Although the MAK did not participate in the Hirak at the start, it later called on its members to raise the flag of the Amazigh people higher than the national flag, both abroad and in Algeria. This caused disputes among those on the demonstrations, and triggered the anger of the Algerian authorities, who proceeded to arrest many protestors simply because they were carrying the Amazigh flag.

In general, diaspora conflicts are informed by a very complex terrain of political, linguistic, cultural and social struggles that are carried over from the country of origin where some of these identity markers have been suppressed (Sullivan 2001). In Algeria, in the post-Black Decade context, the Hirak appears to have served as an imaginary space, giving some in the diaspora the illusion of reconnection with one or other of these different identity markers. The involvement of the organizations mentioned above (Rachad and the MAK) exacerbated assumed differences and caused clashes among the protestors in

2. Rachad is a political movement associated with former members of the FIS.
3. The MAK is a radical separatist movement for Kabyle self-determination—see note 4.

London, Paris and elsewhere, creating rifts in the movement, and was one of the reasons the Hirak began to lose its peaceful character. The young speaker, brought up in multicultural London, urgently wanted to maintain the unity of the Hirak by raising awareness of her attachment to an Algerian identity in all its diversity.

The Hirak's physical protests came to an end on 15 March 2020, partly due to the Covid-19 pandemic. This break gave activists the opportunity to discuss the future of the movement online. Taking place mainly on Facebook or Zoom, many of the debates were dominated by a dialogue between conservatives and progressives, and were mainly rooted in divisions dating back to the Black Decade. The Rachad movement was often at the centre of the debate. Some democratic activists, such as Nadia, accused the movement's leaders of hijacking the Hirak and of playing the democratic card only to achieve their goal of establishing an Islamic state in Algeria.

> Just because the main goal of all [of us] is to change the regime doesn't mean women or democrats should ally with the devil. For my part, I prefer to withdraw and wait, and see what the new government proposes. We must keep the country's institutions standing and not do what Syria or Libya have done with their people. The diaspora will [bear] great responsibility [for] the destruction of the country in the event that this happens.

Louisa, the journalist living in Washington DC, appeared to share this view:

> To me, the real fight is about rediscovering an Algerian identity and a common roadmap, reviewing our national narrative and sorting out our political and historical contradictions, banishing sexism and respecting women, and accepting ourselves beyond biological and cultural differences … So, to me, the real Hirak (or 'revolution') is the one which demonstrates nationalism and should, above all, show more civility … Because boycotting elections and refusing to … play the democratic game will leave the public space to political Islam, and will continue to [portray] men as the absolute masters and first-class citizens.

Loyal to the feminist views she expressed when I first interviewed her in 2012, Louisa declared that she withdrew from the Hirak because she saw Islamists, including some who had been involved in the Black Decade, '*roukoub el mouja*' ('surfing the wave') of the movement.

Conclusion: Seeds of hope

The voices in this chapter are of course not representative of all the women exiled during the Black Decade and its aftermath, but they do reveal certain recurring narrative patterns that have surfaced in the Hirak. They reveal, for example, the unprecedented mobilization of Algerian women, both in Algeria and elsewhere, around the dream of liberating the country from the hands of a government considered obsolete, corrupt and unjust. As mentioned above, the fear inherited from the Black Decade that previously had held many back from openly protesting was banished. Hence, whatever happens next, the Hirak has seeded hope among Algerians at home and abroad. Politics in Algeria is changing—its citizens continue to criticize the ruling elite. In a country in which at least 75% of the population is under the age of thirty-five, Algerians have witnessed the fact that the youth can unite when they need to stand up to what they deem the state's arrogance and disdain.

The words of the women I interviewed here, however, clearly illustrate that difficulties remain, particularly when it comes to maintaining solidarity in mobilizing for the fight for justice, the rule of law and a revival of the principles of the founding anti-colonial revolution. They all consider the amnesty law implemented by Bouteflika's government illegitimate; Lamia in her interview (in Chapter Three) predicted that sooner or later a women's revolt against this 'amnesia' law would take place in Algeria. She, and other women survivors who fled the horrors of the Black Decade, have always maintained that the truth about that bloody decade must be brought into the open and justice for the survivors must be seen. This, they believe, is a necessary condition if they are to return to Algeria, and if the young people in Algeria are to free themselves from 'Salafism' (radical political Islam) and heal from the traumas transmitted to them through their parents. Indeed, it appears from the testimonies of many of the participants in my research that it is these traumas that have so far prevented the peaceful Hirak revolution from succeeding in producing a roadmap that Algerians can unite around, in the struggle to achieve equality for all. Nevertheless, as the continuing debates between women in their online networks testify, the Hirak has revealed new ways of mobilizing Algerians, both in the country itself and amongst those scattered across the world.

6 Final Reflections

Introduction: From networks to a diaspora?

The final section of this book presents the conclusions I have drawn from my research into those highly skilled women who fled Algeria following the escalation in violence during the Black Decade of the 1990s. The book is based around a core case study (Lamia's narrative), supported by an analysis of other participants' accounts, including those of respondents to an online survey, as well as six years of observations. I was able to reveal the existence of networks formed by these women, which I argue can be described as a 'potential women's diaspora'. In particular, I explore the way that the relationships between the members of these networks, as well as their relationships with their adopted countries and their country of origin, are socially constructed. This has revealed the complexities of their personal 'identity reconstruction' and sense of belonging to the societies in which they now live. The resilience, agency and diasporic consciousness displayed by these women need to be mobilized if they are to fully engage both with their transnational locations and with the current social conditions in Algeria, whether they intend to return to live in the country or not. Their participation in the Hirak has clearly demonstrated their support for the struggle for freedom, justice, equality and democracy in Algeria, the lack of which forced them to leave the country in the first place.

The use of the concept of diaspora

In this book I have attempted to reveal the extent to which the lack of freedom of thought, the restrictions associated with the Algerian Family Code, and the increased levels of violence against women during the Black Decade and its aftermath prompted these highly skilled women to flee their homeland. I also investigated the barriers these women have faced in rebuilding their lives in the countries to which they migrated, as well as the barriers preventing many of them from returning to Algeria. This raised the question of whether or not the networks they have formed could act as a diaspora. For this reason, this concluding chapter revisits my decision to use the term, particularly in light of the debate between traditional scholars of diaspora and social constructionists—who understand the concept as a social condition, as well as a heuristic tool with which to explore and better understand the interactions between a group of migrants, their new environment and their country of origin. I have used the term in this book not in a descriptive sense but as a concept permitting the study of the social interactions, identity reconstruction, sense of belonging and mobilization of this particular group of Algerian female migrants.

The reason for my decision to use the concept of diaspora to explore the lives of these women was twofold. First, the highly skilled Algerian women I met (including online) often expressed the urgent need to create an Algerian diaspora. What they meant by 'diaspora' was a network of Algerians who live abroad but are still attached to and interested in its political, economic and social affairs. They believed such a network should also be a space in which the solidarity between members would help them to adjust to and integrate into their new societies. The second reason was the prevalent assumption that there is no solidarity between Algerians living abroad, regardless of gender or level of education. This assumption has been supported by a number of researchers who have concluded that an Algerian diaspora does not exist. Research on Algerian migrants has mainly been conducted in France; however, as this study points out, the post-Cold War situation and the eruption of new conflicts around the world, the emergence of new technologies of communication and the spread of the global market have encouraged and facilitated a surge of population movements. Consequently there is now enough evidence to show that migrants no longer necessarily seek out countries where they have cultural and post-colonial ties, or existing personal or family networks. Given this, I realized it was necessary to also study Algerian migrants in countries other than the traditional locus of Algerian exile, France, and as

I did so, my research yielded some interesting results that do not fully accord with the previous consensus.

The traditional use of the concept of diaspora has been criticized as an essentialist discourse based solely on ethnicity and nationality, and disregarding other identity markers such as gender, age or social class. This is the view put forward by the social constructionists, who argue that a group of people may develop diasporic consciousness and political mobilization based on these other identity markers (Hall 1993; Anthias 1998). I therefore explored the different contemporary definitions and uses of the concept as a social condition and as a heuristic device to investigate the relationships amongst the group of women who participated in my research. As we saw in Chapter One, the existence of three essential criteria is assumed to be crucial when defining a group as a diaspora: first, the trauma behind their dispersal; second, the difficulty in adjusting to new societies; and third, the cultivation of the idea of returning home, whether this be an actually existing homeland or one that is constructed and imaginary. I proposed that the concept is useful in describing the wide geographical dispersal of female intellectuals and other highly skilled Algerian women, and in exploring their process of identity transformation and the reconstruction of their lives in their new societies.

In the absence of official statistics on how many highly skilled Algerian women left the country during the Black Decade and its aftermath, however, I had to first reveal the existence of the group I intended to study and to geographically locate potential participants. To this end, as I explained in Chapter One, I used RDS, a method that combines 'egocentric' and 'snowball' sampling techniques based on referral from individuals to other people to whom they are connected. This method helped me reach 188 participants dispersed throughout eighteen different countries. France, Spain, Canada, the USA and the UK returned the highest numbers.

The focus of the research

Arguably, such an examination of the nature of these women's lives—and how they have attempted to construct new identities in new, sometimes hostile, environments while maintaining some sense of continuity with their country of origin—can help advance our understanding of adaptation, as well as shed light on how attempts to exert agency and resilience in exile relates to the 'myth of return'. It also reveals the way in which a diasporic consciousness can develop through the mobilization of solidarity between the members of a group. To investigate these questions more closely, I focused on in-depth interviews with some of the participants recruited through the RDS method, using a feminist-based ethnographic approach.

My own experience of exile is similar to those of the participants in this research. I am part of the network, and it could be argued that the stories told in this book are the stories of 'us', the highly skilled, secular Algerian Muslim women who experienced family restrictions, social and official discrimination, harassment on the streets and persecution by radical Islamist groups, forcing us to leave our professional jobs, families, friends and homes to flee abroad. Consequently, my research was framed by a feminist approach, allowing the use of both quantitative and qualitative methods to explore the lives of my participants. My political beliefs and emotional empathy were often central to the way I conducted my interviews with them.

Among my interviewees, I found myself most fully engaged by the narrative of 'Lamia' (Chapter Three). Her story speaks of the various different issues experienced by a young Algerian woman graduate who first escaped her small village, and the social and family restrictions preventing her from accessing public space, finding work and exercising her citizenship, to move to the capital, Algiers. Unfortunately, as the country became engulfed in conflict, she found that women's rights and freedoms were becoming equally restricted in the capital. Of all the women I interviewed, Lamia described most coherently the experience of many of the women who lived through the horror of the Black Decade, including the reasons behind seeking refuge abroad. Lamia fled as much from the harsh patriarchal restrictions and the discrimination and harassment she experienced, which she clearly describes as socially embedded, as from the general atmosphere of indiscriminate terror—although she was undoubtedly left with traumatic memories of the violence she witnessed. Given how fully it covers the key themes that emerged from the rest of the research, Lamia's narrative is naturally at the heart of this book. The emotions and feelings shared between us during the interview process were present in my thoughts even during the time spent compiling and analysing the data. Her narrative resonated as one about all of us survivors of the Black Decade.

The elements of diaspora: Trauma, adjustment and the 'myth of return'

There were several post-independence political events that left the majority of Algerian people traumatized in some way even before the Black Decade. Chapter Two examined the legacy of the dysfunctional relationship between the Algerian regime and its citizens, which was exacerbated by the two military coups of 1962 and 1965, as well as by the lack of freedom under nearly thirty years of one-party rule and the annulment of the long-desired democratic process in January 1992. As seen in Lamia's narrative, the assassination of President Boudiaf in June 1992 also left Algerian society with a sense of collective trauma. The murdered president, despite being appointed by the same ruling elite that cancelled the electoral process, had been expected to restore stability and fight the corruption that was rampant amongst the members of the regime.

The rise in violence and insecurity provoked by the cancellation of the first real elections to be held in post-colonial Algeria was also discussed in Chapter Two. It gave an overview of the political and socio-economic environment that predisposed the country towards such conflict: namely, the neoliberal policies imposed by the IMF and the World Bank. These laid down the demand that Algeria engage in a democratic process alongside the introduction of market 'reforms' as a condition for financial assistance, which included the rescheduling of its external debt, estimated at the time to be around $26 billion (Martinez 2000). The government was obliged to restructure national enterprises, leading to a diminishing number of jobs in the public sector (the main provider of employment), intensifying the already existing inequality in society. Anyone without a good network or '*maarifa*' with links to the ruling elite was faced with enormous difficulties in accessing employment, social services or housing. These policies particularly affected women.

The first social explosion triggered by this situation occurred in October 1988. In response, the government amended the constitution to permit the creation of other political parties in a bid to replace the single-party regime. This attempt at pluralism backfired. As a consequence of the dictatorship and the lack of political freedom that had marked the post-colonial era, together with the strong Muslim character of Algerian society, the main beneficiary was the radical Islamist party, the FIS, which won the local elections in 1990 and the first round of national elections in 1991. However, my research also revealed the existence of other identity conflicts, created during the time of French colonization, which the Algerian state had continued to nurture, such as those between Francophones and Arabophones, and between secular and non-secular members of the population, particularly amongst members of the intellectual and professional class. The rise in violence during the Black Decade deepened these conflicts. The cancellation of the electoral process marked the beginning of a war against civilians, with the assassination of intellectuals by Islamist terrorists and the massacre of entire villages, which, alongside the deepening state repression, pushed many hundreds of Algerians to flee their country. It is believed that the tragedy cost the lives of around 200,000 Algerians and many thousands more 'disappeared', while it also severely damaged the country's infrastructure (Le Sueur 2010).

The violence increased the rate of feminization of migration amongst intellectuals and highly skilled Algerians, which was particularly noticeable from the beginning of the 2000s onwards. There were several coercive reasons behind the displacement of the women whose narratives I have recorded in this book, ranging from the general climate of fear and insecurity, and the persecution specifically directed against them or their immediate families, to social and familial repression. Some participants who had initially moved abroad with the aim of enhancing their skills, to take advantage of job opportunities, or to pursue further education were unable to return due to the prevailing climate of terror and insecurity. The fact that their decision to depart (or not to return) took place in an atmosphere of conflict and fear meant that the participants' experience of exile often displayed a traumatic character. This was illustrated by some of these women's interviews, and was particularly well expressed by Lamia's narrative.

The interviews revealed evidence not only of trauma amongst those participants who experienced persecution, either directed against them or their immediate family members, or who witnessed terrorist acts, but also revealed the trauma related to the specific oppression and sexual harassment of women, which increased during the Black Decade. Moreover, both when fleeing the country and on arrival in the receiving country, participants faced the barriers of restrictive asylum and immigration policies. The general flouting of the international law protecting women who suffer gender-based violence, as well as the stigma attached to all newcomers from Algeria, who were frequently regarded as potential supporters of terrorism, made it particularly difficult for women to obtain visas or to be recognized as political refugees. The experience of the international gender-blind asylum process is a traumatic event in its own right. The lack of administrative status for those who decided not to claim asylum was no less so.

Once they were living in their countries of migration, participants deplored the lack of recognition of their Algerian diplomas, as well as an apparent disregard of their efforts to adjust, reinvent new identities and build new lives. Although they showed a remarkable degree of resilience and even obstinacy when it came to rebuilding their lives, particularly their professional lives, it was not without facing a high level of discrimination. The study revealed that women who grow up and live under harsh patriarchal rules bring resilience to any new struggle they face, if only by virtue of their gender. As they experience more personal freedom in the countries they migrate to, their struggle moves from their private to their public lives. The participants were all agreed that they now enjoyed more rights as women, and although the adjustment to their new countries differed from one woman to another, the majority appeared to now enjoy financial independence and to have either widened their knowledge in the field in which they studied and worked in Algeria or requalified in another. It also appeared that due to their settlement in multiple locations, nurturing an idea of a 'homeland' is now negotiated in a transnational space, often virtually in cyberspace. Social networking sites such as Facebook are used to exchange ideas of political resistance, scientific knowledge, music and recipes from Algeria, as well as information on political and social developments in the country. Nevertheless, participants also showed a desire to fully belong to the societies in which they now live, particularly those who live in France, as seen in Chapter Four. However, despite their fluency in the language and the feeling of being fully embedded in the French culture of *laïcité*, or having previously completed their postgraduate studies in France, they appeared to have faced discrimination when attempting to access legal status, work permits and the labour market.

It was during the course of my fieldwork that the full complexity of the relationship between the women I was studying emerged, both in their relationships with each other and in the way they individually attributed themselves an imaginary Algerian identity. Gender, political beliefs and exile certainly added to this complexity—hence my diversion into a brief exploration of the historical context in order to better understand the intolerance and suspicion that often appears to exist among Algerian women, particularly as this is a crucial barrier to sustaining networks and establishing a diasporic consciousness. It has been suggested that this intolerance and lack of trust has been inherited from the experience of harsh colonial rule that excelled in deconstructing the Algerian personality and destroying existing solidarities and networks (Bourdieu 2013). The post-colonial one-party state, often compared to the regime in the former East Germany, continued this destruction (Harbi 1994; Evans and Phillips 2007). Moreover, by making women subject to a discriminatory Family Code instead of a civilian code for all citizens, the post-colonial regime helped create and fuel a sense of separation and intolerance within an already divided society. Undoubtedly, these divisions and suspicions were transported as part of Algerians' emotional luggage during their journey into exile. The preliminary findings of my study revealed that this is evident not only in the context of the complex migration process of Algerian women to France, but is also representative of findings in Spain, Canada, the USA and the UK, countries in which I conducted my in-depth interviews. However, careful attention needs to be paid if we are to draw any viable conclusions, and further research needs to be conducted in other countries to which Algerians fled during the Black Decade. Such research may also need to also include men, as well as those less skilled, in order to better understand how these identities shape the narrative of the Black Decade and the process of resettlement in new societies, as well as the idea of return.

Justice and truth: Healing the rifts of the Black Decade

Lamia's narrative expressed the impossibility of healing—and of thus regaining a sense of positive identification with the 'homeland'—without establishing the truth behind what happened during the conflict and prosecuting the wrongdoers. Other participants emphasized this when I contacted them during the Hirak. It appeared that, for them, official acknowledgement of the truth is an essential prerequisite to restoring dignity to the victims, their surviving families and the nation as a whole. Forgiveness only seemed to be possible for Lamia at an intimate, family level—an important factor in accomplishing her personal process of 're-selving' was the attempt to re-establish a relationship with her father, especially when she learned that he was dying. She forgave him the punitive behaviour she had had to suffer at his hands before she left the country. However, Lamia's narrative, which was supported by those of other participants, showed that she refuses to forgive those responsible for the terrorist acts and other horrors perpetrated during the Black Decade until the truth is revealed and the wrongdoers brought to justice.

This brought to the fore the question of how forced exile relates to the idea of diaspora. Both involve the displacement of people who struggle to retain an identity with their original environment (Sullivan 2001). Diaspora, however, concerns groups of migrants, while exile, as Said (2002: 140) says, 'in a very acute sense ... is a solitude experienced outside the group'. The difference between a diasporic state of mind and an exilic one is that the concept of exile often assumes that individuals hold to fixed, coherent ideas about their new countries and their original homeland, and are often 'cut off from their roots' (Said 2002: 140), whereas the concept of diaspora challenges notions of 'home', borders and nation states, while creating an imaginary homeland and cultivating a 'myth of return'. My research revealed that very often these states overlap.

This book has shown the complexity of the participants' relationships with present-day Algeria and with their peers still living there, whom they often appeared to believe to be either incompetent and corrupt, or too traditional and overtly religious. It seems that they individually attributed to themselves the imaginary Algerian identity—democratic, liberated, secular—that they dreamed of possessing before being forced to flee. As such, it appears that, for the most part, they can only foresee the implementation of women's rights and gender equality in Algeria if the country pursues a policy of secularism. I would argue, however, that this is not necessarily what the majority of women living in Algeria aspire to. In this sense, educational levels, age and political beliefs certainly add to the complexity of imagining a 'new Algeria', as could be seen in the arguments that arose later in the Hirak. Lamia mentioned several reasons why she feels more at home in the UK and could not foresee returning to Algeria, one of them being a residual fear of the security forces, particularly the police. Of the other participants in my research, Nadia also mentioned the fear she felt during her visits to Algeria on vacation when she encountered in the streets the selfsame terrorists who had forced her to leave and who have since benefited from an amnesty applied without accountability. Participants deplored the fact the amnesty was implemented without consultation with those professional and politically involved women who had fled the country.

It appears that, regardless of the politics of race and gender in their new societies, networks of solidarity between Algerian women, when they exist, are not established with a sense of continuity with an Algerian identity. Instead, women have reinvented new selves and a new sense of belonging to a transnational space in which they have learned new life skills and, for now, have found sanctuary and a measure of peace. It has been suggested earlier that the intolerance, suspicion and lack of trust that often occur between Algerians living abroad were inherited from French colonial rule, as well as from the terror directed against civilians in the Black Decade, which destroyed existing solidarities and networks within Algerian society as a whole. In the case of women, there are of course other considerations, which this book has touched upon. Healing the wounds of the Black Decade, however, is an essential first step for any potential reconciliation between Algerians, whether they have left the country or not. Amongst those who fled, reconciliation, tolerance and trust are the *sine qua non* to re-establishing a feeling of continuity with their Algerian identity. It is for this reason that the participants in this research rejected the amnesty law and saw it as an obstacle to their return, since it has not permitted the nation to heal.

In this era of high levels of displacement and population movement, as Maalouf explains in his book *Murderous Identities* (1998), it is those who have succeeded in building a new self, holding to where they come from as well as to who they have now become, who can play the role of bridging different communities, cultures and religions, and building a safe and peaceful transnational space. If the process of 're-selving' is successful, as it appears to have been for the majority of participants in this study, returning home is no longer an overriding concern. Hence, I deduce that both the definitions of diaspora and exile can be applied here, perhaps in the form of an 'exilic diaspora'. Exile culture is located at the intersection of the other cultures in which these individuals have found refuge, and they cannot and perhaps do not wish to be described by one unique identity that restrains them in a culture of 'diaspora'. In this context, the research also noted the beginnings among many Algerians living abroad of the idea of belonging to a global class and partaking in a form of global citizenship that transcends both their original and new cultural locations. It appears that original nationalities can sometimes matter less once a new 'imagined identity' has been created, one that crosses borders and creates its own community.

However, although the process of 're-selving' has given new meaning to the idea of self and belonging amongst participants, their memories appear to have remained to a certain extent embedded in a nostalgia caused by their exile and dispersal, causing them to invent an imagined Algeria—a democratic, secular state in which religious tolerance and gender equality are guaranteed. Returning to Algeria on vacation, visiting online newspapers or interacting via blogs with other women still living in the country, however, made participants increasingly aware that this Algeria not only never existed, but perhaps, for the majority of the Algerian people, is not even on their agenda. By re-electing Bouteflika in April 2014, the Algerian population seemed to express a desire for security and stability above all, regardless of the fact that running for a fourth term was an undemocratic act. Fear of a repeat of the Black Decade still seemed to cast a long shadow. The geopolitical chaos in the region following the suppression of the Arab Spring appeared to have persuaded many ordinary Algerians that democracy, as defined by the West, would bring neither peace nor a solution to their daily struggles for survival. However, all this was disproved in a spectacular fashion when Algerians as a nation rose up against the candidature of Bouteflika for an (unconstitutional) fifth term in office despite his long and disabling illness. Discourses expressing dissent went viral, leading to the beginning of the Hirak in February 2019.

Conclusion: The Hirak and the mobilization of a diaspora

One argument that has emerged throughout this study is that, even in times of conflict or war, there can be no clear distinction between women forced to escape cultures of gender-based violence and harsh patriarchal rules, and those forced to flee by political persecution and violence. As seen most clearly in Lamia's story, and echoed by those of the other women in this book, the reason many of them fled was first and foremost gender-related persecution, and this holds true even for those who also fled targeted political violence and personal death threats. Despite the introduction of gender guidelines in the asylum processes of many countries and by the UNHCR, there is still much work to do to consolidate a recognition in the international asylum system that forms of gender-based violence are grounds for granting refugee status. The participants who did not claim political asylum were for the most part discouraged by the gender-blind asylum regime, although many are aware of the need to bring to wider attention the violence suffered by those women who remained in Algeria.

Apart from the radical insecurity due to the lack of administrative status many women migrants are forced to endure as a consequence of the failure to recognize gender-based persecution, my fieldwork also revealed further obstacles faced by participants in attempting to adjust to lives in their new societies. These varied from the non-recognition of Algerian qualifications and the lack of an organized and supportive Algerian community to more extreme forms of discrimination, often due to their nationality or assumed support of radical Islam and terrorism, as exemplified by Nadia's experience in France. Despite these barriers, participants showed a great deal of resilience, although this needs far more social and institutional recognition, support and nurturing.

Furthermore, despite existing suspicions, mistrust and political divergences among those who migrated during this period, the survey had a high number of participants. Through their participation, these women demonstrated the existence of a wide series of networks, including online networks, amongst those who had fled during the Black Decade and its aftermath. Their engagement with the Hirak and their presence on the streets and online during the months of protests are testament to this. Whether or not such networks can sustain this mobilization remains an open question. However, by taking part in this research and recruiting their peers, these women exhibited a shared interest in the topic of diasporic networks and the potential for mobilization of these networks for political change, not only in Algeria but also in the countries in which they now live. Again, undoubtedly their gender and level of education were key factors in overcoming the aforementioned residual suspicions and divergences, giving credence to the arguments of the social constructionist critics against the classical conception of diaspora.

None of the participants intended to return to Algeria. This finding is not new in itself: research into women's diasporas and migrant women has revealed that, in general, women resist the idea of returning home more than their male counterparts (Abdelhady 2011). However, the main difference here is that these highly skilled migrant women also displayed a detailed awareness of the current problems in their country of origin. Prior to the Hirak, several participants in my research had even returned to Algeria, offering their experience, skills and competence in setting up projects, but had left again because of the bureaucracy, general corruption and, more importantly, the lack of women's rights and the increasingly radical Islamization of society. Participants had very lucid ideas about what in their opinion has gone wrong with the amnesty law implemented in 2005 and the post-conflict peace-building in the country, which they considered a failed process.

Participants have also begun discussing why the Hirak (thus far) appears to have failed to achieve its goal, and why it is critical to continue organizing debates around its ideas in order to support and inspire their compatriots back home. Included in these debates is the belief that many women voiced, that there has been a radical Islamization of Algerian society, which restricts women's freedom and in its conservative beliefs and culture is alien to the traditional Maghrebi practice of a peaceful, tolerant form of Islam. For this reason, many of the participants called for a secular society as the only way for the nation to restore peace and unity, despite the fact that this view was not necessarily shared by all those participating in the Hirak. Many of these women also expressed the view (which Lamia insisted on so forcefully) that it is essential to establish the truth about the Black Decade before there can be any hope of reconciliation, forgiveness or positive change. As such, this book represents a tentative first step towards the establishment of a narrative of the Black Decade as viewed by women in exile from a gender perspective.

The basic requirement of these women is for the Algerian government to ensure the effective implementation of existing laws, and to design new policies and guidelines that will assist women and protect them from the violence and discrimination they still experience in their daily lives in Algeria—particularly as these factors have been identified as one of the main barriers the participants face to returning to the country from which they fled. At the time of writing, the release of the political detainees of the Hirak, including many women activists, continues to be a fundamental demand and a crucial condition for establishing a dialogue between the regime and all Algerians, including those living abroad. The Hirak, whatever its immediate outcome, appears to show us that if this group of women migrants have the capacity to heal from the trauma of the Black Decade, the next generation is likely to evolve into a mobilized diaspora.

Appendix 1: The Author's Place within the Research

In keeping with the feminist framework of my research, I believe it is necessary to explain how my own experiences have informed the research behind this book, as well as how the research affected me in turn. First and foremost, I would describe myself as an Algerian woman of Amazigh origin, a left-wing feminist who, although nurtured in a Muslim culture, believes in the principles of political secularism. My political views are therefore an integral part of this research (Kleinman and Copp 1993; Kirkwood 1993).

I came to social sciences later in life, as a mature student, after my arrival in the UK seeking asylum. My work in Algeria had been unrelated to this field. I studied electronics at Algiers University and worked for seventeen years in the very male-dominated field of non-destructive testing for a research centre related to the Algerian Ministry of Higher Education and Scientific Research. In 2001, I was elected to the National Commission of Women's Rights in the Workplace with the main Algerian trade union, the UGTA (General Union of Algerian Workers), and to the Federation of Higher Education and Scientific Research. However, I and my family were forced into exile, following a traumatic attack on our home, and this experience shaped my subsequent desire to explore the similar experiences of other Algerian women. I embarked on my doctoral research in October 2010 at Swansea University, later transferring to the University of East London.

My first contact on Facebook with some of the women who later agreed to act as the 'seeds' for the RDS research method (explained more fully in Appendix 2) occurred during the second week of December 2010, just a few days before a 26-year-old Tunisian man set himself on fire, triggering what is now known as the Arab Spring. Lina Ben Mhenni, a young Tunisian female blogger, broadcast pictures of the self-immolation on social media, mainly on Facebook and Twitter, that subsequently went viral. Women on Facebook expressed the need to share their experiences of Algeria's Black Decade with their Tunisian and Egyptian sisters. They frequently voiced their regrets that there was not a diasporic space that could be mobilized to present evidence of their experiences and give voice to the collective trauma of the survivors. Although men also contributed to these online discussions, it was the women who created the platforms, blogs and Facebook groups where they shared their concerns and opinions.

Meanwhile, riots started in Bab El Oued, the same area of Algiers where a protest of 20,000 people was bloodily suppressed in October 1988 (see Chapter Two), before spreading to other cities. Unlike 1988, the wave of protests in 2010–12, inspired by the Arab Spring, followed the Algerian government's decision to raise the prices of basic foodstuffs. I observed that the online discourse revealed the active participation of Algerian women living abroad in discussions around these issues, as well as their interactions with women still living in Algeria, as they debated ways of avoiding another Black Decade-style conflict. In this way, it appeared that they were actively creating a diasporic online space in which they could express dissent against the Algerian government. Their online conversations raised the question of how to create a diaspora, by which they meant a network of solidarity linking Algerian women living abroad with each other and with women in Algeria. It was through my participation in this online discourse that I met many women who were actively engaged in discussing the future of Algeria, Tunisia and, later on, the whole region, sharing information and supporting Tunisian, Egyptian and Yemeni female bloggers and online activists. It was during this time that I created a Facebook page, 'Algerian Women Diaspora'. After it was hacked six months later, it became a closed group, discussing issues related to Algerian women living abroad.

My research therefore focused on investigating the existence of a network of highly qualified, professional Algerian women. This included exploring the barriers they face in returning to Algeria. As I was aware that return is more often a dream than a reality, I was interested to know how members of this network built solidarities, and whether they were engaged in making positive changes for women's rights in Algeria or in the transfer of technology, knowledge and remittances. As I started reviewing the existing literature, it quickly became evident that it was necessary to define and confirm (or otherwise) the role of diasporas—particularly diasporas that include women with high levels of education and/or high levels of political consciousness—in providing assistance and support to their peers in their country of origin. Later on, with the beginning of the Hirak, I felt the need to actively support and participate in this movement for democracy, which meant I was able to observe at first hand my female compatriots' engagement with it.

Following my relocation to London, I soon discovered that one positive side of living in the capital was that it gave me an insight into the diversity of the Algerian community. During my research, for example, I also attended *iftar* (the Ramadhan breakfast) at the premises of the Algerian British Connection (ABC), a cultural organization chaired by an Algerian woman. This proved a good opportunity to meet members of the Algerian community from all creeds, and I had many informal discussions on how Algerians interact with each other, as well as the challenges we face living in the UK. The tragedy of the 1990s was always at the heart of any conversation I had with fellow Algerians in both the UK and France. This helped me gain an insight into the different views they hold, and made me realize that London is perhaps the best location in which to learn about how the internal conflict in the 1990s was theorized, and even maintained, outside Algeria.

Later, when the Hirak started in February 2019, I joined the protests in London, Algiers and Paris, where I re-encountered a few of the participants from my original research. I invited this group of women to come together to think about how we could take this opportunity to better negotiate for women's rights in Algeria, and I suggested that we join forces with the Maghreb-Equality 95 Collective. According to Aili Mari Tripp (2019), this group has inspired many gender reforms over the past two decades in Algeria, Morocco and Tunisia; many women living abroad also benefited from these reforms, since the family code legislation in their respective countries also affects these women. Yet, despite these reforms, and the success of Algerian women in many professional and educational fields, women's testimony is still seen as having half the value of men's among the majority of the Algerian population, including many male figures in the Hirak. My suggestion was that we should make our peers aware that our presence and support was indispensable to the success of the Hirak, and so avoid being excluded from the political and social sphere. Of course, women (including those in Algeria) do not hold monolithic views. For example, the aim of some of those who decided to continue marching after the resignation of Bouteflika was, according to one of the regular attendees of the demonstrations in London, to first 'liberate our men from the *hogra* [contempt] of the military regime, then they will liberate us and give us our equal rights'. Therefore, in this book, I have attempted to give equal weight to the varied perspectives of the women I interviewed for my research.

Appendix 2: The Characteristics of the Research Participants

Nearly half (45%) of the research participants who had left Algeria were between the ages of twenty-five and thirty-five, and a further 35% were under twenty-five. Those aged between thirty-six and forty constituted only 13%. Five respondents were aged over forty-five, one of whom was in her sixties. Around a third (42%) left Algeria as university students (with first or second degrees), meaning they were eligible for student visas. Only 12% said they left as labour migrants, 9% as refugees, 3% as undocumented migrants, and a further 9% did not wish to state their reason for leaving the country.

The women who participated in the research held a variety of qualifications from educational institutions, ranging from universities to high schools. Around a third had left Algeria holding a first degree or master's in humanities, 18% held master's degrees in science and technology, and nearly 7% had PhDs in science and technology. In addition, 5% were medical practitioners, 2% of whom were working as specialist doctors in teaching hospitals in Algiers before they left. Nearly half (43%) were willing to give more details about their qualifications and professions, which varied from journalism, law and architecture to medicine, dentistry and pharmacy. Some participants had graduated from prestigious Algerian academic institutions, such as ENA (École National d'Administration), INA (Institut National d'Agronomie), ITFC (Institut de Technologie, Finance et Comptabilité), École des Beaux-Arts and EMP (École Militaire Polytechnique) (formerly ENITA). Nearly two-thirds (70%) said they had been working in Algeria prior to leaving, among whom 15% said they were 'very satisfied' with their jobs and about a third stated they were 'satisfied'.

The participants had migrated to a wide range of countries: the largest group, nearly a third, had settled in France, followed by 21% in Canada, 20% in the UK, 18% in Spain and 7% in the USA. Four participants responded from Belgium; two each from the United Arab Emirates (UAE), Italy and Switzerland; and one each from Australia, Qatar, Germany, Turkey and Tunisia. This shows the efficiency of the RDS method in reaching those who were geographically isolated but still connected to friends or former colleagues. Two women said that their first destination had been France but they had later moved to the USA and Qatar, respectively. One respondent had left for the UAE but later went to the USA; one migrated to East Africa, where she worked for an NGO, and then moved to Canada; and one left for the Canary Isles, later travelling on to mainland Spain. Two left for France but had returned to Algeria at the time of completing the survey. One participant explained, 'I work for a company that moves me every year. I am now here, but when I'm off work, I spend my time between Algeria, visiting my family, and Marseilles, the city I love and where life is good.' In addition, only two participants revealed they wear the *hijab*, and only one revealed her sexual orientation as a lesbian.

Appendix 3: Survey Questionnaire (English Version)

Research on an Algerian Women's Diaspora

Thank you for agreeing to participate in this research project.

About me

My name is Latefa Guemar. I am an Algerian woman who left Algeria in 2003. I am currently a PhD student at Swansea University (Wales, UK) in the Centre for Migration Policy Research, and I am also a Visiting Fellow at the London School of Economics and Political Science (LSE), undertaking my research in the field of Gender and Migration. I have a Master's in Science in Population Movements and Policies, and my dissertation (2011) focused on the impact of forced migration on women's lives. **My supervisors are:** Prof. Heaven Crawley ACSS, Director of the Centre for Migration Policy Research, Swansea University, and Dr Tom Cheesman, Language Department, Swansea University.

What is the purpose of the research?

This research is conducted in order to better understand the experiences of highly qualified Algerian women who left their homeland following the internal political instability of the 1990s. This research aims to make recommendations to international organizations that influence policies concerning the barriers which Algerian women face in rebuilding their professional lives in the country where they live. The research also aims to contribute to the opportunities of women if they decide to return to Algeria: their rights to access pensions and other social protection, and the recognition of their professional experiences. In order to make these recommendations I need your valuable contribution. **Thank you in advance.**

How can you contribute?

First, please complete the survey. The survey asks you about the circumstances of your departure from Algeria, your life abroad, whether or not you belong to an Algerian network and whether or not you intend to return to Algeria.

Secondly, please forward the link to this survey to other Algerian women abroad—at least one, but ideally three or more Algerian women who you know and meet the following criteria.

- Highly qualified: holding a higher education diploma, degree, or equivalent or higher-level qualification, and
- Living abroad, having left Algeria after 1990.

This will help to ensure that the survey reaches the maximum number of respondents. We are interested in the experiences of highly qualified Algerian women regardless of their legal status, profession or country where they are living.

Data collected FOR this survey WILL REMAIN strictly confidential and under no circumstances, your personal information will be disclosed. DATA WILL BE USED for research purposes ONLY.

NB: You may have left Algeria before the 1990s but could not return when the violence started, if so please feel included in this research.

1. Questions about your circumstance of leaving Algeria

1. **When did you leave Algeria?***
   - ❍ Between 1990 and 1995
   - ❍ Between 1996 and 2000
   - ❍ After 2000
   - ❍ Before 1990 but I couldn't return because of the instability in the country

2. **Did you leave Algeria as a:***
   - ❑ Student
   - ❑ Labour migrant
   - ❑ Refugee
   - ❑ Spouse
   - ❑ Illegal migrant
   - ❑ Don't want to say

3. **When you left Algeria, were you:***
   - ❍ Under 25 years old
   - ❍ Between 25 and 35 years old
   - ❍ Between 36 and 40 years old
   - ❍ Between 41 and 50 years old
   - ❍ 51 or over

4. **What was your highest qualification when you left Algeria?**
   - ❍ University degree
   - ❍ Postgraduate qualification in Social Science
   - ❍ Postgraduate qualification in Technology
   - ❍ Professional qualification in Medical Science
   - ❍ Other (please specify):

Please provide detail of your speciality if you wish to do so

5. **Were you working in Algeria?***
   - ❍ Yes (please go to question 7)
   - ❍ No (please go to question 6)

6. **Why were you not working in Algeria?**
   - ❑ Unable to find a job
   - ❑ Family restrictions
   - ❑ Social restrictions
   - ❑ Other (please specify):

7. **Were you satisfied with the job you were doing?**
   - ❍ Very satisfied
   - ❍ Satisfied
   - ❍ Neither satisfied or unsatisfied
   - ❍ Not satisfied
   - ❍ Very unsatisfied

8. **What was your marital status before you left Algeria?***
   - ❍ Single
   - ❍ Married
   - ❍ Divorced
   - ❍ Widowed
   - ❍ Don't want to say

2. Questions about your life experiences abroad

9. **Where do you live currently?***
   - ❍ France
   - ❍ Canada
   - ❍ UK
   - ❍ USA
   - ❍ Other (please specify):

10. **Can you tell us the name of the city where you live?**

11. **Are you working/studying now?***
    - ❑ Yes
    - ❑ No

12. **If yes, what is your profession now?**
    - ❍ Student
    - ❍ Researcher
    - ❍ Reader/Lecturer or Tutor in university or equivalent institution
    - ❍ Teacher or working in high/primary school
    - ❍ Business manager
    - ❍ Community project manager/worker
    - ❍ Doctor/Nurse/Dentist/Pharmacologist
    - ❍ Self-employed
    - ❍ Other (please specify):

13. **Have you ever applied for a course/degree in the country where you live now?**
    - ❑ Yes (go to question 13)
    - ❑ No

14. **Since you are already highly qualified from Algeria, please explain briefly the reason(s) why you had to apply to an additional course**

15. **In your opinion, have you ever not been employed or accepted in a course because of your: (you can tick more than one)***
    - ❑ Gender
    - ❑ Nationality
    - ❑ Age
    - ❑ Religion
    - ❑ Ethnicity
    - ❑ Race
    - ❑ Legal status
    - ❑ Lack of funding
    - ❑ Language barrier
    - ❑ Other (please specify):

16. **What is your marital status now?**
    - ❍ Single
    - ❍ Married
    - ❍ Divorced
    - ❍ Widowed
    - ❍ Don't want to say

17. **What is your highest qualification now?***
    - ❍ Graduate in another field than from Algeria
    - ❍ Postgraduate in another field than from Algeria
    - ❍ Same qualifications than from Algeria

3. Questions regarding your integration in your hosting country

18. **Do you consider yourself as part of an Algerian network/belonging to an Algerian network?***
    - ❍ Yes
    - ❍ No

19. **What does belonging to an Algerian network mean to you?**
    - ❑ Being part of a community
    - ❑ Nothing
    - ❑ Don't know

20. **Do you think that belonging to an Algerian network can help you: (you can tick more than one)**
    - ❑ Meet other Algerians in order to share your experiences
    - ❑ Integrate into the hosting society
    - ❑ Find a job
    - ❑ Create and nurture your idea of return to Algeria
    - ❑ Other (please specify):

21. **Do you go to Algerian events and gatherings?***
    - ❑ Yes
    - ❑ No (go to question 23)

22. **What type of gatherings do you prefer to attend?**
    - ❑ Cultural
    - ❑ Political
    - ❑ Religious
    - ❑ Private/familial
    - ❑ Academic talks/conferences/seminars
    - ❑ Other (please specify):

23. **Do you usually prefer to gather with other Algerians from/of the same:**
    - ❑ Gender
    - ❑ Profession
    - ❑ Age range
    - ❑ Political opinion
    - ❑ Region/city in Algeria
    - ❑ It doesn't matter: they just have to be Algerian
    - ❑ Other (please specify):

24. **If you don't prefer to attend Algerian gatherings at all, briefly explain the main reasons why:**

25. **What is the main language you use when speaking to your family, children and/or Algerian friends now?***
    - ❑ Algerian dialect
    - ❑ Berber
    - ❑ Arabic
    - ❑ French
    - ❑ English
    - ❑ Other (please specify):

26. **What does 'integration' mean for you? (You can tick more than one)***
    - ❑ Exerting citizenship (naturalization, vote etc.)
    - ❑ Having successful family life
    - ❑ Having your qualifications recognized
    - ❑ Finding a job and paying taxes
    - ❑ Rebuilding a successful career
    - ❑ Other (please specify):

27. **To what degree do you feel integrated into the society where you live?**
    - ❑ Strongly integrated
    - ❑ Fairly integrated
    - ❑ Neither integrated or non-integrated
    - ❑ Fairly non-integrated
    - ❑ Strongly non-integrated

4. **Questions regarding communication with Algeria/Algerians**

28. **What is the main tool you use to be informed on national and international news?**
    - ❑ TV
    - ❑ Radio
    - ❑ Internet
    - ❑ Newspapers
    - ❑ Other (please specify):

29. **Do you use the internet to communicate and share information with friends, family and others?***
    - ❍ Yes
    - ❍ No

30. **If yes, what are the main social online network sites you use? (You can tick more than one box)**
    - ❑ Facebook
    - ❑ YouTube
    - ❑ Twitter
    - ❑ Skype
    - ❑ E-mail lists
    - ❑ Other (please specify):

31. **Do you particularly share or forward information that is more related to women's rights in Algeria?***
    - ❍ Yes
    - ❍ No

32. **Do you still have family and friends in Algeria?***
    - ❍ Yes
    - ❍ No

33. **By what other means do you connect with family and friends in Algeria?**
    - ❑ Viber on iPhone
    - ❑ Mobile phone
    - ❑ Landline
    - ❑ Other (please specify):

34. **If you have a Facebook account, how often do you log in?**
   - ❍ Only once a day
   - ❍ Many times a day
   - ❍ Weekly
   - ❍ Monthly
   - ❍ Sometimes
   - ❍ Never
   - ❍ Don't want to say
   - ❍ Other (please specify):

35. **Do you comment online?***
   - ❍ Yes
   - ❍ No

36. **If not, briefly say why you do not comment online.**

37. **Are you a member of any professional e-mail list?**
   - ❑ No
   - ❑ In the country where you live
   - ❑ International network
   - ❑ Algerian only network
   - ❑ Other (please specify):

5. Questions about returning to Algeria

38. **Do you miss Algeria?***
   - ❍ Yes (go to question 39)
   - ❍ No (go to question 40)
   - ❍ Not sure

39. **What do you miss most about Algeria? (You can tick more than one)**
   - ❑ Music
   - ❑ Food
   - ❑ Weather
   - ❑ Family
   - ❑ Friends
   - ❑ Activism
   - ❑ Lifestyle
   - ❑ Don't know
   - ❑ Other (please specify):

40. **When was the last time you visited Algeria?**
   - ❍ Within the last year
   - ❍ Between 1 and 2 years ago
   - ❍ Between 2 and 5 years ago
   - ❍ Between 5 and 10 years ago
   - ❍ More than 10 years ago
   - ❍ Never

41. **Do you think you could/will live in Algeria in the future?***
   - ❑ Yes
   - ❑ No
   - ❑ Don't know

42. **Do you think there are any barriers preventing women like you from returning to Algeria?***
    - ❍ Yes (go to question 43)
    - ❍ No (go to question 44)
    - ❍ Don't know
43. **If yes, please give detail of the barriers you think exist:**
    - ❑ Social
    - ❑ Economic
    - ❑ Political
    - ❑ Familial
    - ❑ Other (please specify):
44. **Do you have any concrete project/job offer to return? Please explain briefly.**
45. **Is there anything you would like to add that has not been mentioned in this questionnaire?**

THANK YOU, I feel honoured that you have accepted to answer my survey.
Please do not forget to forward the survey to other women of your network.
Remember: The country where they live, the legal status they have and their profession are not important, as long as they are highly qualified Algerian women who left following the political instability and the rise of violence during the 1990s.
Please contact me if you have any enquiry about the survey.
Also please email if you would like to receive a copy of my thesis.

Bibliography

Abbot, P. and Wallace, C. (1990). *An Introduction to Sociology: Feminist Perspectives*. London: Routledge.

Abdelhady, D. (2011). *The Lebanese Diaspora: The Arab Immigrant Experience in Montreal, New York, and Paris*. New York and London: NYC University Press. https://doi.org/10.18574/nyu/9780814707333.001.0001

Addi, L. (1991). *L'impasse du Populisme*. Algiers: Enal.

Agger, I. (1994). *The Blue Room: Trauma and Testimony Among Refugee Women: A Psycho-Social Exploration*. London: Zed Books.

Aggoun, L. and Rivoire, J.-B. (2005). *Françalgérie, Crimes et Mensonges d'états*. Paris: La Découverte. https://doi.org/10.3917/dec.aggou.2005.01

Ait Larbi, M., Ait-Belkacem, M.S., Belaid, M., Nait-Redjam, M.A. and Soltani, Y. (1999). 'An Anatomy of the Massacres', in Bedjaoui, Y., Aroua, A., Ait Larbi, M. (eds). *An Inquiry into the Algerian Massacres*. Geneva: Hoggar, pp. 121–160.

Ait Zai, N. (2011). 'Middle East and Northern Africa at a Crossroads: "Arab Springs" Analysed by Key Feminist Actors from the Region'. Published conference paper. *Women's Rights and Gender Equality Amidst the 'Arab Springs'*. 27 and 28 October 2011. Brussels, Belgium. [Online]. Available at: http://crtda.org.lb/sites/default/files/WIDE%20CRTDA%20AC%202011.pdf (accessed 12 January 2015).

Alaoui, M.H. (2010). 'Surmonter l'exil par le militantisme: Le cas des femmes algériennes en France et au Québec'. *NAQD*, 28, *Femmes et Migration, Travail, Bizness, Exil, Asile*, pp. 265–86. https://doi.org/10.3917/naqd.028.0265

Algeria-Watch (2002). 'Le chef d'état-major, le général Mohamed Lamari lors d'une conférence de presse, "L'ANP est une armée républicaine"'. [Online]. Available at: http://www.algeria-watch.org/farticle/sale_guerre/conf_presse_lamari.htm (accessed 30 March2022).

Algeria-Watch (2009) 'Massacre de Bentalha: Le « j'accuse » de Nesroulah Yous'. [Online]. Available at : https://ALGERIA-WATCH.ORG/?P=54784 (accessed 23 April 2023)

Anderson, B. (1998). *Imagined Communities*. London: Verso.

Andrews, M. (2000). 'Forgiveness in Context'. *Journal of Moral Education*, 29(1), pp. 75–86. [Online]. https://doi.org/10.1080/030572400102943

Anthias, F. (1998). 'Evaluating Diaspora: Beyond Ethnicity?', *Journal of the British Sociological Association*, 32, pp. 557–80. [Online]. Available at: http://maxweber.hunter.cuny.edu/pub/eres/SOC217_PIMENTEL/anthias.pdf (accessed 20 July 2016).

Anthias, F. (2001). 'Gendering Migration: The Case of Southern Europe', in Ghatak, S. and Sassoon, A. (eds). *Migration and Mobility*. London: Palgrave Macmillan, pp. 146–67. https://doi.org/10.1057/9780230523128_9

Arkoun, M. (2002). *The Unthought in Contemporary Islamic Thought*. London: Saqui Books.

Arnould, V. (2007). 'Amnesty, Peace and Reconciliation in Algeria'. *Conflict, Security & Development*, 7(2), pp. 227–53. [Online]. https://doi.org/10.1080/14678800701333028

Avebury, E. (1999). 'Foreword', in Bedjaoui, Y., Aroua, A. and Ait Larbi, M. (eds). *An Inquiry into Algerian Massacres*. Geneva: Hoggar, pp. xvii–xx.

Bakewell, O. (2008). 'In Search of the Diasporas within Africa'. International Migration Institute, University of Oxford. Paper accepted for publication in *African Diasporas*, 1(1–2), pp. 5–27. [Online]. Available at: http://booksandjournals.brillonline.com/docserver/18725457/v1n1_splitsection2.pdf?expires=1470848068&id=id&accname=guest&checksum=A9BB1161A01AB36998D4D1F915B8B10F (accessed 20 July 2016).

Balch, B., & Lust, E. (2006). Human Rights and Democratization in Argentina: Truth, Justice, and Reparation. Human Rights Quarterly, 28(4), pp. 1002–1027.

Barbour, J.D. (2011). 'The Consolations and Compensations of Exile: Memoirs by Said, Ahmed, and Eire'. *Journal of the American Academy of Religion*, 79(3), September 2011, pp. 706–34. https://doi.org/10.1093/jaarel/lfr007

Bauböck, R. (2007). 'Citizenship and Migration: Concepts and Controversies', in Bauböck, R. (ed.). Migration and Citizenship: Legal Status, Rights and Political Participation. Amsterdam: Amsterdam University Press.https://doi.org/10.1017/9789048504268

Bedjaoui, Y., Aroua, A. and Ait Larbi, M. (1999). *An Inquiry into the Algerian Massacres*. Geneva: Hoggar.

Begag, A. (2002). 'Les relations France-Algérie vues de la Diaspora Algérienne'. *Modern & Contemporary France*, 10(4), pp. 475–82. [Online]. Available at: http://tandfonline.com/doi/abs/10.1080/0963948022000029556 (accessed 10 January 2016).

Belalloufi, A. (2015). 'AFP Algiers'. *El Arabya* [Online]. Available at: http://english.alarabiya.net/en/perspective/features/2015/02/28/In-Algeria-women-imams-battle-Islamist-radicalization-.html (accessed 19 June 2016).

Belhimer, A. (2014a). 'Violence politique, dialogue et réconciliation nationale en Algerie'. *Human Development Network Algeria*. Algérie: Friedrich Ebert Stiftung Foundation.

Belhimer, A. (2014b). 'Une justice transitionnelle pour la vérité et contre l'impunité est-elle envisageable?'. Unpublished conference paper. *Les politiques de réconciliaton nationale*. 24–25 November 2014. Beyrouth, Lebanon.

Belhouari-Musette, D. (2006). 'Le combat des algériennes pour la citoyenneté'. *NAQD*, 1–2(22–23), *Femmes et Citoyenneté*, pp. 177–92.

Benmayor, R and Stoknes, A. (1994). *Migration and Identity.* Oxford: Oxford University Press.

Bennoune, M. (1999). *Les algériennes victimes de la sociéte **néopatriarcale***. Algérie: Marinoor.

Benrabah, M. (2013). *Language Conflict in Algeria: From Colonialism to Post-Independence*. London: Routledge.

Bouklia-Hassane, R. (2011). 'La féminisation de l'immigration d'origine algérienne: un état de lieux', in *Gender and Migration Series*, Robert Schuman Centre for Advanced Studies (RSCAS), pp. 1–42. [Online]. Available at: http://hdl.handle.net/1814/15617 (accessed 14 June 2016).

Bourdieu, P. (2013). *Algerian Sketches*. USA and New Zealand: Polity Press.

Bourdieu, P. and Leca, J. (1995). 'Non à la ghettoisation de l'Algérie!' *Le Monde* (France), 24 March 1995. Consulted at Bibliothèque Nationale de France Francois Mitterand, Paris on 13 September 2013.

Brah, A. (1996). *Cartographies of Diaspora: Contesting Identities.* New York and London: Routledge.

Brendel, D.H. (2006). 'Psychotherapy and the Truth and Reconciliation Commission: The Dialectic of Individual and Collective Healing', in Potter, N.N. (ed.). *Trauma, Truth and Reconciliation: Healing Damaged Relationships*. Oxford: Oxford University Press, pp. 15–26.

Caldwell, John C. (1982). *Theory of Fertility Decline*. London: Academic Press.

Carr, J. (2016). *Experiences of Islamophobia: Living with Racism in the Neoliberal Era*. Routledge Research in Race and Ethnicity. Oxon and New York: Routledge.

Castles, S. and Miller, M.J. (2009). *The Age of Migration: International Population Movements in the Modern World*. Basingstoke: Palgrave Macmillan.

CEDAW (2006). *Country Report on Reservation.* [Online]. Available at: http://www.un.org/womenwatch/daw/cedaw/reservations-country.htm (accessed 23 February 2016).

Cetti, F. (2015). 'Fortress Europe: The War Against Migrants'. *International Socialism.* Autumn 2015, pp. 45–74.

Chambon, A. (2008). 'Befriending Refugee Women: Refracted Knowledge and Shifting Viewpoint', in Hajdukowski-Ahmed, M., et al. (eds). *Not Born a Refugee Woman: Contesting Identities, Rethinking Practices*. New York and Oxford: Berghahn, pp. 101–10.

Cheriet, B. (2004). 'Gender as a Catalyst of Social and Political Representations in Algeria'. *Journal of North African Studies*, 9(2), pp. 93–101. https://doi.org/10.1080/1362938042000323365

Chomsky, N. (1999). 'Foreword', in Bedjaoui, Y., Aroua, A. and Ait Larbi, M. (eds). *An Inquiry into Algerian Massacres*. Geneva: Hoggar, pp. xiii–xv.

Chomsky, N. (2001). *9-11*. New York: Seven Stories Press.

Christou, A. (2006). *Virtual Networks: Placing the Internet and Consumer Culture*. Routledge

Clifford, J. (1994). 'Diaspora'. *Cultural Anthropology*, 9(3), pp. 302–80. [Online]. Available at: http://www.jstor.org/stable/656365 accessed 20 May 2021.

Cohen, R. (1997). *Global Diasporas: An Introduction*. Seattle, WA: University of Washington Press.

Cohen, R. (2008). *Global Diasporas: An Introduction.* 2nd edn. London: UCL Press.

Cohen, R. (2010). *Global Diasporas: An Introduction.* 3rd edn. London and New York: Routledge.

Cohen, R. (2012). 'Interview with Dr Alan Gamlen'. [Online]. Available at: https://www.youtube.com/watch?v=vTo52DmmlOQ (accessed 26 July 2016).

Collyer, M. (2004). 'Refugee Populations in the UK: Algerians'. London: Information Centre on Asylum Seekers and Refugees. [Online]. Available at: http://icar.livingrefugeearchive.org/navgdalgerians.pdf (accessed 19 April 2023).

Collyer, M. (2005). 'When Do Social Networks Fail to Explain Migration? Accounting for the Movement of Algerian Asylum-seekers to the UK'. *Journal of Ethnic and Migration Studies*, 31(4), pp. 699–718. [Online]. https://doi.org/10.1080/13691830500109852

Collyer, M. (2006). 'Transnational Political Participation of Algerians in France. Extra-territorial Civil Society versus Transnational Governmentality'. *Political Geography*, NB25(7), pp. 836–49. [Online]. Available at: http://www.sciencedirect.com/science/article/pii/S0962629806000941 (accessed 24 February 2016).

Collyer, M. (2008). 'The Reinvention of Political Community in a Transnational Setting: Framing the Kabyle Citizens' Movement'. *Ethnic and Racial Studies*, 31(4), pp. 687–707. [Online]. Available at: http://www.tandfonline.com/doi/pdf/10.1080/01419870701784455?needAccess=true (accessed 15 January 2016).

Crawley, H. (2001). *Refugees and Gender: Law and Process.* Bristol: Jordans.

Dahmani-Lovichi, F. (2006). 'Migration des femmes, une mémoire oubliée. *El-Watan.* 14 February 2006. [Online]. Available at: http://www.djazairess.com/fr/elwatan/36255 (accessed 10 January 2016).

Daoud, Z. (1996). *Féminisme et politique au Maghreb.* 2nd edn. France: EDDIF.

Davies, R. (2007). 'Reconceptualising the Migration–Development Nexus: Diasporas, Globalisation and the Politics of Exclusion'. *Third World Quarterly*, 28(1), pp. 59–76. [Online]. https://doi.org/10.1080/01436590601081823

Dejevsky, M. (1995). 'Bomb Kills 4 People in Paris'. *Independent.* 25 July 1995. [Online]. Available at: http://www.independent.co.uk/news/bomb-kills-4-in-paris-metro-1593213.html (accessed 26 July 2016).

Department for Communities and Local Government: Annual Report 2009. Available at: https://assets.publishing.service.gov.uk/government/uploads/system/uploads/attachment_data/file/228792/7598.pdf. (access 23 April 2023)

Derrida, J. (2001). *On Cosmopolitanism and Forgiveness.* London and New York: Routledge, Taylor & Francis.

Djebar, A. (2002). *Le blanc de l'Algérie.* France: Edition le Seuil.

El Tayeb, S.E.E. (1989). 'The Ulama and Islamic Renaissance in Algeria'. *American Journal of Islam and Society*, 6(2), pp. 257–88. https://doi.org/10.35632/ajis.v6i2.2825

Ellingson, L.L. (1998). '"Then you know how I feel": Empathy, Identification, and Reflexivity in Fieldwork'. *Qualitative Inquiry*, pp. 192–514. [Online]. https://doi.org/10.1177/107780049800400405

Evans, M. and Phillips, J. (2007). *Algeria: Anger of the Dispossessed.* New Haven, CT: Yale University Press.

Fanon, F. (1968). *Sociologie d'une revolution.* Paris: Maspero, pp. 176–80.

Fanon, F. (1986). *Black Skin, White Masks.* London and Sydney: Pluto Press.

Fanon, F. (2001). *L'An V de la révolution algérienne.* Paris: La Découverte.

Farrand, A.G. (2021). *The Algerian Dream: Youth and the Quest for Dignity.* New Degree Press. Washington D.C, United State.

Fenster, T. (2005). 'The Right to the Gendered City: Different Formations of Belonging in Everyday Life'. *Journal of Gender Studies*, 14(3), pp. 217–31. Taylor & Francis Online. https://doi.org/10.1080/09589230500264109

Fisk, R. (2015). *Robert Fisk on Algeria: Why Algeria's Tragedy Matters.* London: Independent Print Limited.

Forbes Martin, S. (2003). *Refugee Women.* New York: Lexington Books.

Gadant, M. (1995). *Le nationalisme algérien et les femmes.* Paris: L'Harmatan.

Ghezali, S. (1999). *Le* rêve algérien. Algérie: Edition La Nation.

Gilroy, P. (1993). *The Black Atlantic: Modernity and Double Consciousness.* London: Verso.

Grenfell, M.J. (2004). *Pierre Bourdieu: Agent Provocateur.* London and New York: Continuum. Available from Google eBook Library at: https://books.google.co.uk/books?id=0MWvAwAAQBAJ&lpg=PP8&ots=A7gx7qaxtB&dq=Grenfell%2C%20M.J.%20(2004).%20Pierre%20Bourdieu%3A%20Agent%20Provocateur.%20London%20and%20New%20York%3A%20Continuum.%20Available%20from%20Google%20Ebook%20Library.&lr&hl=fr&pg=PP8#v=onepage&q&f=false (accessed 13 April 2023)

Guemar, L.N. (2011). *The Challenges of Accessing Mental Health Care for Refugee Women: Case Studies within the Swansea Area.* Swansea: Hafan Books. Available at: www.lulu.com/hafan. (accessed 11 January 2013)

Guemar, L.N., Northey, A.J. and Boukrami, E. (2022). 'Diaspora Activism and Citizenship: Algerian Community Responses during the Global Pandemic'. *Journal of Ethnic and Migration Studies*, 48(9), pp. 1980–97. https://doi.org/10.1080/1369183X.2022.2031924 (accessed 23 April 2023)

Hajdukowski-Ahmed, M. (2008). 'A Dialogical Approach to Identity: Implications for Refugee Women', in Hajdukowski-Ahmed, M. et al. (eds). *Not Born a Refugee Woman: Contesting Identities, Rethinking Practices.* New York and Oxford: Berghahn Books, p. 28.

Hajdukowski-Ahmed, M., et al. (eds). (2008). *Not Born a Refugee Woman: Contesting Identities, Rethinking Practices.* New York and Oxford: Berghahn Books.

Hall, S. (1990). 'Cultural Identity and Diaspora', in Rutherford, J. (ed.). *Identity.* London: Lawrence & Wishart, pp. 222–237.

Hall, S. (1993). 'Cultural Identity in Question', in Hall, S., Held, D. and McGrew, T. (eds). *Modernity and its Futures.* Cambridge: Polity, pp. 273–313.

Harbi, M. (1994). 'Enlisement dans une "sale guerre": l'Algérie prise au piège de son histoire'. *Le Monde Diplomatique*, May 1994, p. 3. [Online]. Available at: https://www.monde-diplomatique.fr/1994/05/HARBI/7290 (accessed 14 June 2015).

Hayward, L., Hajdukowski-Ahmed, M., Ploeg, J. and Trollope-Kumar, K. (2008). '"We Want to Talk, They Give Us Pills": Identity and Mental Health of Refugee Women From Sudan', in Hajdukowski-Ahmed, M. et al. (eds). *Not Born a Refugee Woman: Contesting Identities, Rethinking Practices*. Oxford: Berghahn Books, pp. 196–214.

Heckathorn, D. (1997). 'Respondent-Driven Sampling: A New Approach to the Study of Hidden Populations'. *Social Problems*, 44, pp. 174–99. [Online]. Available at: http://www.respondentdrivensampling.org/reports/RDS1.pdf accessed 19 April 2023).

Heckathorn, D. (2007). 'Extensions of Respondent-Driven Sampling: Analyzing Continuous Variables and Controlling for Differential Recruitment', in Xie Yu (ed). *Sociological Methodology*. Vol. 37. Boston, MA: Blackwell Publishing, pp. 151–207.

Herlihy, J. and Turner, S. (2013). 'What Do We Know So Far About Emotion and Refugee Law?' *Northern Ireland Legal Quarterly*, 64(1), p 47.

Hiddleston, J. (2006). *Assia Djebar: Out of Algeria*. Liverpool: Liverpool University Press.

Iamarene-Djerbal, D. (2006). 'Affaire de Hassi Messaoud'. *NAQD*, 1–2(22–23), *Femmes et Citoyenneté*, pp. 15–39.

InfoMigrants (2021) La parenthèse du hirak «refermée», les Algériens traversent la mer pour atteindre l'Europe au péril de leur vie - InfoMigrants. Available at : http://infomi.gr/1BAq.T (accessed 23 April 2023)

International Organization for Migration (IOM) (2016). *World Migration: Costs and Benefits of International Migration*, 3. IOM Migration Reports. [Online]. Available at: http://iomgmdac.org/global-trends-2015-factsheet/ (accessed 12 May 2016).

International Organization for Migration (IOM) (2020). World Migration Report 2020. [Online]. Available at: https://publications.iom.int/system/files/pdf/wmr_2020.pdf. (accessed 23 April 2023)

International Organisation for Migration (IOM) (2021). Missing Migrants Project – Quarterly Regional Overview – Middle East & North Africa, July 1 - September 30, 2021, pp. 2–6. Available at : https://missingmigrants.iom.int/sites/g/files/tmzbdl601/files/publication/file/MMP_MENA_Q32021.pdf (accessed 23 April 2023)

IREX (2005). *Annual Report 2005*, pp. 3–16. [Online]. Available at: http://unesdoc.unesco.org/images/0015/001520/152010e.pdf (accessed 20 January 2016).

Joffé, G. (2008). 'National Reconciliation and General Amnesty in Algeria'. *Mediterranean Politics*, 13(2), pp. 213–28. [Online]. https://doi.org/10.1080/13629390802127539

Jordan, B. and Duvell, F. (2003). *Migration: The Boundaries of Equality and Justice*. Oxford: Blackwell.

Kabeer, N. (2013). 'Tracking the Gender Politics of the Millennium Development Goals: From the Millennium Declaration to the Post-MDG Declaration'. Event attended at the LSE,

2 October 2013. Available at: http://www.lse.ac.uk/newsAndMedia/videoAndAudio/channels/publicLecturesAndEvents/player.aspx?id=2033. (accessed 16 mars 2020)

Kaci, N. (2010). *Laissées pour mortes: Le lynchage des femmes de Hassi Messaoud.* France: Max Milo.

Kepel, G. (2002). 'Jihad: The Trial of Political Islam'. *International Journal of Middle East Studies,* 36(3), pp. 512–14. https://doi.org/10.1017/S0020743804473073

Kepel, G. (2009). *Jihad: The Trial of Political Islam.* 4th edn. London: I.B.Tauris.

Khaled, K. (2014). 'Ruptures et exils forces des intellectuels algériens', in Ghalamallah, M. (ed.). *L'Université Algérienne et sa gouvernance.* Algérie: CREAD, pp. 57–99.

Khiari, W. (2009). *Nos Silences.* Tunis: ELYZAD.

Kirkwood, C. (1993). 'Investing Ourselves: Use of Researcher Personal Response in Feminist Methodology', in Groot, J. and Maynard, M. (eds). *Women's Studies in the 1990s: Doing Things Differently?* London: Macmillan, pp. 199–210.

Kleinman, C. and Copp, M.A. (1993). *Emotion and Fieldwork.* London: Sage.

Knapp, M.L. and Hall, J.A. (2009). *Non-Verbal Communication.* 7th edn. California: Wadsworth Publishing.

Knauss, P. (1987). *The Persistence of Patriarchy: Class, Gender, and Ideology in Twentieth Century Algeria.* New York and London: Greenwood Publishing Group.

Labdelaoui, H. (2012). 'L'Algérie face à l'évolution de son émigration'. *Revue francaise de reference sur les dynamiques migratoires: hommes et migrations,* pp. 22–37. [Online]. Available at: https://hommesmigrations.revues.org/1872 (accessed 18 July 2016).

Lakhdar, L. (2002). *La femme selon al-ijma.* Tunis: Ceres Edition.

Lakhdar, L. (2007). *Les femmes au miroir de l'orthodoxie Islamique.* Trans. by Abdessamad, H. Paris: Edition de l'aube.

Lalami, F. (2012). *Les Algeriennes contre le code de famille.* Paris: Presses de Sciences Po.

Lazreg, M. (2009). *Questioning the Veil: Open Letters to Muslim Women.* New Jersey and Oxford: Princeton University Press.

Lepinard, E. and Lieber, M. (2015). 'The Policy on Gender Equality in France'. European Parliament manuscript, pp. 13–26. [Online]. Available at: http://www.europarl.europa.eu/RegData/etudes/IDAN/2015/510024/IPOL_IDA(2015)510024_EN.pdf (accessed 16 March 2016).

Le Sueur, J.D. (2010). *Algeria Since 1989: Between Terror and Democracy (Global History of the Present).* Canada: Fernwood Publishing Ltd.

Leftwich, A. (2005). 'Democracy and Development: Is There an Institutional Incompatibility?' *Democratization,* 12(5), pp. 686–703. [Online]. https://doi.org/10.1080/13510340500322173

Lezzar, N.-E. (2006). 'Affaires des femmes de Hassi Messaoud: Le procès du procès'. *NAQD,* 1–2(22–23), *Femmes et Citoyenneté,* pp. 41–46.

Levitt, P. and Jaworsky, B.N. (2007). 'Transnational Migration Studies: Past Developments and Future Trends'. *Annual Review of Sociology,* 33, pp. 129–56. [Online]. https://doi.org/10.1146/annurev.soc.33.040406.131816

Lloyd, C. (2006). 'From Taboo to Transnational Political Issue: Violence Against Women in Algeria'. *Women's Studies International Forum*, 29(5), pp. 453–62. [Online]. https://doi.org/10.1016/j.wsif.2006.07.003

Loughry, M. (2008). 'The Representation of Refugee Women in our Research and Practice', in Hajdukowski-Ahmed, M., et al. (eds). *Not Born Refugee Women: Contesting Identities, Rethinking Practices.* New York and Oxford: Berghahn Books, pp. 166–73.

Maalouf, A. (1998). *Les identités meurtrières.* Paris: Editions Grasset & Fasquelle.

McDougall, J. (2011). 'Dream of Exile, Promise of Home: Language, Education, and Arabism in Algeria'. *International Journal of Middle East Studies*, 43, Special Issue 2, May 2011, pp. 251–70. [Online]. https://doi.org/10.1017/S0020743811000055

Martinez, L. (2000). *The Algerian Civil War 1980–1998.* Trans. by Derrick, J. London: C. Hurt & Co.

Merdaci, A. (2004). 'La Hogra en Algérie: essai de lecture'. *La Tribune.* [Online]. Available at: http://www.algerie-dz.com/article604.html (accessed 16 January 2016).

Merolla, D. (1995). Algerian Regionalism: A Reappraisal. Middle Eastern Studies, vol.31(4), pp. 706–720.

Merolla, D. (1998). 'Communauté et féminité dans *Le Printemps désespéré* et *Illis U Meksa*', in De Ruyter-Tognotti, D. and Strien-Chardonneau, M.V. (eds). *Le roman francophone actuel en Algérie et aux Antilles.* Amsterdam: Edition Rodopi B.v, Amsterdam-Atlanta,vol.34, pp. 53

Moghadam, V.M. (ed.). (1994) *Gender and National Identity: Women and Politics in Muslim Societies.* London: Zed Books, pp. 9–159.

Moghadam, V.M. (2010). *Globalization and social movements: Islamism, feminism, and the global justice movement.* Rowman & Littlefield. Washington D.C

Moghadam, V.M. (2011). 'Algerian Women in Movement: Three Waves of Feminist Activism', in Debra Bergoffen, D., Gilbert, P.R., Harvey, T. and McNeely, C.L. (eds). *Confronting Global Gender Justice: Women's Lives, Human Rights.* London: Routledge, pp. 180–99.

Mohanty, C. (2003). *Feminism Without Borders: Decolonizing Theory, Practicing Solidarity.* Durham, NC: Duke University Press.

Morokvasic, M. (1984). 'Birds of Passage are also Women'. *The International Migration Review, Special Issue: Women in Migration*, 18(4), pp. 886–907.

M'Rabet, F. (1983). *La femme algérienne suivi de, Les Algériennes.* Paris: Francois Maspéro.

Mosteghanemi, A. (2003). *Memory in the Flesh.* Heinemann. Boston, Massachusetts

Mosteghanemi, A. (2004). *Chaos of The Senses.* Trans. by Ahmar, B. Cairo and New York: The American University in Cairo Press.

Mundy, J.A. (2010). *Representation, Civil War and Humanitarian Intervention: The International Politics of Naming Algerian Violence, 1992–2002.* PhD thesis. University of Exeter. [Online]. Available at: https://ore.exeter.ac.uk/repository/bitstream/handle/10036/117792/MundyJ.pdf?sequence=2 (accessed 14 June 2015).

Nyberg Sørensen, N. (2007). 'Living Across Worlds: Diaspora, Development and Transnational Engagement'. *International Organisation for Migration*, pp. 5–14 [Online]. Available at: http://publications.iom.int/system/files/pdf/living_across_worlds.pdf (accessed 15 January 2016).

OECD (2008). *A Profile of Immigrant Populations in the 21st Century: Data from OECD Countries*. Paris: OECD.

Oussedik, F. (2014). Speaking at: Congres International Féminin pour une Culture de Paix, Oran, Algeria. Interviewed by Latefa Narriman Guemar on 29 October 2014.

Papademetriou, D.G. (2012). 'Rethinking National Identity in the Age of Migration (Transatlantic Council Statement)'. *Transatlantic Council on Migration*, pp. 2–5. [Online]. Available at: http://www.migrationpolicy.org/research/TCM-rethinking-national-identity-council-statement (accessed 15 January 2016).

Papadopoulos, R.K. (2002). 'Refugees, Home and Trauma', in Papadopoulos, R.K. (ed.) *Therapeutic Care for Refugees: No Place like Home*. London: Karnac, pp. 9–40. E-book available at: https://books.google.co.uk/books?id=dQlQDwAAQBAJ&lpg=PT8&ots=s8hOAmcEdF&dq=Papadopoulos%2C%20R.K.%20(2002).%20%E2%80%98Refugees%2C%20Home%20and%20Trauma%E2%80%99%2C%20in%20Papadopoulos%2C%20R.K.%20(ed.)%20Therapeutic%20Care%20for%20Refugees%3A%20No%20Place%20like%20Home.%20London%3A%20Karnac%2C%20pp.9%E2%80%9340.%20&lr&hl=fr&pg=PT8#v=onepage&q&f=false (accessed 16 April 2023)).

Papadopoulos, R.K. (2005). 'Political Violence, Trauma and Mental Health Interventions', in Kalmanowitz, D. and Lloyd, B. (eds). *Art Therapy and Political Violence: With Art, Without Illusions*. London and New York: Routledge, Taylor & Francis, pp. 35–59.

Papadopoulos, R.K. (ed.) (2006). *Refugees and Psychological Trauma: A Psychological Perspective*. [Online]. Available at: www.nbc.org.uk/arc (accessed 13 January 2016).

Papadopoulos, R. (2007). 'Refugees, Trauma and Adversity-Activated Development'. *European Journal of Psychotherapy and Counselling*, 9(3), pp. 301–12. https://doi.org/10.1080/13642530701496930

Pearce, L. (1994). *Reading Dialogic*. London: Routledge, Chapman and Hall.

Pison, G. (2015) 'The Population of the World'. *Population & Societies*, 525(8), pp. 1–8. Available at: https://www.cairn-int.info/journal-population-and-societies-2007-7-page-1.htm (accessed 23 April 2023)

Przeworski, A., Alvarez, M.E., Cheibub, J.A. and Limongi, F. (2000). *Democracy and Development: Political Institutions and Well-being in the World, 1950–1990*. New York: Cambridge University Press.

Purcell, M. (2003). 'Citizenship and the Right to the Global City: Reimagining the Capitalist World Order'. *International Journal of Urban and Regional Research*, 27(3), pp. 564–90. [Online]. https://doi.org/10.1111/1468-2427.00467

Ramazanoglu, C. (1992). 'On Feminist Methodology: Male Reason versus Female Empowerment'. *Sociology*, 26(2). Sage Journals Online. Available at: https://doi.org/10.1177/0038038592026002003 (accessed 23 April 2023)

Ravenel, B. (1998). 'La gauche française au miroir de l'Algérie'. *Algeria-Watch*. [Online]. Available at: http://www.algeria-watch.org/farticle/ravenel2.htm (accessed 14 January 2016).

Rebai Maamri, M. (2009). 'The Syndrome of French Language in Algeria'. *International Journal of Arts and Sciences*, 3(3), pp. 77–89. [Online]. Available at: http://openaccesslibrary.org/images/Malika_Rebai_Maamri.pdf (accessed 12 January 2016).

Roberts, H. (2003). *The Battlefield: Algeria 1988–2002: Studies in a Broken Polity.* London and New York: Verso.

Roy, O. (2016). 'Exclusif. Djihadisme: Olivier Roy Repond a Gilles Kepel'. *Bibliobs*. [Online]. Available at: http://bibliobs.nouvelobs.com/idees/20160406.OBS8018/exclusif-djihadisme-olivier-roy-repond-a-gilles-kepel.html (accessed 30 July 2016).

Saad, L. (2014). 'The "40-Hour" Workweek is Actually Longer by Seven Hours'. Gallup. Available at: http://www.gallup.com/poll/175286/hour-workweek-actually-longer-seven-hours.aspx (accessed 23 April 2023)

Saada, E. (2000). 'Abdelmalek Sayad and the Double Absence: Toward a Total Sociology of Immigration'. *French Politics, Culture and Society*, 18(1), pp. 28–48. [Online]. Available at: https://doi.org/10.3167/153763700782378193 accessed 20 May 2020).

Safran, W. (1999). 'Comparing Diasporas: A Review Essay'. *Diaspora: A Journal of Transnational Studies*, 8(3), Winter 1999, pp. 255–91.

Said, E.W. (1991). 'Diasporas in Modern Societies: Myths of Homeland and Return'. *Diaspora: A Journal of Transnational Studies*, 1(1), Spring 1991, pp. 83–99.

Said, E.W. (2000). *Reflection on Exile and Other Essays.* Cambridge, MA: Harvard University Press, pp. 173–86.

Said, E. W. (2002). Reflections on Exile and Other Essays. Harvard University Press

Samraoui, M. (2003). *Chronique des années de sang: Algérie Comment les services ont manipulé les groupes islamistes.* Paris: Editions Denoël.

Sandoval, C. (2000). *The Methodology of the Oppressed.* Minneapolis: University of Minnesota Press, pp. 41–66.

Sayad, A. (2004). *The Suffering of the Immigrant.* Boston, MA and Cambridge, UK: Polity Press.

Schiller, N.G. (2009). 'A Global Perspective on Migration and Development'. *Social Analysis*, 53(3), pp. 14–37. [Online]. https://doi.org/10.3167/sa.2009.530302 (accessed 12 May 2016).

Schulhofer-Wohl, J. (2006). 'Algeria (1992–Present)'. *University of Virginia, CIWAW01C.* [Online]. Available at: http://faculty.virginia.edu/j.sw/uploads/research/Schulhofer-Wohl%202007%20Algeria.pdf (accessed 12 June 2016).

Seeley, K.M. (2008). *Therapy after Terror: 9/11, Psychotherapists, and Mental Health.* Cambridge: Cambridge University Press.

Sidhoum, S. (2003). 'L'intelligence qu'on assassine'. *Algeria-Watch*. [Online]. Available at: http://www.algeria-watch.org/fr/mrv/mrvrap/sidhoum_intelligence.htm (accessed October 2014).

Sidi Moussa, N. (2019). 'Algeria: A Historic and Ambivalent Movement'. *Brooklyn Rail.* [Online]. Available at: https://brooklynrail.org/2019/05/field-notes/Algeria-A-Historic-and-Ambivalent-Movement (accessed 23 April 2023)

Smail Salhi, Z. (2010). 'The Algerian Feminist Movement Between Nationalism, Patriarchy and Islamism'. *Women's Studies International Forum*, 33(2), pp. 113–24. [Online]. https://doi.org/10.1016/j.wsif.2009.11.001 (accessed 15 March 2022)

Smail Salhi, Z. (2013). *Gender and Diversity in the Middle East and North Africa.* London: Routledge.

Smith, B.G. (2008). 'Eroticism', in *The Oxford Encyclopedia of Women in World History*, Vol. 1. Oxford: Oxford University Press, pp. 190–92.

Solomos, J. and Wrench, J. (1996). 'Racism and Migration in Western Europe'. *Canadian Journal of Sociology/Cahiers canadiens de sociologie*, 21(2), pp. 295–98. [Online]. Available at: http://www.jstor.org/stable/3341995 (accessed 12 May 2015).

Souaïdia, H. (2006). 'Dans la République de la peur, le viol est une arme de guerre'. *Algeria-Watch.* [Online]. Available at: http://www.algeria-watch.org/fr/article/tribune/souaidia_arme_guerre.htm (accessed May 2012).

Soysal, Y. (2000). 'Citizenship and Identity: Living in Diasporas in Post-War Europe'. *Ethnic and Racial Studies*, 23(1), pp.1–15.

Stephens, J.D., Rueschemeyer, D. and Stephens, E.H. (1992). *Capitalist Development and Democracy.* Chicago: University of Chicago Press.

Stone, M. (1997). *The Agony of Algeria.* New York: Columbia University Press.

Sugiman, P. (2008). '"Days You Remember": Japanese Canadian Women and the Violence of Internment', in Hajdukowski-Ahmed, M., et al. (eds). *Not Born a Refugee Woman: Contesting Identities, Rethinking Practices.* New York and Oxford: Berghahn, pp. 180–240.

Sullivan, Z.T. (2001). *Exiled Memories: Stories of the Iranian Diaspora.* Philadelphia, PA: Temple University Press.

Talahite, F. (2000). 'Economie administrée, corruption et engrenage de la violence en Algérie'. *Revue du Tiers-Monde*, 41, p. 161.

Tamzali, W. (2014). Congres International Féminin pour une Culture de Paix, Oran, Algerie: https://www.youtube.com/watch?v=3tr8wiYgeAI (accessed 23 April 2023).

Taylor, J.A. (2008). *The Construction of Identities Through Narratives of Occupations.* PhD thesis. University of Salford. Available at: http://usir.salford.ac.uk/1946/1/Whole_thesis_Final_version.pdf (accessed 12 July 2016).

Tölölyan, K. (1991). 'The Nation-state and Its Others: In Lieu of a Preface'. *Diaspora*, 1(1), pp. 3–7.

Tölölyan, K. (1996). 'Rethinking Diaspora(s): Stateless Power in the Transnational Moment'. *Diaspora*, 5(1), pp. 3–36.

Tölölyan, K. (2011). The contemporary discourse of diaspora studies. Comparative Studies of South Asia, Africa and the Middle East, 31(1), pp. 83–87.

Transparency International Report (2016). 'TI and the Algerian Association Against Corruption Call on Algerian Government to Put a Stop to Press Freedom Violations in Algeria'. [Online]. Available at: http://www.transparency.org/news/pressrelease/transparency_international_and_the_algerian_association_against_corruption (accessed 10 January 2016).

Tremlett, G. (2005). 'Spain Grants Amnesty to 700,000 Migrants'. *The Guardian.* 9 May 2005.

Tripp, A.M. (2019). *Seeking Legitimacy: Why Arab Autocracies Adopt Women's Rights.* Cambridge: Cambridge University Press.

UN Human Development Report 2002. [Online]. Available at: https://hdr.undp.org/en/content/human-development-report-2002. (accessed 23 April 2023)

UNDP (2009). 'Overcoming Barriers: Human Mobility and Development', in *Human Development Report.* [Online]. Available at: http://hdr.undp.org/sites/default/files/reports/269/hdr_2009_en_complete.pdf (accessed 10 December 2015).

UNHCR Report on Refugee Women. [Online]. Available at: http://www.unhcr.org/uk/women.html (accessed 16 July 2016).

UNHCR (2021). 'Figures at a Glance.' [Online]. Available at: https://www.unhcr.org/uk/figures-at-a-glance.html. (accessed 23 April 2023)

Van Hear, N. (1998). *New Diasporas.* London: UCL Press/Routledge.

Vertovec, S. (1997). 'Three Meanings of "Diaspora", Exemplified by South Asian Religions'. *Diaspora,* 6, pp. 573–82.

Vince, N. (2014). '1960s Algeria: Women, Public Space and Moral Panic'. Talk organized by the Society for Algerian Studies in collaboration with the Middle East Centre, LSE. 12 November 2014.

Weinstein, E., Lira, E. and Rojas, E. (1987). *Trauma, Duelo y Reparacio'n (Trauma, Mourning and Reparation).* Santiago de Chile: FASIC/Interarnericana.

World Bank. (2021). *Algeria's Economic Update—Fall 2021.* Available at: https://www.worldbank.org/en/country/algeria/publication/algeria-economic-update-fall-2021(access 23 April 2023)

Yous, N. (2000). *Qui a tué à Bentalha ? Algerie: chronique d'un massacre annoncé.* Series libres. Edition La Decouverte.Paris

Yuval, N., Gross, R. and Marshall, R.D. (2006). 'Mental Health in the Wake of Terrorism: Making Sense of Mass Casualty Trauma', in Yuval, N., Gross, R., Marshall, R.D. and Susser, E.S. (eds). *9/11: Mental Health in the Wake of Terrorist Attacks.* Cambridge: Cambridge University Press, pp. 3–14.

Yuval-Davis, N. (1997). *Gender & Nation.* London: Sage.

Yuval-Davis, N. and Anthias, F. (1989). 'Introduction', in Yuval-Davis, N. & Anthias, F. (eds). *Woman-Nation-State.* New York: St Martins, pp. 2–15.

Zachar, P. (2006). 'Reconciliation as Compromise and the Management of Rage', in Potter, N.N. (ed.). *Trauma, Truth and Reconciliation: Healing Damaged Relationships.* Oxford: Oxford University Press, pp. 67–82.

Index

Abdelkader, Namia 152
Agger, Inger 13, 68, 88, 95
Alaoui, M.H. 29, 43–4
Al-Banna, Hassan 39
Algerian British Connection (ABC) 76, 145, 188
Algerian intellectual female diaspora 44–8
Algerian International Diaspora Association (AIDA) 145
Algerian Sketches (Bourdieu) 52
Algerian Solidarity Campaign (ASC) 145
Algerian women in exile 101–2
Algerian women's forced migration in 1990s 42–55
  Black Decade impact 42–4
  brain drain of Algerian women 45
  causes and patterns of 42–55
  Family Code, 1984 54
  Law of Reconciliation 54
  legal and social situation 48–55
  political and economic crisis of 1980s 47
'Amnesia Law' 94
Anderson, Benedict 161
Anthias, Floya 5, 21–3
Arab Spring xvii, 19
Arkoun, Mohammed 139
Army of National Liberation (ALN) 90
Arnould, Valerie 91
Avebury, Lord 9

Bab El Oued riots 187
Bakhtin, Mikhail 26
Barbour, John 32
Battle of Algiers, The (Pontecorvo) 145
Bauböck, Rainer 17
Bedjaoui, Youcef 73
Belalloufi, Amal 110
Belhadj, Ali 38–9
Belhouari-Musette, Djamila 69
Belriadouh, Abdelhak 111
Benmayor, Rina 24
Bennabi, Malek 40
Bennoune, Mahfoud 46
Berber Cultural Movement (MCB) 41, 106
Black Atlantic, The (Gilroy) 21
Black Decade xvii, 1–2, 6, 9, 11–12, 15, 17, 19, 25, 27, 29–31, 101–71
  healing the rifts of 179–82
  impact on women 42–4
  women of 147–71
  see also fragmented narratives of Black Decade
Boudiaf, Mohamed 176
Bouhired, Djamila 151
Bouklia-Hassane, R. 55
Boumediene, Houari 51
Bourdieu, Pierre 9, 52, 59, 105
Bouteflika, Abdelaziz 109, 148, 151–3, 155, 169
Brah, Avtar 22
Brendel, David 92
Brooklyn Rail, The 160

Caldwell, John 35
Carr, James 4
Chambon, Adrienne 15
Cheriet, Boutheina 40
Chitour, Fadela 151
Chomsky, Noam 3–4, 9, 43
Christou, Anastasia 18
Clifford, James 5, 20, 25
Cohen, Robin 4–5, 17–20, 22, 89, 146
collective trauma 63–8
Collyer, Michael 6–8, 75
Communist Party (PCF) 115
Convention on the Elimination of All Forms of Discrimination Against Women (CEDAW) 48
Crawley, Heaven 81, 105

Dahmani-Lovichi, Fatiha 49
Daoud, Zakya 48, 51
de Beauvoir, Simone 125
democracy 35–8
  Western definition of 36
Derrida, Jacques 9, 105
de-selving 27, 30–3
dialogism 26–33
  de-selving 27, 30–3
  re-selving 27, 30–3
  women's identity transformation 26–33
diaspora(s) 1–33
  concept of, use 172–4
  data collection 13–14
  elements of 176–9
  feminist framework 9–11
  fieldwork 14–15
  interviews, transcribing 15–17
  from networks to 172
  non-verbal communication 16
  perspectives on 141–6
  research methodology 12–17
  research on 192
  sampling the network 12–13
  social constructionist definition of 21–5
  traditional use of 174
  victim diasporas 20
  see also Algerian women's forced migration in 1990s; women and migration
diasporic consciousness 17–21
Djaout, Tahar 123
Djebar, Assia 25, 45–6
Double Absence, The (Sayad) 32

'egocentric' sampling techniques 12
Ellingson, Laura 14
European Union, 'refugee crisis' at 2
Evans, Martin 53
exile, Algerian women in 101–2

Fanon, Frantz 28, 45, 125
Farrand, Andrew 161
feminist framework of diaspora 9–11
feminization of Algerian migration 34–56
  democracy and women's rights 35–8
  political background to 34–56
  radical Islamist movement rise 38–42
  seeds of conflict 34–5
  see also Algerian women's forced migration in 1990s
Fenster, Tovi 60
Fisk, Robert 94
Forbes Martin, Susan 81
fragmented narratives of Black Decade 101–46
  discrimination and violence, links between 103
  identity, transnational space and belonging 101–46
  integration, language and identity 121–5
  'myth of return' 131–41
  narratives of regaining selfhood 125–31
  persecution and the decision to leave 102–13
  rebuilding lives and a sense of self 113–31
  regionalism in 144–5
Française, Académie 46

Gilroy, Paul 21

Hajdukowski-Ahmed, Maroussia 26, 30–1, 33, 85, 87
Hanoun, Louisa 69–70
Hassi Messaoud event 7
Hayward, Lynda 117
Heckathorn, Douglas 12
Herlihy, Jane 79
Hiddleston, Jane 46
Hirak movement 19, 147–71
  course of 148–54
  Covid-19 pandemic and 170
  hopes and fears for 158–63
  and mobilization of diaspora 182–5
  spirit of, sustainability 163–70
  women in diaspora during 154–8
  women of 147–71

Ibn Badis, Abdelhamid 40
Immigration and Asylum Act 1999 6
InfoMigrants 1
Inquiry into the Algerian Massacres, An (ed. Bedjaoui) 43, 73
International Committee for the Support of Persecuted Algerian Intellectuals (CISIA) 105–6
International Federation of the Algerian Diaspora (FIDA) 145
International Organization for Migration (IOM) 2
Islamic Salvation Army (GIA) 90
Islamic Salvation Front (FIS) 34

Jasmine Revolution 162
Jaworsky, Nadya 17
Joffé, George 91, 93

Kaci, Nadia 7
Khaled, Karim 129
Kherata protests 148
Khiari, Wahiba 67
Khider, Mohamed 41
Kichk, Abdelhamid 41
Knauss, Peter 45, 51

Labdelaoui, Hocine 47
Lakhdar, Latifa 49, 139
'Lamia's' story 57–100
  1951 Refugee Convention in 81
  1984 Family Code 72
  arrival in UK 75–8
  claiming asylum in UK 78–85
  emotional impact of migration 85–7
  migration process 71–85
  'myth of return' 95–7
  negotiating a new identity 97–100
  personal reconciliation 87–9
  post-traumatic stress disorder (PTSD) 94
  reaching UK 71–5
  reconciliation and forgiveness 87–95
  reconciliation in Algeria 90–5
  terrorism and women's oppression 68–71
Language Conflict in Algeria: From Colonialism to Post-Independence (Mohamed) 123
Larbi, Mokrane Ait 73
Lazreg, Marnia 140
Leca, Jean 105
Lefebvre, Henri 60
Left for Dead: The Lynching of Women in Hassi Messaoud (Kaci) 7
Levitt, Peggy 17
Loughry, Maryanne 59–60

Maalouf, Amin 123, 136–7, 181
Maamri, Malika Rebai 122
Ma'arifa (networking) 58
Madani, Abbassi 42, 150
Mellah, Salima 9
Merdaci, Abdelmadjid 98
Mhenni, Lina Ben 187
Milestones (Qutb) 41
Moghadam, Valentine M. 25, 46, 61, 81, 91
Mohamed, Benrabah 123
Mokadem, Malika 45, 47
Mosteghanemi, Ahlem 123
mourshidates (Islamic guides) 110
Moussa, Nedjib Sidi 160
M'Rabet, Fadéla 45–6

Murderous Identities (Maalouf) 181
'myth of return' 176–9

Nasser, Gamal Abdel 40
National Algerian Centre (NAC), 145
National Independent Authority
of Elections (ANIE) 153–4
National Liberation Front (FLN) 34–7
non-verbal communication 16

Ouattar, Tahar 123
Our Silence (*Nos Silences*) (Khiari) 67
Oussedik, Fatma 69

Papadopoulos, Renos K. 27, 29, 59, 79, 85, 99, 112
personal trauma 57–100
gendered sociopolitical origins 57–63
terrorism and counter-terrorism experience 63–8
see also 'Lamia's' story
Phillips, John 53
political actors, women as 158–63
Pontecorvo, Gillo 145
Professional and Linguistic Assessments Board (PLAB) 120
Purcell, Mark 60

Qutb, Sayyid 40

radical Islamist movement rise in Algeria 38–42
Ravenel, Bernard 115
Reflections on Exile (Said) 32
1951 Refugee Convention 102
re-selving 27, 30–3
pseudo-re-selving 31
respondent-driven sampling (RDS) 12
return 131–41
Roy, Olivier 39

Saada, Emmanuelle 32
Safran, William 18, 20
Said, Edward 32
Samraoui, Mohamed 67
Sartre, Jean-Paul 125
Sayad, Abdelmalek 10, 32, 114
Schiller, Nina Glick 4
Schulhofer-Wohl, Jonah 58
Seeley, Jan 64
social constructionist definition of diaspora 21–5
Socialist Party (PS) 115
Sørensen, Ninna Nyberg 18–19
Souaïdia, Habib 68
Soysal, Yasemin Nuhoglu 22, 24
Stephens, John D. 36
Stoknes, Andor 24
Stone, Martin 124
Suffering of the Immigrant, The (Sayad) 32
Sugiman, Pamela 31
Sullivan, Zohra T. 154
survey questionnaire 192–205

Tamzali, Wassyla 139, 139n4
Taylor, Jacqueline 128
Tebboune, Abdelmadjid 157
'Third World' feminist movements 45
Tlemçani, Salima 49
Touat, Dalila 152
transnational populations 17
trauma 176–9
Tripp, Aili Mari 188
Turner, Stuart 79

Van Hear, Nicholas 4
victim diasporas 20
Vince, Natalya 52

Weinstein, Eugenia 60
Who Killed at Bentalha? (*Qui a tué à Bentalha?*) (Yous) 9
women and migration 1–5
feminization of 2
Hassi Messaoud event 7
post-Cold War 3
socio-economic circumstances 3

women in Algeria 48–55
identity transformation, feminist approach 26–33
legal and social situation of 48–55
as political actors 158–63
women's rights in 35–8
see also Algerian women's forced migration in 1990s
Women in the Mirror of Muslim Orthodoxy (*Imra'atuI'ijmâ*) 49

Yous, Nesroulah 8
Yuval-Davis, Nira 25

zawiya (Islamic Sufi order) 109
Zéroual, Liamine 90